DEBT TRAP

DEBT TRAP

Rethinking the Logic
of Development

Richard W. Lombardi

PRAEGER SPECIAL STUDIES • PRAEGER SCIENTIFIC

New York • Philadelphia • Eastbourne, UK
Toronto • Hong Kong • Tokyo • Sydney

Library of Congress Cataloging in Publication Data
Lombardi, Richard W.
  Debt trap.

  Bibliography: p.
  Includes index.
  1. Debts, External—Developing countries. 2. Economic
development. 3. International economic relations.
4. International finance. I. Title.
HJ8899.L65   1985   336.3′435′091724   84-18303
ISBN 0-03-003007-2 (alk. paper)

Published in 1985 by Praeger Publishers
CBS Educational and Professional Publishing
a Division of CBS Inc.
521 Fifth Avenue, New York, NY 10175 USA

56789 052 987654321

Printed in the United States of America
on acid-free paper

To my father and to his

Preface and Acknowledgments

This book started out as a description of the impact of multinational banking in the Third World, that is, as a discussion of the international banks and their poorest clients. From the start, it was realized that our banks are but the instruments of a broader economic and political world order operating North-South—or rather, disorder. It seemed important, then, to discuss firstly the tragic disorder and, secondly, the banks. This I have done in Part I of the following text. Throughout the book my efforts have been to go beyond an anecdotal, financial whodunit and to reveal the root causes behind the presently disguised but persistent financial anarchy that marks, in tragic dimension, the scarred landscape connecting the First World with the Third.

Our present world order has a specific cause that is theoretic (a failure in human reasoning) before it is ideological, economic, or financial. "It is manifest," as we are told by the French philosopher, Étienne Gilson, "that the end corresponds always to its principle."

In Part I, entitled "The Third World Question," we shall see how a specific first principle dictates subsequent Third World development theory; how a one-dimensional development theory determines economic model building at the World Bank and the International Monetary Fund; and how the economic models have set the stage for commercial bank lending practices in the Third World. These lending practices have led the rich nations and the poor to the quite frightening brink of bankruptcy, moral as well as financial. As a result, Third World development has come to a virtual standstill (poverty is on the increase), while the major powers turn to force rather than to money in their efforts to preserve our existing political orders.

In Part II, entitled "The Western Question," we will review the seminal ideas, the worldview behind our existing world order. In a deliberate manner, we will reason more strategically rather than continue to shock the reader with examples of the trenchant realities of global poverty reinforced by the costly failures of bank management and aid policy. Hence, Part II is admittedly more abstract.

"The Western Question" deals with a crisis in self-identity, with the identity of the bankers, diplomats, and businessmen participating in the development process itself. Without a better understanding of the Western question, the Third World question could well direct all of us, North and South alike, into the senseless match for the destruction of a second Troy.

Already, the much acclaimed North-South dialogue has been diverted into an increasingly sterile polemic instead of constructive negotiations related to a changed global order. Without a more meaningful dialogue, pending financial and economic disorder will become a fact measurable in terms of men and of arms.

I would like to thank the First National Bank of Chicago for granting me a leave of absence for the preparation of this book and the School of Foreign Service at Georgetown University for inviting me to serve as a Research Associate and Thursday Fellow within the Karl F. Landegger Program in International Business Diplomacy. Special thanks go to Francis X. Winters, S.J., and to Peter F. Krogh, dean of the School of Foreign Service.

I likewise am indebted to a number of academics, bankers, economists, and financial journalists who helped me to see where I wanted to go and who made valuable suggestions to the text. Special acknowledgment is extended to Edward Mendelson of Columbia University and to George P. Brockway, a regular contributor to the *New Leader* and, until recently, chairman of W. W. Norton and Company. This book would not have been completed without their guidance and support. A special note of thanks goes to Lawrence Malkin of *Time* magazine, whose capacity to reduce complex issues to simple verities served as an example in my own more humble efforts at drafting the following text, and to Sidiki Diakité of the Philosophy Department at the University of Abidjan, who pointed out convincingly that modern man seems to have broken away from his metaphysical moorings.

Before ending these acknowledgments, I would like to extend my gratitude to the library staffs at Georgetown University, at the Atlantic Institute in Paris, and at the Fondation Nationale des Science Politiques (Paris) for their many kindnesses during my research. Kate Lewin, a research assistant at *Time* magazine, provided timely information of press coverage on the debt crisis. Lastly, special acknowledgment must be directed to my wife, Elisabeth, who generated initially my interest in the project—and then stuck by it.

It is sometimes noted—and should be repeated—that our life-support systems are a reflection of the "kingdom of the mind." We will attempt to judge what Western political leaders and bankers have done with this kingdom. The kingdom has become planetary in its dimension for Western man has wedded himself, through his finance and technology, to the globe in its entirety.

In not a few instances, however, Western politicians, bankers, and international civil servants no longer are convinced of the importance of the kingdom of the mind. Nor are they familiar with the responsibility of their recent marriage. Part I deals with the marriage and Part II with the kingdom.

Richard W. Lombardi
Longpont, France, August 15, 1984

Contents

Introduction: The Second Holocaust

Despite the present conviction of our political leadership, a grow-ing number of informed citizens appear to be realizing that the in-creased tension, even fragmentation, within our global orders origi-nates not in East-West competition but rather in what currently passes as North-South cooperation. We shall demonstrate how this "cooper-ation" has led the First World and the Third on a collision course one with the other. The trajectory leads in a straight line from post-World War II development theory to its manifestation in the de facto bank-ruptcy of a number of our leading multinational banks and their largest Third World clients.

Yet if we hope to gain an adequate perspective on the entirety of the trajectory, we will need to step out of our normal bias. Indeed, as Pierre Teilhard de Chardin, anthropologist, priest, and poet, noted at the twilight of his career: "What is decisive is not always where one is looking but where one is looking from."[1] This maxim is particularly relevant for people concerned with international finance and Third World development or, with its correlative, world stability.

The maxim does not represent an idle abstraction nor an enigma. Teilhard de Chardin was restating a conviction that, until recently, has found clear resonance throughout the history of Western thought. Simply put: one's worldview determines one's method of problem solving. In the end, one's paradigm dictates discovery.

Facts do not make their own decision, notwithstanding Citibank's dictum to the contrary.[2] Information brings us but to the brink of knowledge. What really matters is being able to change our vision when the facts no longer correspond to reality, when the model is no longer relevant. What matters is "where one is looking from." Statis-tical series, in the words of the Secretariat of the Organization of Economic Co-operation and Development (OECD), represent, in the end, but mental constructs.

When we look at the precarious state of our global systems, what counts is our capacity to change our vision. Without a fundamental shift in worldview, our existing laws of nature—particularly in finance, in trade, and in economic development theory—could well lead us to ultimate political apoplexy. Indeed, it is not too much of an exaggeration to say that we are almost there.

We live in the face of two holocausts. The first is the nuclear threat —what our poet, T. S. Eliot, prophetically called the "bang." The second is starvation, a sort of "whimper" to which we seem to have grown accustomed. The first is potential, the second actual. We are witnessing today what some experts call "a Hiroshima every five days,"[3] a sort of holocaust in large but silent doses. We accept this second holocaust, mass starvation, because it fits our worldview. The second holocaust, however, could well trigger the first. Increasingly, we can recognize that the two inevitably go together. We confront today what T. S. Eliot could only intuit. Violent North-South disequilibrium has become the focal point of East-West tension.

Already, the vital interests of the developed countries are defined on the periphery, at the Straits of Hormuz (where the U.S. government has threatened to use its nuclear arsenal), at the Horn of Africa, in Central and South America, on the subcontinent of Asia. There is little coincidence, of course, that these expanding vital interests are located precisely at those points where our global systems are at their weakest, where the whimper of abject poverty is the loudest.

At the tactical level, the major problem might be seen as one of allocation of global resources, natural, technological, and financial. At present, 75 percent of the world's wealth is produced for the benefit of 25 percent of the world's population. This figure comes from Robert S. McNamara, recent president of the World Bank.[4] The data indicates in economic terms the degree of separation between the Western world and the Third World. The data likewise signals at best a delicate adjustment period ahead for the globe in its entirety.

If we are to believe however, Teilhard de Chardin and the body of Western thought that he represents, then the tactical issues, the hard facts as they present themselves, must take second place to our capacity to change vision.

At the moment, our vision on global economic order is giving us a false view of reality. We stand, as it were, before the control panel at Three Mile Island just before the hydrogen explosion could occur to uncover the core reactor. The computers cannot give us a measure of the heat in the containment building because an accident of the sort taking place was not supposed to happen. The program did not cover such an eventuality.

An example of a similar situation in political economy might be summarized as follows: our current worldview permits us to accept the fact that the earth can be divided logically into developed and developing countries. The terms themselves, however, speak of a specific value judgment, of a given preconcept that serves to distort, even to denature, the very problem that quite clearly needs more careful analysis.

Seen from a global point of view, economic development since World War II has been as distorted as it has been dangerous. Indeed, one might argue that there are few developed countries, only a minority of states that are hyperdeveloped or falsely developed and a majority of states that are economically underdeveloped. In fact, given the financial tensions and economic disparities in our current world order, we might say, along with some thoughtful strategists, that most countries are simply maldeveloped.[5] To do this, however, we need to change our worldview, or, more fundamentally, we need to change our concepts about what makes the world turn. What are these concepts? What is the basic premise that underscores the Western world's current attitudes on development theory? For the premise, as we shall see, determines subsequent trade and financial flows as well as political alliances. The premise, or first principle, likewise preordains the system's stability, its duration, and its meaning.

THE WORLDVIEW

We in the North today possess a vision of reality wherein we presume that nature is hostile rather than harmonious. To speak in more philosophical terms, we can no longer say, along with our forefathers, that by definition opposites are mutually exclusive, that there is no proportion between order and chaos, that chaos is inimical to creation and to life. Our modern metaphysics tells us that conflict is rooted in the laws of nature. Being and non-being, chaos and order, are one (Hegel).[6]

This vision of the world inspires our art, our politics, our modern management techniques, and, at its center, our Third World development efforts. As Parmenides said in the fifth century B.C.: the parts make a whole.

Geopolitical strategy assumes conflict as the start and finish of foreign policy. Economic development theory posits comparative advantage over threshold cooperation between the weak and the strong as the source of growth and material well-being. As we shall observe, the "Law of Comparative Advantage"[7] serves as the singular driving force behind North-South trade and finance. The conviction of structural disharmony in nature has been lifted whole into economic model building. In the end, modern man is held hostage to a worldview that consents to the irrational and to its future. Even our art has become disharmonic, not to mention our banking systems.

The logic, however, that gives direction to our current global order has led us to the precipice. In economic strategies, disparities have been encouraged, even legitimized, in the name of *growth*. In sum, the pattern of Third World development has come to resemble the underlying paradigm wherein discontinuity is considered as normal and where growing destitution is taken as the necessary spinoff of what we dare to call "development." The results: even poorer debtor nations matched by a gradual but real paralysis in our banking system (See Chapters 9 and 10). In geopolitical strategies, our worldview tells us that the next war might be definitive. Indeed, definitive several times over.

In parallel with our economic theory and with the finance that backs it up, our destructive potential represents a sort of ultimate homage to our current worldview. For if man is structurally conflictual, in keeping with our current interpretation of nature, then total destruction of one's enemy rather than defense of legitimate national interest becomes not only a logical possibility but, in fact, an imperative. Our nation states share in this imperative. In short, our "kingdom of the mind" is in anarchy.

Our vision of reality, as one-dimensional as it is blind-sided, carries yet further into our assumptions about global economic order. We thus reinforce an already dangerous geopolitical strategy with a terrible fatalism in economic model building. That is, we accept absolute poverty as consistent with the natural order of things. We fail to make a distinction between poverty brought about by an error in human reasoning and poverty brought about by nature. Nature is easier to blame. We even accept structural disequilibrium as a *precondition* to growth (See Chapter 4). Our assumptions fit our paradigm. In turn, the worldview that backs it up explains development logic and the banking that follows, a banking system that has contributed to its own demise because the bankers have not questioned the operative premise of their own Third and First World activities.

THE PLANNING OF GLOBAL COOPERATION

In more concrete terms, the Brandt Commission report, one of the most prestigious and comprehensive documents to date on North-South relations, speaks of the Third World as an "engine of economic growth." The full title of the report, *North-South: A Program for Survival*,[8] underscores the immediacy of establishing a "New International Economic Order" (NIEO) in light of growing interdependence among nations. The document was prepared for the World Bank by an independent commission of development experts and by world famous political leaders serving in their capacity as private citizens. The members of the commission were mobilized from the Western world and from Third World countries. Willy Brandt, former West German chancellor, chaired the committee. Other well-known members included Edward Heath, ex-prime minister of Great Britain; Olof Palme, president of Sweden; the late Pierre Mendès-France; and the U.S. banker, Peter M. Petersen.

While the mixed commission proved eloquent in its capacity to identify the flash points in our global economic system, the report itself ultimately fails to render a justification and meaning for economic cooperation; that is, the justification leans on a dated worldview and, in the process, mixes freely the concepts of growth with those of development. By extension, the logic of the report denies the hope of any real change in direction, a change that is badly needed if we are to establish a political, economic, and financial order appropriate to our elementary needs in the twenty-first century.

In identifying the Third World as an engine of economic growth, the experts assume that our existing systems are working, that we simply need to extrapolate our current worldview and our current know-how southward. Our leaders, however, are gliding on a too facile solipsism. Even cooperation ultimately is explained in terms of larger markets, in terms of a more competitive economic environment, and, finally, in terms of the survival of the fittest. In this situation, the Third World will be the first to lose. The gaps will widen. As a consequence, our mechanism for growth will surely derail.

DEVELOPMENT LOGIC

When we describe Third World development as an engine or locomotive of growth, we should realize that, simultaneously, the train is out of control. Growth in economic terms has virtually nothing to do with balance, with proportion, nor with distribution. Growth means an increase in production. Growth is measured in terms of gross national product, regardless of what the product is—arms, matches, or wells.

On the contrary, development as a first order of priority concerns itself with composition. Development increases our potential to make conscious choices. Growth is linear, development diffuse. Growth measures output; development is a measure of man's capacity to govern, to organize his universe.

We must be careful, then, not to speak only about locomotives, this mechanical approach to development. Our national leaders, our international bureaucrats, our bankers, and our planners will need to address the more vital problem of people, their specific goals, their capabilities, their cultures, and their intentions. Inevitably, our decision makers will have to concern themselves not with the survival of the fittest in a so-called competitive marketplace, but rather with the survival of the species. The two are not reconcilable, despite the dictates of our current worldview. Our worldview, however, prevents us from seeing this obvious verity.

For example, the trickle-down theory of current development policy is not working, particularly in the Third World. Our numbers tell us as much once we are able to look at them from a different vantage point. Since World War II, whenever the Third World became richer by $1 per capita, the industrialized world became richer by $268 per capita.[9] For a number of Less Developed Countries (LDCs), average income per capita by 1980 did not exceed $450 per year, a destitution wage. Therefore, a $1 per year increase represents just a little more destitution, or rather, a little more abject poverty.

Development does not trickle down like water. Development grows rather like a flower, upward, once a given set of variables are brought together at the base. As we shall see, one of the most critical variables is a relevant aid and banking system.

Thus far, we have tied together two issues that touch our life-support systems. The first deals with our so-called defense posture. The second issue deals with mass starvation and with its twin, frenetic disequilibrium in North-South trade and finance. Both issues are interrelated and are symptomatic of a deeper reality. Indeed, the "whole" reflects a set of values, a vision of the world, or "ways of being a man." For the moment, these ways of being a man are not flattering. Not only are a number of our banks failing but, there are about 25 people in the world dying each 60 seconds as a result of absolute poverty.[10] The World Bank describes "absolute poverty" as a condition where one's physical, even genetic potential cannot be realized due to insufficient food, shelter, and health care. Most of the victims are children under the age of ten.

The average reader can hardly visualize this tragedy. We would prefer to abstract the problem. All of us would prefer to call death by starvation a natural disaster, which of course it is not. Modern technology, whether in banking, in agriculture, or in communications prevents us from blaming starvation on the weather or on the gods. Indeed, the only excuse we have is indifference or a vague feeling of helplessness.

Given the dimensions, however, of this tragedy we hardly have the right to discuss the issue of aid, of finance, and of abject poverty if we cannot propose an alternative approach to our current methods of problem solving. For surely, mass starvation in our time represents more than a mere symbol of inconvenient but temporary economic disequilibrium, a method that has momentarily failed us. If we are to believe this argument, then we are back in the Dark Ages of Thomas Malthus and of his good friend, David Ricardo. We might recall that Malthus' "Iron Law" of wages condemned entire generations of European workers to a subsistence wage in order to limit population. Ricardo used the same principle in order to explain capital accumulation according to his Law of Comparative Advantage. In other words, destitution explained profit, growth, and the "natural" control of population.

Famine, however, in our own age of such large proportion, represents a breakdown in our capacity to react intellectually, morally, and emotionally to one of man's most fundamental rights: his right to share.

Hence, what we must look for is a new schema, or model, in what today is called "the development business." Without a new model, we risk to experience a redoubling of what we have seen to date, that is, a significantly weakened financial structure in the West compounded by insupportable sociopolitical tensions elsewhere. These tensions, in turn, undoubtedly will have their ripple effect in the Western world.

THE BANKS AND AID AGENCIES

Despite obvious satisfaction with existing systems, we must ask: How can the community of nations design a development process commensurate with real need? Likewise, how can the First World bring its own aid programs and the banking system more effectively into the process? For if intentions do not coincide with financial resources, or rather, if the two do not complement one another, then the planet is headed for a difficult passage indeed. Already our banking system is bending under the weight of poorly conceived Third World lending programs, while aid donors are losing their political constituencies. The result: stagnation in development and a loss of hope. This loss of hope has led to a suppressed state of conflict, both internal and external to the Third World.

The following, then, is written not only for policy makers and bankers but for all those who want to participate in an issue central to our times. The issue is not simply finance but a heritage or concomitant value system that we will be leaving to future generations of our own peoples and to those of less happy circumstances.

The topics of development, of aid, and of banking are but convincing surrogates for discussing the broader issues of international cooperation and threshold balance in the distribution of global resources.

The Revolution of Rising Expectations probably will not wait for the year 2000 to bring the full weight of its presence to our doorsteps. In anticipation of its arrival, we might want to know what can be done to confront the issue of structural underdevelopment in the Third World. One way of doing this is to judge how those in the finance and development business conceptualize their activities and then to proffer alternatives. To be sure, Third World economic development cannot take place without an adequate financial system operating in tandem with development goals. This means that we need adequate banks and, more importantly, adequate bankers who understand their role in Third World development. To date, we have witnessed a singular lack of both. To the extent that we are not sensitive to the issues at hand, we are foreclosing on our potential to shape in a constructive way our destiny as we enter the twenty-first century.

The banks and the poor have been entwined into a single web of debt and underdevelopment. It remains to discover the geometry of the web and, thereby, to propose an exit. The geometry can be discovered through careful reasoning. The exit can be reached by applying the right amount of method and money. All three elements can be used to reorder the development priorities that now result in such notorious human tragedy and, in the process, save our biggest multinational banks from the pending crack in our worldwide financial system. The two go together. To be sure, finance and development, like the rich and the poor or the North and the South, share today a common destiny. That destiny can only be ignored at the risk of prolonged and furious disorder in our global systems, in banking, in commerce, and, most importantly, in our daily lives. These remarks should become self-evident as we take firstly a brief look at the broad socioeconomic problem at hand.

Part I
The Third World Question

Spontaneity and chance are posterior to intelligence and nature.

Aristotle, *Physica, Bk. II, 6*

1
The Rich Nations and the Poor Nations Revisited: A Macroeconomic Overview

Of 900,000 million children under the age of 15 now living on the planet, 90 percent of them live in the Third World. [1] Meanwhile, global gross national product (GNP) by the fourth quartile of the twentieth century is said to have reached $6,000 billion. Of this amount, the North accounted for $5,000 billion. The balance ($1,000 billion) is shared by the entirety of the Third World, including the so-called rich Arab OPEC countries.

The figures become even more pertinent when we recognize that average per capita income in a number of Third World countries has stagnated, for all practical purposes, at levels already described as a condition of absolute poverty. The so-called poverty belt will soon encompass about 1 billion members of the human family, a family increasingly at odds with itself as the rich get ostensibly richer and the poor, poorer.

Moreover, economic growth rates for a large part of the developing world could well decline for the balance of the next decade. This means that absolute poverty will become more absolute unless adequate measures are taken to reverse the trend. Likewise our banking systems will continue to fragment as trade and financial flows contract.

For the moment, however, the measures being taken to reverse the trend seem to have had the opposite effect. In fact, one might argue that the New International Economic Order, as presently structured, serves to underdevelop a significant portion of the world's population. The underdevelopment is both *psychological* and *material*. Psychological in the sense that local values are almost systematically ignored

3

in the race for economic take-off. Material in the sense that growth favors a relatively small minority of the Third World population.

The results are at once concrete and significant. Of $1,000 billion in Third World gross national product, more than 70 percent has accrued to less than 80 percent of the Third World population. [2] This gap is not circumstantial. It would appear that the inspiration as well as the structure of existing growth models encourages inequality of income, a separation of life-style, and perhaps more importantly, a fragmentation of value systems. The cost of this fragmentation has yet to manifest itself in its full dimension upon the world stage. In not a few instances, relative poverty has become absolute even for those participating in the modern sector of many Third World economies.

For example, during Pakistan's most successful development period (the 1960s), unemployment increased, while real wages in the industrial sector—the only sector where development was taking place —actually declined by about one-third. [3] But Pakistan, with a population at the time of about 160 million people, is only one example among many. Over the past two decades, Brazil, Latin America's largest economy, has experienced an average annual growth rate of 6.8 percent. This growth rate would indicate a remarkable success in development planning. As it turns out, however, 90 percent of Brazil's newly created wealth has accrued for the benefit of the richest 10 percent of the population. [4] The bottom 40 percent, the marginal men, have been, in the language of development theory, bypassed. That is, they have become just a little more destitute.

Similar anomalies exist in other large, newly industrialized economies (NICs). A sample listing would include Egypt, India, Mexico, Nigeria, the Philippines, Saudi Arabia, and Zaire, to name but a few of the more strategic Third World powers. Both capitalist and centrally planned development models have led to serious economic dislocation. At the same time, the safety net provided by traditional value systems and by indigenous social structures has been swept away by the fiat of national leaders anxious to accept Northern patronage coincident with Northern development theory, money, and arms.

In the end, even where the development models have succeeded on their own terms, the results have been growing unemployment, poorly conceived foreign debt, urban sprawl, reduced agricultural production, a breakdown in social values, and, in some instances, national disintegration. In other words, economic growth without development. In fact, when one gets behind the confusing figures on growth rates and debt, one discovers that for about two-thirds of humanity, the increase in per capita income in real terms over the past three decades has been, on balance, nil. This last observation comes from Mahbub ul Haq, made when he served under Robert McNamara as director of policy planning at the World Bank.[5]

The exceptions to the rule are few: South Korea, Taiwan, possibly Israel, the Ivory Coast, and Panama. In the case of these smaller economies, trade-led growth has been supported by enormous per capita foreign resource transfers, undertaken largely for political reasons. In addition, each country has been given exceptional First World market access, again for political reasons. Thus, the development model has been transferred into fairly homogeneous societies with the attention, the patience, and the sacrifice not likely to be made available to larger, more heterogeneous nation states.

For instance, over the past 20 years, Taiwan and the Ivory Coast have increased their export volume by more than 1000 percent. If India were to export cheap labor-intensive products on the same order as Taiwan, or if West Africa were to export agricultural goods on the same order as the Ivory Coast, then the North would be awash with unwanted imports. In other words, our global development models and associated finance have worked in a sort of test-tube environment. Where they have not worked, the results have been pernicious for some and clearly tragic for others.

We might argue that development theory (and action) stands at an impasse. At the center, the advanced economies grow, but with little real value—mostly arms, aerospace, government employment, and growing trade wars, which could test the very foundation of existing political order. On the periphery, the latecomers, the newly industrialized countries, face a sort of de facto bankruptcy as foreign debt payments sap remaining strength out of faltering domestic economies. In the Fourth World, development has meant falling below a subsistence wage in the so-called struggle for life, a struggle worsened by our planning models.

By example, we should recall that farming remains the chief source of income for nearly two-thirds of the world's population and especially for those living within the poverty belt. Ironically, among the rural poor, in the Fourth World participation within the international economy has meant growing hunger, sometimes unto starvation. Cash crops earmarked for Northern markets have replaced local food production. Remaining food production has been monetized, with the terms of trade as well as with the transportation networks shifting in favor of the urban population. As a result, in a number of countries, global economic integration according to Northern models has served to worsen the conditions of poverty rather than to ameliorate what we have termed, perhaps polemically, "The Second Holocaust." North-South economic development has resulted in the irony of the Third World producing nonedible cash crops such as cocoa, soybean, coffee, rubber, jute, manioc, and tapioca in exchange for more expensive, not-always-available imported foodstuffs such as wheat, corn, or rice financed at subsidized rates. Even worse from a structural point of view, the terms of trade have been negotiated directly between farm export lobbies in the North working closely with urban interests in the South—to the overall disadvantage of the rural poor. The sorry results (flagrant and widespread malnutrition) were not intended. The results, however, are consistent with the development models that have been proposed by the international development community and with the underlying logic on which they are based.

By 1980, the worldwide food crisis had become sufficiently awesome that a U.S. presidential commission on the dynamics of hunger sounded the alarm: "World grain trade is so tightly integrated," says the report, "that a crop failure anywhere in the world may adversely affect the most remote villages . . . the lives of 800 million estimated to be living in absolute poverty are put at risk every time there is a drought in Kansas, or floods in India, or a late frost in the Ukraine."[6]

This warning makes reference to only one of the variables affecting Third World food security, namely, the most distant, that is, natural catastrophe. Over the past three decades, however, other variables have had a more immediate impact on infant mortality rates, on genetic insufficiencies, on epidemic disease, and on related tragedies associated with malnutrition. These variables include deteriorating terms of trade, volatility of bank credit, commodity speculation, uncontrolled foreign exchange movements, and the charity, *in extremis*, of private volunteer organizations concerned with the problem of starvation. In sum, the major variables are human rather than endowed by nature.

The same argumentation applies equally well to other fundamental human needs such as minimal shelter, affordable health care, and a relevant educational system. In a word, the problem of Third World poverty cannot be reduced in its totality nor in its sweep and its density to the simple mechanical formula: "overfertile woman and underfertile soil."

Carelessly the Third World seems to be swapping its cultural identity and a goodly portion of its physical wealth against high-rise buildings with elevators, sophisticated medical equipment for the urban elite, and know-how (on credit) that mirrors the image of distant civilizations. For those without access to modern services, however, economic progress has meant little more than a plastic washbasin, synthetic clothing, temporary shelter, mounting foreign debt and, from time to time, a food handout at prices fixed by central government. Thus, the exchange North-South seems to be one way, i.e., in the direction of future financial, social, and political upheaval. As a result, the once acclaimed Revolution of Rising Expectations could become, in the near term, a revolution of a different nature.

For after three or more decades of intense Third World development effort, economic growth appears to have enriched the rich and the powerful at the risk of pauperizing not all but a vast number of the "coping" poor. In a related sense our finance and trading systems have become distended, while makeshift, new Third World credit is proposed not simply as an inadequate palliative to poverty but in an open effort to bail out our largest multinational banks. The taxpayer, meanwhile, is being asked, in the words of California Congressman Jerry Lewis simply to "pay and pray."[7] Debt relief and debt reschedulings (private and public) since mid-1982 have exceeded $150 billion. This amount does not include the related Continental Illinois Bank bailout, another $8 billion dollars plus. Unhappily if nothing is done to change our development model then both the payments and the problem could represent only the first installment of an indefinite, long-term credit plan to save a fundamentally insolvent program.

The origin of the dilemma can be found in the worldview that inspires post-World War II development theory. In turn, the theory makes comprehensible subsequent development models. The models themselves shape foreign aid and multinational banking policy. In short, method follows the logic of a specific economic paradigm. What is this paradigm and how does the logic manifest itself within the context of our global economic system? The paradigm, the model, and the method are interrelated in the following manner.

2
The Origin of the Development Process: The Paradigm

At the end of World War II, the international economic order was constructed around a seemingly obvious, well-understood law: the Law of Comparative Advantage. Simply put, the theory (not a law) tells us that the specialization of land, labor, and capital should track comparative economic advantage proposed presumably by nature. In this way, growth follows the simplicity of the economic imperative. The Law of Comparative Advantage subsequently has played a determinant role in the shaping of aid policy, trade flows, and, ultimately, in the complexion of bank credit to the Third World.

As we know, at the end of World War II, most of the so-called economic advantages were lodged firmly—where they remain—in the hands of the North. Thus, it should hardly come as a surprise that the new global compact has served to promote structural disequilibrium among a large portion of the human race. This disequilibrium is manifest not simply between the North and the South but, more precisely, between the North, its mimetic agents in the South, and the vast majority of urban and rural poor, that is, the new "indigent population."

Ironically, the advantages at play (the economic imperatives) have very little to do with natural endowment, with labor costs, or even with the manufacturing process itself. To prove this latter point, we simply would note that most industrial components enjoy a life cycle of about ten years, based on commonly accepted amortization tables. Hence the Law of Comparative Advantage is not an economic "Law" but rather a political theory both in inspiration and in application. For real advantage consists of what the economists, in almost platonic fashion, blithely call "the invisibles." The invisibles include technology,

8

shipping, communications, insurance, distribution, markets of scale, and, most importantly, *finance*, the heart of the economic system. Accordingly, advantage turns out to be almost wholly organizational, that is, political before it is economic. As a result, comparative advantage naturally plays into the hands of the powerful—for better and for worse.

In sum, the economic imperative established at the end of World War II has fooled policy planners. The Law of Comparative Advantage has served to shield, if not perpetuate, structural imbalances within our international orders. As a result, the rich have gotten richer (not a bad thing in itself) and the poor, poorer. This is despite sustained and costly efforts to arrest the drift toward threshold imbalances.

Indeed, one might even argue that absolute poverty has been induced by our reasoning process. Obviously, this was not meant to be the case. The results, however, inevitably follow the logic of the model. The theory of comparative advantage is taken from an eighteenth-century worldview that assumes conflict rather than cooperation, competition rather than reason as the primary (and certainly the most efficient) source of motivation: the start, as it were, of the development process. As we shall see in more detail in Part II this worldview was first schematized by Thomas Hobbes and is based on the proposition "That the condition of mere Nature . . . is Anarchy and the condition of Warre."[1]

Beginning with David Ricardo, the father of economic science, economists have subsequently domesticated the eighteenth-century worldview by proposing that each person and each nation produce according to his particular advantage. Economic advantage is simplified into quantitative terms, with international market prices serving as the final arbiter for what constitutes value.

The Law of Comparative Advantage has shaped post-World War II development policy—and the finance that follows, at least on a North-South basis. Unfortunately, it is precisely on the North-South axis that dissymmetry between the weak and the strong is greatest and where competition risks, in practice, to be less than loyal, balanced, or productive, particularly for the disenfranchised.

In other words, in devising a new Global Compact, the international development community at the end of World War II looked backward rather than forward and reconstructed for the twenty-first century what already had been constructed (and destructed) for the eighteenth and the nineteenth. Since 1945, the North simply has displaced the model to include the globe in its entirety.

Despite the worrisome results of three decades of development, the Law of Comparative Advantage remains fundamentally unchallenged by those financiers primarily responsible for the development process. For example, following his appointment in 1982 as president of the World Bank, A. W. Clausen addressed a prestigious group of commercial bankers assembled in Vancouver for the annual International Monetary Conference in the following manner:

> Fortunately, the actions we can take together to benefit people in the developing countries stand to benefit the rest of the world, too. Prosperity in the developing countries means higher exports and value-for-money imports for the industrial countries—more jobs and lower inflation. Prosperity in the developing countries also makes for more secure trade in crucial resources and, in general, a stabler and less troubled world.[2]

Mr. Clausen, in making an articulate appeal to enlightened self-interest, defends as he defines the international economic order based on the Law of Comparative Advantage. For the past 40 years, this law has been applied with unfailing vigor across the better part of the Southern hemisphere. The results Mr. Clausen himself describes with careful nuance: "In summary, economic performance of developing countries has been varied but, in more places than not, it's been *dynamic*."[3] [my italics]. The very term "dynamic" fits the mechanical, linear nature of the Western world's reasoning process since the eighteenth century, a reasoning process that has reached the absolute limits of its usefulness. For dynamic, is not a synonym for development. Clausen continues:

> Just now, the economic resilience of the developing countries is being tested again—perhaps as never before. Slow growth—if not actually a recession—in the global economy is costing them export revenues. The index of commodity prices fell last year to the lowest level in real terms since 1945.[4]

As a banker by training, Mr. Clausen is not given to overstatement. This "lowest level in real terms" hides, so to speak, the real problem. With a bit more urgency, we might argue that the division of land, labor, and capital has led, all too often, to the marginalization of the disadvantaged. This marginalization of a geopolitical dimension is what we should be calling "underdevelopment," that is, a regressive evolution in the quality of life—in some instances, the regression of life itself. This regressive evolution would seem patterned within our global orders, our logic, our life-styles, and our consumption habits.

A DOUBLE STANDARD

Ironically, our method of development has served to "envelop" the Third World in an economic process that the advanced economies themselves are able to escape when necessary. Indeed, the specialization of labor and of the productive process exists primarily between the rich and the poor and not between the rich countries themselves. Competition in the North takes place among fairly equal partners according to carefully defined ground rules. As a result, North-North competition is reasonably balanced and minimal harmony respected.

For example, every major industrial power in the West, including Japan, maintains an important and productive agricultural base as well as a reasonably integrated manufacturing capacity. In order to protect this agricultural base, the developed economies in the West collectively spend about $35 billion a year on direct and indirect domestic price support of importable primary commodities. This compares with about $28 billion per year in Overseas Development Assistance or foreign aid.[5]

In manufacturing, the member states of the Western Alliance maintain tariffs on imports between themselves at a rate of about 50 percent less than tariffs on manufactured imports from the Third World.[6]

Perhaps more revealing, by the end of the 1970s, the Third World earned some $30 billion from the export of their 12 major commodities (excluding oil). After processing in the First World, these same goods were sold on world markets at an estimated value of some $200 billion.[7] The difference ($170 billion) represented "value added" in favor of Northern enterprise. The chocolate in a chocolate bar, for example, represents about 10 percent of its retail value. The producers know this, but given tariff and nontariff barriers, there is little that they can add to value through local processing. The producer's specialization has been reduced to the bean itself.

Hence, the Law of Comparative Advantage (the supposed dynamic of economic progress) might have served to worsen the conditions of poverty rather than to reverse them. On the periphery, the latecomers, the newly industrialized countries, recognize the real cost of their dependence: a mountain of foreign debt, a dissatisfied labor force, and worse, a loss of cultural identity. Balance has given way to an economic theory that hides an alien worldview, alien to local culture and certainly alien to any rational, that is, human definition, of the term "development." Among the poorest of the poor, the human condition risks to slip below tolerance levels of human survival, causing some thoughtful First World analysts to recommend that the Fourth World isolate itself against outside economic interests. Thus, the separation between the rich and the poor, between the West and the Third World, could become complete, a manifest denial of hope in man's common destiny and of order in our global systems financial, economic, and social.

Yet the Law of Comparative Advantage has served—and continues to serve—a more insidious purpose than merely freezing existing advantage in favor of the powerful, or worse, exaggerating existing discrepancies. More fundamentally, the law rationalizes production as the primary goal of the economic process. It is here that we come face to face with the treachery of the logic at its starting point.

The Law of Comparative Advantage accepts production as the end, the telos of economic life, not its start. In the final analysis, our international economic order (and disorder) springs from an intellectual confusion between mechanical cause and finality—at least, North-South, that is, production precedes purpose. By extension, production escapes the notion of measure, of limit, and, finally, of meaning.

The theory of comparative advantage, with its single-minded concern for output, denies a more necessary preoccupation with a way of life, with the totality of a culture, with goals. The emphasis concentrates on quantity over quality, on production at the expense of purpose, and on specialization at the risk of sacrificing self-respect. Work exceeds judgment rather than vice versa. In fact, work becomes annex to human life.

To simplify, we accept as quite normal the concentration of the synthetic fibers industry in South Korea as a replacement for cotton textile production in Africa. The comparative advantage of one is understood, at least in the long run, as an advantage to all. The means justify the end: the end is production. In the meanwhile, it makes only partial difference if indigenous African populations are marginalized or if synthetic fiber in a tropical climate represents a real substitute for cotton. But fibers represent a sort of feigned caricature of a much more serious dilemma. As we argued earlier, the substitution of imported cash crops for local food production represents to quite credible observers the single most important source of malnutrition in the Third World today.[8] Our development model could have condemned a portion of the human family to contrived hunger and to premature death.

Yet the single-minded emphasis on production and specialization at the cost of development should not divert our attention away from a long-term dilemma equally important to that of growing impoverishment among the weakest of the weak. Specialization of the productive process among the so-called successful Third World countries—Taiwan, Korea, the Ivory Coast, Egypt, Cameroon, and others—might well have brought on a cultural pauperization, the results of which we are unable to calculate.

A sort of dualism or split personality has been established at the national level of many Third World countries. Local production has virtually nothing to do with local consumption. Accordingly, there exists no subjective nor objective relationship between what is produced and what is used. This dissymmetry is even more obvious among certain oil-producing nations such as Saudi Arabia, Indonesia, Nigeria, and, more recently, Mexico. Dissymmetry at the national level oftentimes manifests itself as an acute case of schizophrenia: e.g., Iran.

Some development theorists have referred to the problem at hand as one of "economic and/or financial extroversion."[9] The extroversion, however, goes further and deeper and might best be described as cultural, even ontological in nature. It is this ontological extroversion that we should be calling "underdevelopment." For underdevelopment does not mean poverty per se. Poverty can be justly described in terms of inadequate shelter, structural malnutrition, poor health care, and, more fundamentally, the lack of a sociopolitical consensus capable of sharing these problems. Instead, underdevelopment represents, as it were, a metaphysical loss of footing.

Poverty takes place within the context of a specific spatio-temporal setting with which the poor are familiar, although to which they are seldom resigned. Underdevelopment is introduced and represents a deliberated mental blackout. Underdevelopment occurs when economic and material structures bypass intellectual and spiritual values. Poverty is an economic condition; underdevelopment, a loss of identity. Our economic models would seem to introduce this loss of identity to the Third World in the name of development by free trade.

FREE TRADE AND ECONOMIC EXTROVERSION

One does not argue, of course, that international trade is wrong per se nor that the theory of comparative advantage makes no sense. Quite obviously, trade and international commerce based on specific national endowments serve to bridge cultures, even conflicting ideologies, as well as to fill gaps in the supply/demand equation. After all, pepper does not grow in the Northern hemisphere nor walnuts in

Upper Volta. But this argument only serves to sidestep the more critical issue of development. International trade, like growth in output, should be understood as a by-product of the development process not as its objective. When trade and production based on the theory of comparative advantage become the goal of global development policy, then the necessary balances are destroyed. Harmony at the national, regional, and global levels becomes an impossibility in theory and in fact.

Ironically, as we claim to be entering the post-industrial age, civilization has submitted itself to an eighteenth-century economic imperative based on the Law of Comparative Advantage. This manifestly one-dimensional imperative transits our development models, aid policy, and commercial bank lending practice in that order. For the moment, suffice it to note that both the imperative and the law fit perfectly our prevailing worldview and, by extension, our notion of cause.

In terms of our worldview, advantage is exploited rather than shared by virtue of what we consider to be a hostile universe, hostile not only in relationship to man but hostile at the very roots of reality itself. On this basis, modern man, in good conscience, is able to wage an unlimited war not only on the environment but on himself and on his species. We agree with Hegel when he remarks that contradiction is at the root of all movement and of all life. *Homo faber* has come to adore two principles simultaneously: force, and its opposite, counterforce. Progress becomes identified with power only. The source of this aberration is not complicated, but it is abstract. In terms of our notion of cause, the "how" replaces the "why" as the primary inspiration for growth. The result: hyperproduction in the North and growing misery in the South. The Latins would call the situation from which we presently suffer, "magnus chaos," an enormous gap.

Should the gap continue to widen or our logic persist, we risk to be swallowed up, each of us, not only in the second holocaust, but in the first as well. For our *"know-how"* has clearly outstripped our *"know-why."* Comparative advantage determines product and personhood.

In the call for a New International Economic Order, the South implicitly has endorsed the productivist economic models proposed by the North.[10] With few exceptions, the new elite in the Third World has yet to question the overall *raison d'être* of the program. The South perceives its development options as limited between private or state production according to imported definitions of development. The same can be said for the logic that underscores these modes of production.

Accordingly, the development models which have been proposed will continue to prosper until such time as the system cracks. Based on current debt figures, on growth rates, and on the indicators coming from Amnesty International, that time might well be upon us. Development has come to resemble that "horrible pagan god who wished to drink nectar only from the skull of his fallen enemies." Development has meant the wholesale destruction of existing life-styles in the name of production and free trade. Production overtakes purpose, while free trade separates the strong from the weak, the living from the dead.

In conclusion, our existing global compact distills into economic formula a quite specific worldview that modern man, particularly the politicians, the bankers, the aid people, and their constituencies, have yet to put under cross-examination. Production has become not only the goal of the development process but the single measure of its success. Production can best be augmented by taking care of one's comparative advantage in the struggle for life.

In the end, not only does development become synonymous with output and with competition but output is thought to be a function of natural endowment, of power, of historical process, of the past rather than the future. At the end of the twentieth century, we remain blocked within the confines of our existing paradigm. The growing gap between the rich and the poor is justified morally by a precise and arbitrary premise on which subsequent method and action and finance depend.

The theory of comparative advantage makes comprehensible subsequent development models. As we shall see, in each model, development policy reflects a worldview where advantage rather than thought, force rather than design, mechanical rather than final cause determines our policy options. Meaning becomes subordinate to action; reason, to advantage; and a sense of proportion or of limit, to unlimited power.

The 1983 (OECD) *Report on Development Cooperation* captures, in a single paragraph, the essence of the case. The argument is unambiguous:

> Trade is also a driving force for growth and progress. Trade opportunities and the dismantling of obstacles to trade are a strong stimulus to seek out new sources of supply and markets and hence to invest and to develop economic activity. Trade goes hand in hand with competition; and competition is the most effective spur to progress.[11]

Ironically, this single-minded preoccupation with production, with competition, and with trade rather than with development has served to separate rather than to integrate our global economic orders. Indeed, the logic tends to weaken the parts at the expense of the whole. According, the whole is in peril.

THE POLITICS OF DEVELOPMENT

As the First World shrinks to less than 10 percent of the world's population, development efforts (and associated finance) will need to shift from production to purpose, from competition to minimal cooperation, from comparative advantage to coexistence. Without more coherence in our global orders, one party's gain will continue to be another party's loss. The gap between the rich and the poor, between the hyperdeveloped and the underdeveloped will continue to widen. The same is true for the gaps in the balance sheets of our major multinational banks.

In order to bring about a shift in development policy, development specialists will need to operate from a different premise and with a different set of intellectual tools, both of which presume a wider range of policy objectives. The premise must posit *homo rationalis* as the center and not the end product of his universe. The intellectual tools for dealing with *homo rationalis* are not the social sciences, including economics, but, as we will argue, the art of politics (See Part II). Politics as an art does not assume that man as a social animal can be reduced to a set of scientific laws that are at once necessary, universal, and unchanging. Politics assumes value judgment at the heart of all political order. In this manner, the world, instead of being determined, is chosen. And this brings us to the question of objectives.

Development objectives should be recognized as wholly political in nature rather than as economic. In addition to survival, the objectives include the real invisibles, that is, a sense of proportion, an acknowledgment that human values precede price value and a conviction that production, like productivity and solvency, ultimately springs from cooperation, choice, and intelligence rather than from conflict. The North should emphasize these values rather than deny them at the heart of its global compact. Based on these values, means cannot be confused with ends, production with development, tyranny with civil government.

Yet, for the moment, mankind still believes that production means progress and that productivity alone can erase poverty. We seem trapped, as it were, in the intellectual machinery, the nuts and bolts, the steam and vapor, left to us by our immediate forefathers. Our minicomponents do not hide the logic. They simply augment the risks. Our technology makes more subtle the worldview in which we are confined. Steam has been replaced by the atom. Our goals, however, remain the same. Only the danger has increased.

As a result, it is not an overstatement to say that world development policy, along with the attendant banking system, has reached a figurative dead-end street. Beyond, however, lies not the unknown, a reasonable challenge for humanity, but rather a series of convulsions both within and outside of our existing economic orders. These convulsions would seem integrated, as it were, within our current method of problem solving. Accordingly, it remains to change the method. A brief review of recent development history might convince us of this latter necessity. As we shall see, our current dilemma, a sort of economic Armageddon, did not just happen. Our plight has been designed both in theory and in structure. Likewise, the structure has a specific historic setting. The setting is the United Nations and its various agencies, especially the World Bank and the International Monetary Fund (IMF). The key players are hidden behind their theories, their delegations, their banking networks and, ultimately, behind their worldview.

3
Three Decades of Global Development: From Concept to Concrete

The First United Nations Development Decade was ushered in if not by fiat then with a figurative drum, with cymbal, and with undaunted optimism. President John F. Kennedy, using the platform of the UN General Assembly, announced in 1961 a new era of global cooperation and development.[1] President Kennedy's development strategy reflected a consensus shared by the Atlantic Community in general. Likewise, the strategy condenses into a whole prevailing views on the causes of Third World poverty and on the methods necessary to bring about a better distribution of the world's wealth.

The causes of Third World poverty were perceived to be first, a lack of money and second, a lack of modern technology. In addition, it was understood that a better distribution of wealth could be brought about by the specialization of the factors of production, land, labor, and capital according to the Law of Comparative Advantage.

The developing countries lacked neither labor nor natural resources. Accordingly, the North would supply capital and technology in return for access to more economic (that is, cheap) labor and land.[2] The proposed marriage was one of manifest self-interest, of generosity, and of hope.

As the plan would have it, the exchange of the factors of production according to existing advantage would at once increase world trade, provide for larger markets—North as well as South—and, most importantly, bring the Third World into the mainstream of Northern economic activity. The overall objective was to increase world economic activity (output) and thereby alleviate Third World poverty.

18

Not only did there appear to be a happy convergence in the factors of production. Equally important, there was a convergence of political interests and a successful model on which to formulate development policy.

By 1960, the industrial capacity of Europe had largely recovered from the unprecedented devastation of World War II. In fact, by 1965 industrial capacity, in not a few sectors, would begin to exceed overall Western market demand. This so-called "miracle" of post-war reconstruction was brought about through planning, know-how and money that now was to be applied southward.

We might do well to recall the major features or mechanism that produced the so-called economic miracle in Western Europe, a miracle the end of which we are unable as of today to judge. Firstly, of course, there was the Marshall Plan. In an expression of unprecedented generosity and enlightened self-interest, the United States transferred abroad, between 1949 and 1952, capital and services equivalent to nearly $22.5 billion, or some 4.5 percent of overall GNP. These bilateral transfers were reinforced by the flow of private capital from the United States to Western Europe.

Second, Western Europe set out to create what now constitutes by value the single largest trading block in the world, the European Economic Community (EEC). Coincident with the development of the EEC, the United States and Western Europe negotiated a reduction of tariff and nontariff barriers within the Atlantic Community as a whole. Negotiations eventually were institutionalized under the General Agreement on Tariffs and Trade (GATT), now a permanent UN Commission located in Geneva, Switzerland.

Third, in order to augment as well as to protect capital and trade flows both within and between the European Community and North America, a third pillar was added to the edifice of post-World War II development planning. The third pillar became known as the Bretton Woods institutions and includes the World Bank and the International Monetary Fund. With the United States as the largest single shareholder, both organizations played a key role in the reconstruction of the post-war economy—the World Bank through project lending and the IMF through the swapping of international currency reserves for trade purposes.

Thus, experience indicated that the problem of development was largely technical in nature, one of amassing the right combination of variables—mostly money, markets of scale, and modern technology—in order to reach takeoff into sustained economic growth.

At the start, however, of the First UN Development Decade the happy convergence between interest in larger world markets for surplus industrial goods and method were only two elements that influenced First World development efforts. The final and perhaps the key factor was clearly geopolitical in nature. Indeed, by 1961, France and Great Britain had largely completed their pullback from colonial empire. There existed widespread recognition in the West, firstly that the former colonial powers owed a debt to their ex-colonies and secondly that a potential political vacuum could be filled by Soviet design.

Put differently, at the moment of President Kennedy's UN General Assembly address, development had become a clear-cut economic and political imperative. The means for Third World development were, with minor nuance, to follow those already employed for the reconstruction of Western Europe. The personnel necessary for the task were available from the Marshall Plan, from the World Bank, and from the foreign offices of the ex-colonial powers, Britain and France. Thus the symmetry between the reconstruction of Western Europe and the Third World was nearly complete. It sufficed to transfer the method, the model, the machinery, and the money.

The method consisted of the Law of Comparative Advantage. The model was the industrial one already established in the North. The machinery consisted of the World Bank, the IMF, GATT, and a number of export guarantee agencies. The money was to come from the individual member states of the OECD, or, that failing, from the world's major multinational banks, which in fact, is what happened.

At the time, few people were prepared to admit that the Law of Comparative Advantage between the rich and the poor might possibly turn the development process quickly into a parody. Nor was it anticipated that the production model, when proposed on a turnkey basis, would break, in the Third World, the necessary linkages between the past and the future. Finally, no one projected that most Third World countries would borrow abroad not as much money as they needed but rather as much money as was available on the inflated international capital markets.

The new password was "development"; the means, money; the method, comparative advantage; and the goal, production or output within the context of Northern industrial models. Thus, means and goals became indistinguishable one from the other. The result: a degree of induced destitution and bankruptcy never known in the history of mankind. Some have called this dual problem the result of progress.[3]

THE FIRST UN DEVELOPMENT DECADE: A BRIEF HISTORY

Following President Kennedy's 1961 UN General Assembly address, the United Nations, later in that same year, voted a formal resolution naming the 1960s as the First Development Decade. With Western support, development goals were identified and ground rules endorsed, as President Kennedy had put it, "to accelerate progress toward self-sustaining growth of the economies of all independent nations."[4] Self-sustained growth, however, became unsustainable economic extroversion.

The stated objective of international development efforts for the First Development Decade was defined as reaching a growth target for the Third World of 5 percent per year by 1970. Development, of course, was to be measured in terms of GNP, the standard economic yardstick. Within this narrow definition of development, no sectorial growth objectives were established, for example, industry versus agriculture, versus services, versus government administration. With the advantage of hindsight, we can say with confidence that during the First Development Decade, development or progress was associated unilaterally with smokestacks, steel, glass and cement. In like manner, distribution of growth across the economy was thought to resolve itself automatically as overall economic activity in the modern sector increased. At its origins, then, product instead of proportion, industrial production instead of balance, set the pace for Third World development policy.

In order to reach the 5 percent growth target cited above, the First World was to undertake the annual transfer of development capital to the Third World equivalent to 1 percent of combined First World GNP. The Kennedy administration was one of the first to endorse this objective, originally proposed by the World Council of Churches. The burden itself seemed fitting, particularly for those countries, England and France, whose ex-colonies made up the majority of newly emerging Third World states. Thus, the 1 percent aid target enjoyed rather wide public support in the North and served as a sort of post-colonial catharsis.

The capital transfers in question were to consist of tied export credits, of bilateral foreign assistance (grants), and of loans through multilateral agencies. In turn, these transfers would serve the triple purpose of promoting Northern exports, of utilizing the competitive factors of production in the South, and of spreading wealth. By the end of the First Development Decade, the first two objectives had been realized. North-to-South trade increased to $58 billion in 1970 from \$28 billion in 1960. Likewise, the overall GNP growth target of 5 percent had been realized—to nearly everyone's surprise! All of the growth, however, had taken place in the industrial, in the mining, or in the service sectors of the economies in question.

In the meanwhile, the third objective, that of spreading wealth, had not occurred. International monetary reserves continued to accrue largely in favor of the North.[5] The trading profits that filtered down to the South accumulated principally to burgeoning central governments and, through these governments, to the powerful or to the new elite. The process of nation building all too often turned out to be but a caricature of political models taken, like arms and money, from the West or from the Soviet bloc countries. This same caricature spilled over into investment patterns and consumer habits that only the rich could either profit from or could afford. With considerable and bitter hindsight, the World Bank subsequently noted that the benefits of economic development do not trickle down automatically in less than egalitarian societies, especially in poor countries with only a masked sense of nationhood. Nor do the benefits trickle forward to future generations.

Worse yet, given the industrial model that had been pursued during the First Development Decade, the domestic terms of trade shifted against the largest part of the Third World population, that is, against the poorly organized rural population producing the food. As a result, food production per capita actually decreased in the developing world between 1963 and 1970, with but minor exception.[6] In other words, while monetized GNP was going up, the same could be said of hunger. While ambitious GNP growth targets were being met, abject poverty was on the increase. Indeed, the confusion of means with goals, of economic rationalization with survival, resulted in the irony of the international development community obtaining its GNP growth targets while, at the same time, creating a human tragedy of uncommon parallel. This tragedy continues unabated today throughout the better part of the Third World.

Lower domestic food production has been accompanied by the inevitable exodus of the rural poor to the urban centers, an exodus associated with a breakdown in social fabric, widespread destitution among the landless poor, political foment, insurrection, and, eventually, a costly intervention by one of the two superpowers, causing the entire schema to turn in a vortex of increasing violence. The examples form the rule: Cambodia, Ethiopia, Haiti, El Salvador, Nicaragua, Angola, Chile, Afghanistan, Zaire, Iran, Syria, Liberia, Iraq. And how many prospective candidates are on the list? Brazil, Morocco, Indonesia, or possibly even Egypt and/or Saudi Arabia, where fundamentalist insurrections have come within a short distance of success.

Most ironically, political leadership in the majority of Third World countries, like their respective sponsors in the North, including the banks, remain mesmerized by output and production, by GNP growth figures, 5 percent, 3.4 percent, 7 percent, and the like. In fact, Third World development planning in any number of countries might be characterized as more First World than similar plans in the North, rather like Russia just prior to its revolution of 1917. Output overshadows meaning. Economic momentum is propelled by (and receives most of its force from) a chronic case of mimesis, reinforced by an abundance of careless money.

Not only has First World development theory been accepted with little nuance in the Third World but, equally important, so have the specific development models that derive from this method. As we now shall attempt to demonstrate, both the method and the models derive from the identical premise. Thus, before moving to the Second Development Decade, a review of our development models (mechanistic in inspiration) will enable us to appreciate more fully the intellectual structure, the logic in which the development community is currently embedded. For the mistakes of the First Development Decade have been extended into the Second and the Third. Meanwhile, as the mistakes accumulated, so did the money.

4
From Method
to Model:
The Big Push

We might do well to recall that at the beginning of the First Development Decade, the First World already had entered, with great fascination and enthusiasm, what we now routinely call the "Space Age." Both the United States and the Soviet Union were prepared to land a man on the moon. The technicians had predicted that the job could be done—and they were right. Accomplishment of the task was largely a question of time, of money, and of the refinement of existing technology. In other words, a question of choice, not of method.

Likewise, with similar fascination and enthusiasm, development strategy was being formulated in space-age terminology. Unfortunately, so were the goals and the expectations. In the latter case, however, the prognostications of development strategists, bankers and their regulators turned out to miss the mark altogether. For hidden behind the rhetoric of the First Development Decade stood the assumption that development was a mechanical problem, that is, technical, financial or economic in nature, rather than a human and political challenge of much more subtle and complex dimension. Put differently, there existed little appreciation for the fact that development policy demands a range of objectives, some of which are clearly outside the reach of economics as a policy instrument. Thus, it should not come as a surprise that the model for Third World development was capturing false or irrelevant information.

Development became associated with a move across a specific linear trajectory. The central question was posed in the following manner: How does one get from A to B to C, from a gross national product per capita of less than $200 to an annual per capita GNP of

$600? At $600, inequality of opportunity was thought to wash out of the system.

Based on this last assumption the Noble Prize winner for economic science, Arthur Lewis, backed a growth model first articulated at the World Bank. He proposed a "big push." "In planning growth," Lewis explains, "one looks first to two or three industries whose rapid expansion is going to give drive to the rest of the system."[1] The purpose of the "big push" was to create as broad an industrial base as possible. In this way, a new economic order would replace old balances, what Lewis referred to as "underdevelopment equilibrium."

Arthur Lewis was less predisposed than most of his colleagues to the imperatives of a global market system. He argued that "infant industries" should be protected by tariff legislation, at least in the early stages of development. The model, of course, assumed an important deployment of capital. The thrust or capital necessary to push the economy off the launching pad would come in the form of private and public investment, largely from abroad. Limited domestic savings could be harnessed through revised tax policy, or, as turned out to be the case in most Third World economies, by turning the domestic terms of trade against the peasant. The shift in the terms of trade was justified arithmetically by the then famous Kuznets U-Curve, a statistical formula devised originally to describe growth in the developed economies.[2]

In brief, the formula argues that incomes would need to go down —way down if one were already living at the poverty line—before going up. The results of this slide, this roller-coaster effect, can be seen today from downtown Kinashasa to the hinterlands of Brazil.

Experience, of course, quickly demonstrated that capital accumulation alone could not launch the model, even when local industry enjoyed certain natural or contrived competitive advantages. By the mid-1960s, Pakistan, Ghana, Turkey, Egypt, Brazil, and others had undergone the experience and failed. Each country was in the throes of a debt crisis and/or of a change in government.

Some economists already had recognized that a big push in investment was only one element necessary for getting the model into orbit. Hopes were quickly dashed for getting over such obstacles as lack of physical infrastructure, missing cultural incentives, education, land tenure, and the like. One alternative was to ignore them.

The optimism inherent in the big push model was persuasively challenged by the Harvard economist, Albert O. Hirschman. Hirschman enjoyed on-line experience as a development consultant to several

Latin American governments. He proposed a more modest, hard-nosed approach to the thorny problem of Third World development. "Unbalanced growth" or "gaps," he argued, serve as a source of motivation, an "energizing effect," on society as a whole. Governments, to the extent that they participate in the planning process, should provide for "unbalancing" of existing "linkages." The balancing function should come after the fact. Likewise, "It is the role of foreign capital" writes Hirschman, "to enable a country to set out on the paths of unbalanced growth." As a sort of prelude to the debt trap, Hirschman argued that foreign capital seems "better equipped than domestic capital alone to take the first 'unbalancing' steps in growth sequences."[3] —à la Mexico, Argentina, and Brazil. In other words, "big bucks" and "unbalancing" were consciously promoted.

More recently, Herbert Kahn has developed the same theme in a 1979 report from the Hudson Institute. Kahn repeats the metaphor that gaps serve as an engine of growth. He then ingeniously recalls (out of context) John Kennedy's phrase borrowed from Winston Churchill that "a rising tide floats all ships." In his report, *World Economic Development*, Kahn argues that the growing gap between the rich and the poor "is in reality a force for transferring the benefits of economic development to the poor."[4] Kahn mirrors the *mis*concept not only of his predecessors in development thinking but of the politicians, technicians, and bankers that have followed.

During the first two Development Decades, the development process as well as foreign aid policy and bank lending practice fell in line with changing development theory and with the models that the theory produced. The "big push" gave way to unbalanced growth, which, in turn, evolved into a more aggressive strategy of "creative destruction." Creative destruction, as a development model, promotes "contrived imbalances" that serve to break the "vicious circle" of poverty. Destruction comes from the outside, from big government or from big allies. The instruments employed include the international aid agencies (the method and the model), multinational banks (the money), and foreign universities (the know-how). Equally important, outside entrepreneurs with new products, new management techniques, and new organizational models arrive to provide the final *coup de grace*. The object of destruction is production according to the Law of Comparative Advantage.

FIVE STEPS TO NOWHERE

The idea of creative destruction, of the big push and of contrived imbalances was initially synthesized by President Kennedy's economic aide and a noted development theorist, Walter W. Rostow. "It is possible," writes Rostow, only a few months prior to President Kennedy's UN address, "to identify all societies in their economic dimensions as lying within one of five categories: the traditional society, the preconditions for takeoff, the takeoff, the drive to maturity, and the age of high mass consumption."[5] Rostow assumes at the heart of his logic (and in the program that follows) that all societies are destined to move from the preconditions for takeoff, across a fixed linear path, into the age of high mass consumption. In a slight change of metaphor, we might conclude (with hindsight) that modern man is moving not into a world of space but rather into a world of things.

Rostow categorizes "traditional society," or the first stage of economic development, as pre-Newtonian, that is, as not capable of manipulating nature. As we shall see, this fateful and costly arrogance springs full born from the seventeenth and eighteenth-centuries, from Bacon, from Descartes, from Hobbes, and from David Hume. Indeed, for Rostow, as for his peers, progress originates in tangible force, in manipulation, in mechanical necessity at the obvious risk of excluding intentionality, that is, wholeness or limit. Naturally progress becomes the domain of the technocrat, the "realist:" he who is able to manipulate nature and the presumed inevitable violent forces that are pitted against man. For Rostow as for his peers, development apparently began with Newton's discovery that the apple falls at a rate proportional to its mass and to that of the earth.

If we wanted of course, to be hasty with Walter Rostow's chronology as well as with his logic, we simply would note that pre-Newtonian society included the Republic of Venice, the Egyptian dynasty of Ramses II, Athens in the third century B.C., Rome under the Republic, and Paris at the construction of Notre Dame. Each of these societies was pre-Newtonian. Each of these societies possessed a slightly different notion of cause, and, by extension, a different definition of nature, its design and purpose. Each of these societies—the Egyptians, the Greeks, the Romans, and the French in the thirteenth century—would oppose the Age of Mass Consumption. For the notion itself includes no concept of limit. As Aristotle cautioned in the so-called golden age of Greek civilization: "There is no ratio in the relation of the infinite to the finite, whereas order always means ratio." (*Physica, Bk. VII*) Without a clear understanding of this principle, we are liable to return to a city without lights, not to mention to an economy without banks. In other words, force without design, leads to what Aristotle called an "infinite plurality," a notion anathema to human reason and to common sense.

In *Fathers and Sons*, Bazarov, the hero of Turgenev's prophetic novel, expresses Rostow's problem differently: "We have nothing to boast about but the sterile knowledge of understanding, up to a certain point the sterility of what exists." Within this sterility resides modern man's most highly esteemed value, namely, force. Turgenev anticipated, by about one hundred years, modern development theory —both North and South—and the crack in the logic. He called it "nihilism."

Rostow's second stage of economic development, "the Preconditions for Takeoff," can be reached when a country enjoys access to the insights of modern technology. Access, the author agrees, also means adaptability of culture, of attitudes, and of political orientation. Subsequent emphasis on technology without limit accounts for much of the economic dislocation that has been experienced to date in Third World development planning. Nasser's Aswan Dam is one of the better (more costly) examples. Zaire's Inga-Shaba transmission line—the longest in the world and practically unused—another. Both projects were built with Northern know-how, tax dollars, bank credits, and material. Both projects represent unmitigated "development disasters." In other words, technology and money are without meaning unless the technology and money in question are reduced to human needs and made proportionate to political value and individual purpose. The planning models, with their one-dimensional emphasis on output, make this marriage between technology, money, and purpose almost impossible. This is doubly true when output follows faithfully —as is usually the case—the contours of comparative advantage.

Our development process seems to admit that the world pursues no end. As a result, technology overwhelms intentionality, and with it, freedom. The dichotomy between technique and freedom, as fatal as it is for man himself, characterizes Third World development policy, its logic, its method, its money, and even its metaphor.

"Take-off," Rostow's Third Stage of Economic Development, occurs when "the forces making for economic progress come to dominate society" so that "growth becomes its normal condition."[6] The intention seems to be in the nature of a leap outside of the earth's gravitational forces—all too often a leap without identifiable objectives.

In order to facilitate the "take-off," Rostow proposes that a "new elite," a new leadership, be created and "given the scope to begin the building of a modern industrial society." A 'new elite' presumes the collapse of the old, a technological euphemism for a radical shift in political power. Should we call this "creative destruction"? In any case, the shift included not only the men but the model as well. "Sociologically," Rostow argues this new elite must—to a degree— "supersede in social and political authority the old land-based elite."[7]

In brief, the South should be prepared to follow the same trajectory or lunar orbit as that covered by the North during the past 200 years of its own development, a strategy that was based on different needs, different resources, and different goals. Rostow continues: "A society predominantly agricultural—with in fact 75 percent or more of its working force in agriculture—must shift to a predominance for industry, communications, and services."[8] This shift in sectorial production becomes (and in fact became) the *sine qua non* condition for take-off.

Hence, "take-off" represents not a space trip into the twenty-first century but rather a mutation into the nineteenth. This mutation we have had the pretension to call "development." Seen, however, from a Third World point of view, the development process can be understood not as a challenge but rather as a condemnation, a condemnation to repeat the success and the errors of others. On this basis, the development process and its horizon look bleak indeed. For the errors of the First World, when repeated in the South, take on added dimension—witness Mexico City, Lagos, Teheran, even Tokyo. *Odium Fati*!

Rostow's fourth stage in the development process, "the Drive to Maturity," is reached when some 18 percent to 20 percent of national income is available for reinvestment in future production. At this stage of development, output, according to the mathematical models then available, should exceed population growth.

More precisely, the argument is based on what was considered to be the empirically reliable Harrod-Domar growth model. The model equates the rate of growth in output to the ratio of savings to income divided by the capital-output ratio. Capital, that mysterious source of wealth, is described, in its classical form, as savings available for productive reinvestment.

Like the Kuznets U-Curve cited earlier, Harrod and Domar took their statistical data (input) from economic experience in the United

States and Europe.[9] Expectations, then, were falsified from the start. Neither input nor output were especially relevant to the manifold sociopolitical "nettles" associated with Third World development.

Nonetheless, along with a number of his contemporaries, Walter Rostow applied the findings of the Harrod-Domar model—and its logic—southward. In the manner of capitalist and of communist development theoreticians alike, Rostow writes: "Increase the rate of investment over 10 percent of national income—and the job is done."[10] The machine is in orbit.

Unfortunately, both for the poor and their bankers, during the First Development Decade, development did not follow a specific trajectory from A to B to C. While the spacecraft enjoyed plenty of thrust, the astronauts aboard lacked direction. Each conceptual model focused on economic growth versus development. Each model presumed that development would occur by mechanical force, by a big push, by creative destruction, or by contrived imbalances to reach takeoff. Each model was oriented around a concept of development synonymous with industrialization per se or, more recently, with the industrialization of agriculture according to Northern example. Finally, each model inclined to the underlying logic and method of the Law of Comparative Advantage, that is, to production for production's sake.

Rostow tells us that as a "pre-condition for take-off," the population at large must be prepared to accept training for . . . and then to operate an economic system whose methods are subject to regular change, and one which also increasingly confines the individual in large, disciplined organizations allocating to him specialized, narrow, recurrent tasks."[11] In a figurative sense, Detroit was to be transferred to downtown Dakar, or to the suburbs of Dar es Salaam. "Take-off" for some undoubtedly could be construed as a second-class subway ride to the fifth stage of economic development, the "Age of High Mass Consumption." In order to buy the fare, the South was to become—as turned out to be the case—the workhouse for labor-intensive manufactures and the supplier of raw material to the North. The North was to shift gradually its own productive apparatus—as is happening— to high technology, services, and leisure. This division of labor—this chasm—inevitably will lead to division of a more traumatic nature. As we shall observe our logic already is spinning back on itself, and with it, our finance and trading systems.

Ironically, the models and the method proposed by the North have been endorsed in the South by national leaders anxious to accomplish in the post-colonial era what the previous masters had apparently failed to do. Perhaps this imitative faculty comes from the fact that most Third World leaders not only were educated in the North but educated at our modern universities in the faculties of the so-called value free social sciences. That is, like so many of our modern managers, they have been formed rather than educated. At the center of this formation, man has become the object rather than the subject of his universe. He is fast becoming that "conscious automata" prescribed by Charles Darwin's prolific and faithful disciple, Thomas Henry Huxley.[12]

In summary, in both the North and the South, decision makers in general, and our political leaders in particular, seem unwilling to admit that development has more to do with cultural evolution than with economics or social engineering and that the principal way of conducting or encouraging this evolution would be by transmitting values, values that will not permit goals to be confused with means nor justice with comparative advantage.

Unless this fundamental transition in thought process can be undertaken, development risks to be—even in a geopolitical sense—a take-off to nowhere. Our development models continue to be pushed from behind without clear definition of goals. Therefore, the models, like the money, are without balance, without proportion, and, finally, without limit.

As with nature, modern man seems capable of manipulating development and the money that backs it up without bringing the process down to his measure, that is, down to his own most fundamental needs as a species.

5
The Second and Third Development Decades

The logic and the subsequent development models proposed for the First Development Decade launched the global economy into the Second and Third. Given the ostensible success of the First Development Decade (a GNP growth rate exceeding 5 percent per annum by 1969), the plan for the 1970s and the 1980s became just a bit more ambitious.

The strategy for the Second UN Development Decade targeted a 6 percent blended growth rate by the end of the 1970s: 8 percent in manufacturing and 4 percent in agriculture.[1] Unlike the First Development Decade, growth targets were divided by sector in order to account for potential trouble spots now appearing on the screen. The trouble spots included: (1) poor nutrition associated not with poverty but with change, (2) the growing dichotomy between the urban elite and the rural poor, a rural poor now migrating toward the cities, (3) the vulnerability of the Third World to a deterioration in the terms of trade, (4) disequilibrium in factor prices, and (5) the lack of protective food production. In other words, in the rush for "take-off," severe problems had arisen which the development models themselves had mistakenly considered as ancillary. In fact, the move from "big push" to "unbalanced growth" to "creative destruction" quite possibly had unbalanced the development process itself. The causation was cumulative and the empirical results all too obvious.

Halfway into the Second Development Decade, the Third World accounted for less than 10 percent of the world's modern economy. The growth in GNP that had been registered over the previous 15 years of development measured neither distribution nor employment nor the full impact of changing agricultural production. A careful review of each category revealed serious problems in development methodology. Distribution was skewed, unemployment had grown in direct proportion to urban migration, and food production had declined as a percentage of overall population.

At the same time, Third World debt going into the models had increased from $7.6 billion in 1960 to $166 billion in 1975, with built-in momentum that was to reach $650 billion by 1980 and nearly $1,000 billion by 1985.[2] Today, default on interest payments alone could collapse a number of our major multinational banks. The increased debt burden was related, of course, to production patterns in the South, which required a growing need for foreign exchange and for foreign technical advisers. These needs were financed by big banks in search of foreign markets and encouraged by their regulators in keeping with the "free trade" model. Meanwhile, the terms of trade, with the exception of soft minerals, had turned against most Third World commodity producers.

By the late 1970s, stagflation in the North had more than redoubled in the South. Particularly squeezed were those already living at the poverty line. Finally, local ownership of the production process itself had shifted to big government, to big business, or to outside investors.

Worse yet, in each of the categories just listed, the tendencies were —and remain—more disturbing than the facts themselves. What we have described as mechanical development models had led away from meeting a number of fundamental social, political, even economic needs. Process had excluded relevant purpose.

Early in the 1970s, certain Third World political leaders, encouraged by a new generation of development theorists, began to question the structure of existing economic and political order. Some strategists recommended a decoupling and others a pulling down of the "poverty curtain" against what was perceived to be a predatory global economic system. Dialogue and action became particularly aggressive; the most obvious example: oil. Dissymmetry had become structural. Likewise, the structure itself began to rupture.

Nonetheless, in keeping with the plan a number of developing countries were able to meet the 8 percent growth rate in manufacturing output programmed for the end of the Second Development Decade. These countries were located largely in the Far East. Not a single country in the developing world met the much more modest 4 percent agricultural growth target. The results should have been anticipated.

However, for two consecutive development decades, the real picture remained hidden behind the logic, the models, and the self-congratulatory rhetoric of the development program itself.

The bottom line reads as follows: From 1960 to 1980, food production within the Third World increased by 2.8 percent per year, while population increased by 2.4 percent annually; that is, food production per person increased by less than 10 percent in 20 years for the developing world as a whole. Nearly all of this growth took place among Second World countries. For the bottom quartile of the world's population—about one billion people—food production increased 2.5 percent during the 1960s and 2 percent during the 1970s. This latter figure translates in the aggregate as an actual decrease in food production of 0.4 percent per person per year during the 1970s.[3] This negative growth rate represents what we have referred to earlier as the "whimper" of mass starvation, as distinguished from the related but very real menace of a nuclear exchange. The two realities go hand in hand for they both assume a common ground of value. The first is simply a fact and the second, a possibility. By the end of the Second Development Decade, it has been estimated that 12 million children under the age of five died prematurely in a single year due to starvation and directly related diseases.[4] Ironically, that same year, 1979, had been declared the UN Year of the Child!

By way of understanding the exact spatiotemporal context of this tragedy, some precise historical perspective is in order. The three continents of the Third World exported ten million tons of grain in the 1930s, were self-sufficient in the 1950s and imported 70 million tons of grain by the end of the Second Development Decade. Grain imports are expected to increase to 76 million tons by 1985 and could well exceed 140 million tons at the end of the century.[5]

In all, our development models have launched the Third World into a global economic system where survival could hinge not on national cohesiveness nor on commonly accepted political goals but rather on the terms of exchange. When the terms of exchange move against the poor (as they surely must, based on our current logic) the rich nations have the option of increasing aid (a temporary palliative) or of watching our global systems fragment. In both instances, the longer term results are the same: growing destitution among the weakest of the weak matched only by a more generalized politico-financial paralysis of global, perhaps even permanent, dimension.

6
The Third
Development Decade
and Beyond

The Third Development Decade commenced on January 1, 1981, after four years of high-level, increasingly acrimonious, conference diplomacy between the North and the South.

Negotiations leading up to this compact took place at a number of poorly understood, costly, international forums including: the United Nations Conference on Trade and Development (UNCTAD) in Nairobi (1976) and later Manila (1979) and at the United Nations Industrial Development Conference (UNIDO) in Lima (1975) and New Delhi (1980).

These conferences were supplemented by ongoing policy initiatives taken at the more specialized UN agencies such as the International Monetary Fund, the World Bank, Gatt, and the Food and Agriculture Organization (FAO). Within these agencies, program design evolved out of an increasingly restless dialogue between the 125 member states from the developing world and those international civil servants representing the 24 industrialized countries of the West.

In addition, the Western powers continued to coordinate aid policy and long-term development strategy through the OECD, the so-called Rich Man's Club. The South, for its part, attempted, sometimes successfully, to speak with a single voice under cover of the Group of 77, a coalition now made up of some 120 nonaligned Third World states.

A final development strategy for the 1980s and beyond was drafted in joint committee at the United Nations in New York during the last days of 1980.[1] The development program was presented for voice vote at the UN General Assembly between Christmas and the New Year.

On balance, the strategy for the Third Development Decade calls for more of the same. Even the plan's inspiration remains identical with development policy pursued during the 1960s and the 1970s. In light of a deteriorating economic climate, tactical positions simply hardened and/or became more strident.

The litany of issues and proposals is familiar. The detailed strategy document for the decade argues in favor of an increase in international liquidity through the creation of additional Special Drawing Rights (credits at the International Monetary Fund) as well as a doubling of the IMF's capital. In addition, better multinational control of trans-national corporations (particularly banks) is thought to be worthy of further attention. Control would come after the gathering of more complete information on unit costs. The arms race is singled out correctly as a significant impediment to further global development.

Finally, an eloquent plea is made in favor of accelerated growth in the North. A "hyping" of the growth rate, so the argument goes, would provoke a tunnel effect and drag with it, in its wake, the world's most destitute economies. We might call this "trickle-down economics" with a different metaphor.

In the end, the documentation supporting the UN resolution on Third World development for the 1980s follows the broad outlines of the Willy Brandt report, *North-South: A Program for Survival*. While some recurrent Third World claims are left aside—for example, a global development tax or the automatic transfer of financial resources to the Third World—the logic remains the same. Economic growth fuels development. "Take off" is restricted by lack of capital, lack of physical endowment, lack of trained personnel, lack of trading opportunities, and, in the final analysis, by a lack of food. The problem is posed as if all of these factors precede rather than stem from an acceptable notion of progress, or, more fundamentally, from a development model that works.

In terms of objectives, the plan proposed an increase in average GNP growth targets from 6 percent in the 1970s to 7 percent annually by the end of the Third Development Decade. Industrial growth objectives were augmented once again, in this instance, from 8 percent to 9 percent. The growth target for agriculture remained the same at 4 percent reflecting, of course, poor performance during the previous decade.

The means brought to bear to accomplish the plan's goals are likewise familiar. They include the intensification of trade and of technological transfers, an increase in capital flows southward, and more open access to Northern markets for light manufactured goods and for processed food products.

According to the program, or rather, the mix of objectives, the Third World should account for 25 percent of world manufacturing by 1990, up from current levels of less than 10 percent. As in previous North-South negotiations, this latter objective was defended vigorously by the Group of 77.[2] The argument employed has a standard ring and is based on the ever-present Law of Comparative Advantage. We learn from the Group of 77 that trade-led growth should reduce inflation in the North, increase global productivity and, thereby, stimulate world economic dynamism.

Development remains synonymous with the dynamics of international trade. Once again, we are caught, in this instance on a global basis, in the myth of a purely mechanical universe where progress depends on aggregate economic output and where output remains a function of comparative economic advantage. Thus, the South as a group has opted for a Northern growth strategy—a strategy not necessarily fruitful on Southern soil if we are to judge from existing evidence. In the case of the South, of course, the ability as well as the willingness to compete hinges largely on the availability of cheap labor. One wonders how many First World and Third World citizens are fully aware of the terms of the option chosen.

As a further part of the development contract, the South continues to accept its position as a net importer of capital, of industrial goods, and of technical services from the North for the balance of the Third Development Decade. These imports are to be offset partially by the export of raw materials and of labor-intensive manufactures: textiles, shoes, electronic components, household goods, Christmas tree lights, and the like, nearly all of which are produced for foreign markets and for foreign tastes.

The growth targets established for the Third Development Decade were to be funded 28 percent internally, with the balance (72 percent) coming in the form of foreign aid and commercial bank loans. In aid terms, once more the North is called upon to make available on a best-efforts basis the 1 percent of GNP proposed at the start of the First Development Decade but never met. Likewise, Arab-OPEC aid donors are encouraged, by a coalition of First and Third World countries, to increase their soft lending programs and to lengthen maturities on overseas development loans.

THE FOURTH WORLD

A series of separate growth targets are established for the weakest members of the global community. These targets simply expand, quantitatively, existing development logic. That is, the strategy pursues for the least developed countries the same reasoning process and methodology proposed for the developing world generally. Only the industrial growth target changes. It is increased from 9.0 percent to 9.5 percent. Likewise, the internal funding requirement for the poorest of the poor shifts to 30 percent from 28 percent. The need to save presumably is greater in direct proportion to the degrees of poverty. Savings, of course, are to accumulate primarily in favor of industry. Industrialization continues to be proposed as a palliative for hunger.

Classical post-war development planning has seemed to ignore, until it was too late, the unambiguous historic fact that in the United States, in England, in France, or for that matter, among every major industrial power, agricultural development has preceded industrial development rather than vice versa. The space-age development process quite possibly has overlooked both the principle of gravity and the primacy of Mother Earth.

In defining overall planning policy for the Third Development Decade, specific development objectives have become attached to the more obvious marcoeconomic goals just noted. These development objectives include (1) the elimination of famine through the improved use of food and water resources, (2) a lengthening of average life expectancy to 60 years, (3) a reduction of the infant mortality rate to no more than 50 per mil (currently three per mil in the North), (4) an increase in Third World literacy, and (5) full employment by the year 2000, which today means unemployment at less than 10 percent.

These noneconomic, that is, purely developmental goals are thought to flow automatically from the macroeconomic objectives just defined. Thus, what we are party to is an economic strategy disguised as a development plan.

From the start, development logic turns in circles, in furious circles, for action and output replace meaning. Without exaggeration, one might argue that the global development community has been making history at the risk of not thinking accurately. Yet the risk that is being courted is not simply of a logical order. Faulty reasoning accounts for subsequent disorder.

Even our growth imagery reflects a development logic that can only serve to hide, without impunity, a more fundamental philosophic imperative. As Albert Camus points out: "A times comes when deception transforms patient hope into furious disillusionment and when the ends, affirmed with the mania of obstinacy, demanded with ever increasing cruelty, make obligatory the search for other means."[3] Ironically, other means will not begin to come into focus until the development community has consciously shifted its development goals.

For the moment, development goals lead back to a number of economic growth models, all of which assume the free trade model, or its corollary, production for production's sake, as a universal necessity.

One might be tempted to argue that the development community is trapped within the confines of a Ricardian universe. It would be much more accurate to recognize that this Ricardian universe is but the reflection of an underlying worldview, a notion of progress that denies intention in nature and the supremacy of intelligence within man and society. Out of this notion of progress has grown modern development theory.

For example, some planners and futurologists consider the crisis of malnutrition (brought on by contrived economic dislocation) as a "second generation problem,"[4] the measure of success, as it were, of the development process. The rural exodus, the sprawling shantytowns, and the brain drain have served to augment global industrial production and to rationalize farming. Medicine and modern delivery systems have pulled down the death rate.[5] Both of these arguments in favor of existing development methodology assume that people cannot take care of their own or that the challenge of development is one of mere survival. Here we are back to the messianic and naive vision of mechanical progress as handed down to us by Thomas Malthus, his predecessors, and his heirs. Success breeds problems of adaptation. The strongest or the fittest will survive. In the end, the problems are resolved by nature. We used to call this sort of progression "progress" or "evolution." Today we call it "development."

VISION VERSUS KNOW-HOW IN THE 1980s

Experts at the World Bank have estimated that it would cost about $380 billion, plus recurrent charges of $28 to $40 billion per year for a decade, to assure delivery of basic human needs to the planet's Third World population. The annual charges represent about 0.3 percent of the world's GNP, that is, only 5 percent of the world's yearly expenditure on arms. Put differently, annual transfers would represent less than 1 percent of the developed nations[6] output of goods and services. At the occasion of the Marshall Plan in Europe, the United States gave away about 5 percent of its own GNP for five consecutive years. Today we praise the results.

In the case of the Third World, however, the emphasis on money, on the automatic transfer of resources, and on the demand capacity of the rich represents an inadequate response to the crisis at hand. In fact, the emphasis might even serve to disguise the problem.

It is clear, of course, that the industrial powers in particular need to free up money, energy, and talent in order to arrive at a different —less costly and dangerous—global compact. As Barbara Ward has pointed out: "A 10 percent cut in arms expenditure would release sufficient funds for development on a proper scale and do so from the most inflationary of current uses."[7]

But money, energy, and talent are only three elements and perhaps the most irrelevant (that is, mechanical and self-serving) for solving the immense problem of holding the planet together as we enter the twenty-first century. More importantly, we need to change our approach or to free up our imagination. To do this, our bias must shift. At its heart, this implies a change in our understanding of what causes progress. This accomplished, the rest will follow.

For the moment, our understanding of development, the blind confidence in power at the expense of intention, flies in the face of our most primitive needs as a people—whether North or South. Likewise, our current ideology and our bias produce sufficient empirical evidence to enable us to question its premise. Our notion of cause corresponds neither with the discoveries of modern science nor with the art of successful global management. We think that goals are ancillary to means.

Thus far, we have attempted to demonstrate the manner whereby our worldview has shaped subsequent development models. We now want to see how this worldview transits aid policy and multinational banking practice, in that order.

By getting behind the mechanism, the stubborn facts that mark aid and bank policy, we will propose a financial program based on an alternative logic. For the moment, let us summarize the existing argument. Development is not natural nor dependent on economic law. Rather, development is artificial by definition, or, like all human activity, a question of "knowing, making, and judging," (W.H. Auden). On this basis, modern man cannot escape his responsibility to survive not only as a species but to survive in minimum human dignity. In brief, we want to insist on the distinction between *homo faber* and *homo rationalis*, that is, between doing and judging. As we shall witness, this distinction has not always been made in formulating aid policy and bank credit. Instead, the financing of the development process has reflected the models proposed by an overworked and perhaps outdated reasoning process. The end result is insolvency.

7
Aid Policy
and
Third World Development

The financing of post-World War II development policy has been structured around two principal centers of gravity. The centers in question are not found at the extremes of East-West tension—the polarity of the Bear and the Eagle. Rather, they both are located at or near H Street N.W., Washington, D.C. As every international civil servant and commercial banker knows, the H Street address identifies the premises of the World Bank and, around the corner, its sister organization, the International Monetary Fund.

Around these two agencies has evolved, in practice, the paradigm of Third World development policy. The World Bank provides the *structure* for development, that is, the project funding, and the IMF the *stability*, that is, protection of the international payments system. The World Bank, then, is concerned primarily with infrastructure or with bricks and mortar, and the International Monetary Fund with trade equilibrium, that is, with currency convertibility. The two functions are complementary. For, in each instance the organizing principle, the pole around which development takes place, is production for an international marketplace according to the Law of Comparative Advantage.

The two organizations, the World Bank and the International Monetary Fund, now account for capital resource flows to the Third World in excess of $50 billion per year.[1] The direction and intended impact of these resource flows reflect changing development theory and practice. Around this theory follows bilateral aid policy and, eventually, commercial bank credit.

Accordingly, the World Bank and the IMF represent, as it were, the primary focal points of North-South dialogue and action. Both institutions are UN agencies, the only two with a significant amount of money at their disposal. Both institutions are controlled by their largest shareholders—the Western powers. In fact, both institutions reflect Western know-how, Western method, and Western manners. For, unlike the other UN agencies, voting authority at the Bretton Woods institutions is weighted according to approximate order of subscription size, rather than "one flag, one vote." Hence, it might be appropriate that we look in the glass and draw some lessons from a Western critique.

THE IMF AND THREE DECADES OF DEVELOPMENT

Walter Bagehot warned some one hundred years ago that "money doesn't manage itself." The same can be said for trade. The International Monetary Fund was founded to manage both. Obviously, this task has proven difficult to accomplish. . .not only in *theory* but likewise in *fact*.

In theory, the Ricardian paradigm determines the Fund's charter and, by extension, the breadth of its activities. The IMF has been structured to operate on the assumption that political, social, and economic well-being automatically go hand in hand with a growing and unobstructed system of international trade whether between the strong and the weak or the rich and the poor. In the first of the Articles of Agreement, we read that the IMF was organized "to facilitate the expansion and balanced growth of international trade and to contribute thereby to the promotion and maintenance of high levels of employment and real income and to the development of the productive resources of all members as the primary objectives of economic policy."[2] This is conference speak for saying that the Law of Comparative Advantage represents the single most effective method for promoting international economic order. In turn, the construction of the international economic order has become identified, or rather, confounded with, development. At its origins, the solutions for Third World poverty were cast—largely as a self-evident convenience—in terms of growth in international trade rather than development, or in economic rather than in political terms. Accordingly, the solution has become not merely part of the problem but, more fundamentally, an extension of the paradigm.

The IMF's structure and methodology are, by now, fairly well understood. The IMF represents a pooling of a portion of the currencies of its 146 member states (originally 45). These currencies are available for distribution in tranches to those subscribers unable to maintain their position within the international payments system. Lawrence Malkin of *Time* magazine has spoken of the IMF as an international credit union, owned by countries instead of people.

In the case of need, each country is allowed, under standby agreements, to draw in four successive tranches up to 450 percent of its initial subscription, also known as "quotas." These quota drawings are taken down in hard currencies from the common fund. Drawings under the first credit tranche are automatic but cannot exceed one-quarter of a member country's subscription. Subsequent drawings are tied to increasingly strict, oftentimes contested, IMF conditionality clauses. These latter borrowings all take place within a preordained stabilization program, known alternatively as "the international adjustment process."

The purpose of the international adjustment process is to shore up a member country's deficit balance of payments position—in other words, to keep the country alive within the international trading system. It is for this reason, and others, that the IMF has become known alternatively as a "lender of last resort," as an "international safety net," or, more simply, as the "international gendarme." In short, the IMF serves as a sort of multilateral overlord responsible for protecting exchange rate stability and for stabilizing balance of payment deficits. As the trading system reaches the limits of its internal logic, the tactics of the overlord become all the more forceful—and, in one sense, all the more stereotyped. Action reflects the mandate. In this case, action reflects the IMF Articles of Agreement. More recently, the Articles of Agreement have been interpreted to allow the IMF to serve as a safety net for commercial banks and suppliers lending and selling into Third World markets.

The Case for IMF Riots

The IMF stabilization program, or the *international adjustment process*, consists of exchanging hard currency against a national austerity program. The austerity program generally includes a series of preordained measures designed to correct balance of payments (BOP) disequilibrium. The causes for BOP deficits are perceived to be two in nature: firstly, temporary or cyclical due to a fall in commodity prices, poor harvest, or some other natural event not likely to repeat itself. The remedies include drawing against the first or low conditionality credit tranche or, alternatively, having access to the Compensatory Financing Facility (CFF). The CFF window, it should be noted, functions outside of the original quota system and was introduced in 1963 to compensate, at least partially, export shortfalls beyond a country's control.

The second source of payments deficit is deemed more fundamental—as are the remedies. In this instance, IMF management is confronted by structural disequilibria occasioned by overexpansive domestic and/or monetary policy. In the Third World, the symptoms are an excessive import bill, a "bunching" of foreign debt payments (as external borrowing has usually been used to bridge budgetary deficits/ overspending), and virulent inflation. High conditionality, then, hinges on measures to correct both the symptoms and causes of, among other things, nonpayment of foreign debt. The measures, that is, the adjustment process, typically would include any combination of the following: a devaluation of local currency to reduce import demand, a rescheduling of foreign debt, tighter control over credit expansion, wage and/or price freezes, a reduction of public sector spending, higher taxes, and a redirection of investment into those sectors of the economy producing for export. The measures are consistent with the mandate.

In sum, the program, subsequent policy action, and quantitative targets are constructed, all of them, with the intention of making progress toward the growth of international trade as agreed upon at Bretton Woods. In *Finance and Development*, a joint publication of the World Bank and the International Monetary Fund, we read: "Thus, in time, the practices of conditionality came to encompass all general aspects of economic policies that influence the demand for and the supply of resources, *so that imbalances could be redressed without resort to restrictions on trade and payments*" [my italics].[3] Unless we can accept the proposition that trade automatically spawns development (a dubious premise, indeed), then we should understand that the IMF was founded to maintain a specific system of exchange rather than to address the more fundamental and tragic issue of widespread and growing absolute poverty. In other words, the international adjustment process does not directly confront the most salient features of development, namely, the problem of income distribution, employment, cultural identity, food dependence, and regional life-style. Herein resides a built-in, unresolved conflict, a conflict increasingly difficult for the well-intentioned and talented managers of the IMF to manage. In fact, as the system continues to expand, the conflict can only continue to grow, both in the minds of management and in the maintenance of global order.

The system to be maintained by the IMF is founded on the Law of Comparative Advantage. The system might have been appropriate for the consolidation of the Atlantic community, for the creation of larger, more homogeneous markets within the Northern hemisphere. The needs, however, of the newest members of the IMF—particularly its weakest members—have very little to do with advantage. Rather, their real needs clearly relate to assistance and caring outside the dimensions of a competitive marketplace.

This contradiction between the system and current reality probably accounts, even more than the breaking away from fixed exchange rates in 1971, for the present unthreading of our international economic order. Free trade, as we have pointed out, is not a panacea for poverty. Competitive advantage can be used on a selective basis as one vehicle among many for solving certain problems of economic scarcity. The "law," however, should not be allowed to inspire, let alone overwhelm, the development process itself. Unfortunately, this is exactly what has happened in the drafting of the IMF charter, in subsequent methodology, and in its application. Accordingly, systems maintenance would seem to be increasing systems risk.

For this reason—and for others less legitimate—a number of developing countries do not want IMF help. In confronting local political and economic mismanagement, the IMF's first reflex is to condition the local economy to outside markets. In not a few instances, the results lead to what have become known as "IMF riots"—Jamaica, the Dominican Republic, Egypt, Turkey, Peru, Ghana, the Sudan, Zaire, and others. These countries did not come to the IMF in time, and, when they did, the standard medicine was applied. In his book, *The Money Lenders*, Anthony Sampson vividly describes the case of Chile. After the overthrow in 1973 of Marxist President Allende, the IMF redoubled efforts to redress an otherwise shattered economy, which the old regime had left, as a heritage, to the new. Allende's successor, General Pinochet, eventually agreed to the terms of a new stabilization program. Given the nature of Pinochet's government compliance was assured in advance. The IMF's first loan was taken down in January 1974. Sampson writes:

> The "shock treatment" . . . had its shocking effects: in 1975 the gross domestic product fell by sixteen percent, unemployment went up to

twenty percent, industrial output went down by twenty-three percent. Workers' wages went down further and many small businesses went bankrupt. But the IMF welcomed the policy of lowering import duties and opening up Chile to the rest of the world as a "major achievement of Chilean economic policy."[4]

To make matters worse, Pinochet's acceptance of the terms of the IMF, Standby agreement provided a green light to foreign commercial banks, which subsequently lent to the Chilean government nearly $10 billion over the five-year period following the Stabilization Program. These debts already have been renegotiated because the Pinochet government was unable to repay the banks. In addition, the bank borrowings were used to finance imports in accordance with comparative advantage. In turn, these imports ruined a goodly portion of Chile's local industry and severely hurt not a small percentage of the middle class.

For their part, the commercial banks—not shrewdly but conveniently—have followed the signals of the IMF's now famous stabilization programs. In nearly every Standby Agreement, the program calls for a renegotiation of foreign bank credit and for a lengthening of loan maturities. This serves both as an accommodation to hard-pressed Third World borrowers and also allows the banks the right to continue to carry the loans on their books as earning assets. In the long run, the accommodation also incites the banks to take advantage of the system. The cycle would seem to be self-perpetuating. The IMF now finds itself in the undesired position of functioning at once as a sort of supranational collecting agent, the financial sheriff, and as a lender of last resort. In a telling issue of the *Financial Times* dated February 7, 1983, we read: "The efforts of the IMF to prevent the collapse of the world's financial system have so far depended, like a game of poker, on a combination of shrewdness, brinkmanship and sheer good luck." This report comes from the *Financial Times'* highly regarded economics correspondent, Anatole Kaletsky.

Currently, the International Monetary Fund is involved in a task of massive patchwork from Mexico City to Seoul, South Korea. With some $35 billion a year in available resources, the IMF attempts to enable clients facing bank debt of around $850 billion to stave off default. We might call this a Herculean task or wishful thinking, particularly given the current dynamics of our international economic order.

Holding the System Together

As the Bretton Woods payments system came under increasing pressure in the early 1970s firstly because of the unpegging of the dollar to gold, then a redoubling of inflation in the West, then a corresponding hike in oil prices, the IMF attempted to compensate its member states in the following manner: First, the Fund increased international liquidity through the allocation of a Special Drawing Right (SDR), or paper gold. The first allocation, equivalent to about $10 billion, took place between 1970 and 1972. These allocations were made not according to need but in accordance with the size of member state's quotas. A Special Drawing Right allocation is a book-keeping entry at the IMF serving as an official instrument of international payment between IMF countries. In other words, the SDR represents an extension of credit without payment in kind. Allocations are made without conditionality. Cumulative allocations now stand at about $30 billion.

Second, it was recognized by 1974 that certain member states, co-incidentally the weakest, were suffering from external shocks to their domestic economies. These "external shocks" are to be distinguished from the earlier sources of BOP payment problems, namely, a cyclical downturn in export receipts or fundamental disequilibria. The "external shocks" included oil price increases redoubled by price hikes on imported capital goods from the North. To give some perspective on the problem, the prices of manufactured goods actually outpaced oil price increases between 1975 and 1979. In addition, inflation in the North spread quickly to the South. Subsequent tight money measures in the United Kingdom and the United States had an equally nefarious effect, both in terms of the South's capacity to compete and in terms of its capacity to service debt. Every 1 percent increase in interest rates, fixed in London or New York, adds about $3 billion to the Third World's cost of money.[5] The inflation shock and subsequent oil shock gave way to a debt shock nurtured by an interest rate shock.

Individually, the "external shocks" were considerable. Taken together, the shocks were judged to have a *structural* impact on the economies concerned. In response, the IMF, midway into the Second Development Decade, opened an additional borrowing window known as the Extended Fund Facility (EFF). Unlike the more modest IMF standby facility, which aims merely at correcting temporary balance of payment disequilibria, the EFF attempts to change the *structure* of the economy in question. The overall goal of the program is to adjust domestic policy in accordance with a changing external environment. Like the Standby Facility, the EFF operates within the parameters of the IMF Stabilization Program and is subject to similar conditionality clauses. Unlike the Standby arrangements, drawings under the credit tranches are repayable at a maximum tenure of ten years rather than three. The ten-year duration gives the IMF yet more leverage in dealing with recalcitrant member states. Thus, the medicine remains the same; the dosage merely increases. The palliative, however, does not cure the disease.

According to an internal IMF staff paper prepared in 1978, of 75 Stabilization Programs reviewed for performance, 18 resulted in an increase of international reserves—or no improvement in 76 percent of the cases. Inflation (in 29 programs) came down in seven cases, for a miss ratio once again of 76 percent. In the meanwhile, growth in GNP went down 53 percent of the time despite record increases in global GNP during the period under consideration.[6]

The question remains: Can the International Monetary Fund operate within the context of its existing charter and still make a positive contribution to world economic recovery, let alone to development? The response is by no means obvious and this despite the quite talented people located at the Washington headquarters or stationed at various missions around the world. For the moment, IMF program policy is designed to promote global economic integration at the risk of suppressing regional human development. Development, let alone the alleviation of wide-scale regional destitution, becomes the anticipated spinoff of the growing exchanges of goods and services between the rich and the poor. We might argue that our eighteenth-century Western paradigm has become vitrified in the institution of the IMF. This vitrification needs somehow to be undone.

DOUBLE JEOPARDY

Under current circumstances, the staff at the IMF finds itself working at the same time for and against the system. For the system, in the sense that program design reflects the preconception that progress depends on the Law of Comparative Advantage, or on the survival of the fittest in an open marketplace. Against the system, in the sense that on-line management attempts, whether through moral persuasion, conditionality, or a technological fix, to protect the weak from the strong. Protection comes in aiding governments in contract negotiations, in controlling spendthrift heads of state, or by providing bridge finance in the event of rapidly falling export receipts.

In the first instance, the corollary is production for production's sake; in the second, maintenance of minimal harmony among nations. When the two come in conflict, the Articles of Agreement are weighted in favor of the first. Our paradigm takes precedence over purpose. As a result, not only is financial order in grave peril, but so is world political stability.

Development has become the stepchild of economic order. Economic order is based on competition, not within countries, but between countries. IMF program lending protects this order—especially between the weak and the strong. The longer the order lasts, the weaker become the weak. Eventually, a void develops that no increase in IMF quotas can hope to fill. In the final analysis, the North cannot count on buying its way out of the problem.

Since 1980, Third World payment deficits have exceeded $100 billion in all but one year. Even with a doubling in IMF quotas, the growing gap between the rich and the poor will continue to expand. Accordingly, the efforts of the IMF to prevent the collapse of the world's finance and trading system will continue to depend, like a game of poker, "on sheer good luck."

According to current guidelines, the IMF may lend up to 150 percent of a member country's quota on Standby Agreement for any one year, or up to 450 percent of quota over three years for structural adjustment. To put these figures into perspective, Mexico's quota is SDR 802 million. This means that the IMF can lend the government of Mexico up to $1.3 billion over a one-year period. Mexico's BOP deficits, however, were running on the order of $15 billion per year. This gap, a difference of $13.7 billion needed to be bridged by additional foreign bank credit, by bilateral aid, and/or by a reduction of imports. Like Mexico, Argentina's quota is SDR 802 million, with an external deficit in excess of $3 billion. Nigeria has been allocated a quota of SDR 540 billion versus a current account deficit of some $4 billion. With a quota allocation of SDR 225 million, Morocco, like the Ivory Coast, confronts a BOP deficit of ten times that order.

We might conclude that the Third World is living not only on borrowed money but on borrowed theory as well. Given the IMF's own incapacity to service the system that it was designed to protect, the polemic surrounding the IMF's future mandate has grown both in volume and in number of participants.

On the right, the Reagan administration has accused the International Monetary Fund of statist solutions to international economic problems and of interference with free market forces. For the purists on the new Right, the IMF only delays, at considerable cost to the U.S. taxpayer, the *adjustment process* that the weakest members of the world community must make in order to compete profitably on international markets. Here, the Darwinian worldview enjoys ample realization—both logically and in fact. As remarked earlier, the adjustment process often entails wide-scale immigration, a too rapid and costly change in consumer habits, a loss of identity, and, eventually, a loss of political order.

To prove the seriousness with which the administration believes in its own logic, on arriving in office, Beryl Sprinkel, a high-level U.S. Treasury official, suggested that the U.S. Government sell to the general public its share in the International Monetary Fund and the World Bank. This remark predictably sent its own share of "external shocks" through the usually well-cushioned halls of the IMF and the World Bank.

On further reflection, the Reagan administration eventually agreed to go along with the proposed 50 percent increase in IMF quotas scheduled to be completed by 1985. The agreement has nothing to do with the survival of the weakest but rather with the survival of the strongest. The accord was obtained during the Mexican debt crisis at the urging of Donald Regan and George Shultz. The 50 percent increase was seen as the absolute minimum necessary to keep the Bretton Woods system afloat—and with it, our major international banks. Secretary of State Shultz later explained before the Senate Foreign Relations Committee that the U.S. government has a major interest in assuring that "the lesser-developed countries have sufficient capital to pay for imports of goods and services that will enhance productivity and contribute to world economic expansion."[7] And service bank debt.

On the left, the most credible defense of the IMF and its activities has come from the Brandt Commission. In its most recent report, *Common Crisis*, the commission argues for a doubling of IMF quotas, for a $40 billion increase in SDR allocations over a three-year period, for a shift in conditionality clauses to allow more time for adjustment, and, finally, for an increase in the Compensatory Financing Facility.[8] The report also endorses a U.S. "safety net" proposal and recommends that the idea be realized through an enlargement of the IMF General Arrangements to Borrow (GAB). Under GAB, the Group of Ten industrial countries lend through the IMF to each other in order to forestall or cope with an impairment of the international monetary system. The Brandt Commission suggests that this First World financing facility, the safety net, be increased and expanded to include the least developed countries as well. This has been done with caveats.

The Brandt Commission endorses not only the maintenance of our existing system of free trade but its active *management*. For its part, the new right would have the system manage itself. The right enjoys the virtue of consistency and the left of compassion.

In the realm of the real, both parties come together on common ground in support for a common program: production based on the international division of land, labor, and capital according to the Law of Comparative Advantage. Hence, the dialectic is closed. As a result, the machine tumbles forward on its own singular momentum—a momentum that is leading us to an enormous void. The growing cleavage between the weak and the strong, the rich and the poor, the productive and the unproductive represents a common contagion. This *common crisis*, this contagion, springs from our underlying paradigm.

One of antiquity's most widely read economists, Aristotle, pointed out in the fourth century B.C. that a small error in the conceptualization of a problem leads to a large error in its resolution. Given the state of our trading and finance system, management at the IMF might want to think about Aristotle's dictum. For the crisis that the Brandt Commission so deservedly is concerned about relates not to a lack of money, nor of quotas, nor even of goodwill. The *common crisis* relates to a lack of logic. The international development community has been attempting to make a *whole* without sufficiently respecting the *parts*. This failure in logic has created a grave fissure in our economic and political orders North-South. This failure also transits the IMF's international adjustment process. The adjustment process consists of conditioning the local economy not to national nor to regional endowment but rather to the international order, an order that relates at best only marginally to local mores, to local talent, to local tastes, and, finally, to local needs.

In searching for a more suitable IMF lending methodology, some of the more important questions to be posed might conveniently be summarized under three general categories.

Firstly, what are the practical limits of world economic integration and the timing of same? Would it not make more sense to strengthen, on a regional basis, the weakest parts of the system first and only then attempt to integrate the regions with the whole? To encourage this formula, macroeconomic planning at the IMF would need to be broken down on a truly regional basis and, likewise, the adjustment process. For development purposes, the Third World might be divided into five relatively homogeneous groupings or markets. These *parts* already have been suggested by the late economist and humanist, Maurice Guernier.[9] They include with some minor change in detail:

- Sub-Sahara Africa (black Africa) from the Ivory Coast to Kenya, from Ougadougou to Cape Town
- The Muslim world from Morocco to Iran
- South and Central America, including the Caribbean
- Asia, including the Philippines, Indonesia, Japan, and Singapore
- The Indian subcontinent

The process would simply mean that if the Indonesians are going to manufacture typewriters, then they would need to know how to use them. Or if the Tunisians want to make blue jeans, then, likewise, they should want to wear them.

The timing of subsequent global economic integration would follow the harmonization of regional groupings rather than vice versa. Once the structure is established, one could reasonably envision integration on a more universal scale within five decades. Given the advances in modern technology and communications, this integration is already under way and will not be reversed. In the meanwhile, the poor need economic protection, not just aid. This protection needs to be *systematized* (as it already is in the North) and well understood. There is enough talent available at the IMF and the World Bank both to adjust the system to current needs and to sell it. In brief, protection could go hand in hand with development. Meanwhile, rational protection, reinforced by a change in the development paradigm, might serve to bring the debt balloon down slowly before it pops.

The second most urgent question that needs to be posed relates to the logic of the production process itself. In the West, we still believe as a society that output is coincident with progress. This logic has been conveyed to the Third World via Northern aid programs and the development models that these programs have sponsored. The programs have come back to the West in the form of unwanted consumer goods and, perhaps more damaging, in the form of unloyal competition, especially from the Far East. In effect, those wage earners employed in threatened industries in the North are advised that they should live and work like Asians. We hear this incessantly from not a few hard-nosed bankers, multinational corporations, and their apologists at the IMF and the World Bank. The logic itself, as we shall explain, finds its source in the West, in the Post Renaissance concept of nature and of reality. Since the seventeenth century, Western man has interpreted nature (a small error in the premise) as fundamentally hostile and, therefore, to be exploited rather than loved. This premise gives way to the economic notion of comparative advantage, i.e. production for production's sake. This notion, or rather, its premise, is not wrong per se. It is not wrong historically, nor intellectually, only morally—especially in the Third World. We might argue further that the premise, not by coincidence, is also wrong geopolitically.

For in the Third World, the necessity for structural harmony between man, society, and nature plays a much more important role than in the First World. For example, the layer of humus in the tropics measures two to ten centimeters even in the dense forest regions versus several meters on the plain in the temperate zone.[10] *Exploitation*, then, can have immediate repercussions not only on the local economy but on the surrounding ecosystem as well. Overcutting of tropical rain forests in the Ivory Coast alone is said to be the principal source of renewed drought conditions in the grasslands farther north. In the South, one is quick to notice that man does not live in a universe but in a biosphere. Accordingly, economic development policy must seek not to exploit nor to dominate nature but rather to take her as a bride.

When given the reality of a fragile resource base, output according to comparative advantage does not serve to orient production according to short-term necessity, let alone long-term needs. In order to solidify this resource base, the South will need to follow a gradualist development policy, one that protects not only the environment but also man's relationship with this environment, that is, his civilization. Regional development policy undertaken at the IMF would reinforce the reciprocal relationship between man, society, and nature.

Likewise, a turning away by the IMF from a development policy of production for production's sake according to the pretended exigencies of a global marketplace would not represent a deliberate slowdown of economic activity. Quite the contrary. For what is at issue clearly is not the limits to growth but rather the direction of change. The change under consideration would limit the distance—and the rivalry—between the rich and the poor. Competition would be established proportionate to regional needs, talents, resources, and goals. In other words, competition, like nature, would be rendered intelligent or, should we say, "loyal." The same holds true for production.

And this brings us to the third, perhaps fundamental question to be examined. Under current circumstances, the West is (and will remain for the foreseeable future) the globe's preeminent economic power. The complexion and the methodology of IMF management testifies to this simple fact. The West's position—and its responsibilities —could be tested only in the event of a major economic and political breakdown of global order, a sort of leveling brought on by a common crisis that we cannot now imagine. This crisis, however, is in the making. We find evidence of the problem in the size and purpose of bank credit to the Third World, in our statistics on starvation, or by looking closely at Northern defense budgets, their size, and justification.

Yet the crisis does not come from the outside, from competition from the South, and, even less so, from competition East-West. The crisis relates to our worldview. The worldview tells us that force is a more important element than thought in the organization of our global systems whether natural or social. For this reason, the International Monetary Fund, like its sister organization, the World Bank, has been founded to protect an economic order based on the theory of unlimited free trade and open-ended competition. As we have attempted to demonstrate, this theory has reached the limits of its usefulness, at least as a transmission belt for Third World development. The theory is also testing our ecosystem, not to mention man's most fundamental definition of himself and of his purpose. Given our inability to establish a notion of limit, the testing already is at the outer limits of the possible.

We need to ask ourselves: Is our worldview working? And if not, can it be somehow altered to allow within our international orders some happy compromise between force and thought, production and purpose, mechanical cause and telos.

For the moment, we are living on the intellectual momentum of our immediate forefathers. To preserve our culture as well as the full range of our intellectual heritage, we shall need to shift momentum. We might start with those agencies charged with protecting the international economy from chaos.

In 1975, the Brookings Institution published the most extensive, independent study of the Bretton Woods institutions ever undertaken. At the start, the authors, Edward Mason and Robert Asher, make the following observation, a form of summary statement:

> Looking back, with the benefit of twenty-five years of hindsight, on the events leading to the formation of the International Bank for Reconstruction and Development and the International Monetary Fund, one is struck by both the magnificence of the achievement and the lack of prescience of the founding fathers.[11]

The "magnificence of the achievement" relates to the contribution that the Bretton Woods institutions made to the reconstruction of economic order within the Western Alliance. This contribution was largely the work of the International Monetary Fund, the agency responsible for assuring a system of unfettered multinational trade among approximately equal partners.

The authors are not so clear about the "lack of prescience of the founding fathers." We might conclude that this lack of prescience was first made manifest when the Bretton Woods system was enlarged in the late 1960s and its method applied, without significant modification, to North-South economic relations. The international development community had taken economics as a science and assumed that its laws, including the Law of Comparative Advantage, were applicable universally, i.e., North-North and North-South.

In the face of existing danger, the necessary modifications to the Bretton Woods system cannot be undertaken by the management of the World Bank nor the IMF without a corresponding change in consensus on the part of the principal shareholders, notably, the United States. Thus, ultimately the problem can be localized not in the domain of economic theory but rather in the upper echelons of political decision making. The politicians, for their part, cannot reach a new consensus without a change in paradigm, or a way of looking at the world and its future. In other words, our political leaders need to *revision* international economic and financial order. A review of World Bank and commercial bank Third World lending practices should make this statement obvious.

8
The World Bank: From Process to Project Lending

Like the IMF, the International Bank for Reconstruction and Development (the World Bank) opened its doors for business during the heady days following America's defeat of Hitler in Western Europe. "The Bank," as the World Bank is known in finance circles, was designed to further the *Pax Americana*. Or better, to construct it.

While the IMF is concerned with macroeconomic management, that is, with *process*, the World Bank is concerned with *project* finance, that is, with microeconomic development planning. The two functions have operated in tandem to create the development programs that follow our paradigm. The IMF has defended, and at times imposed, the method. The World Bank has funded the matter. Both method and material have gone into the creation of a global production process based on the Law of Comparative Advantage. For three consecutive development decades, the World Bank has shared the logic of this law and has supported its consequences. During this period, construction pursued the industrial models proposed by the North: "the big push," "unbalanced growth," or "take-off." Development indicators were established to fit these models. Bank investment followed the indicators—and commercial bank money, the investment.

The development indicators originally adopted in World Bank project analysis reveal the process, the program, and the premise. They included: (1) efficiency of local resource use vis-à-vis competitive outside suppliers, (2) comparative rates of return, both economic and financial, (3) impact on private and public savings, (4) impact on national and per capita income (GNP), (5) relative capital/output ratios, and (6) indicators to measure balance of payment results. In other words, the indicators patterned (and reinforced) both the program and its methodology.[1]

Not by coincidence, the development indicators reflected the World Bank's mandate and the development philosophy of its early management. The development indicators ignored such *nonmaterial* considerations as public participation, relevant technology, life-style, or a sense of identity as well as such clearly *material* considerations as employment, training, food security, shelter, environmental impact, rural versus urban development, and equity-with-growth. Output was the optimal development measure; capital savings and investment, the composite indicator for progress. Likewise, the World Bank shared the conventional prejudice that agriculture was not the first step to development. This is despite the cumulative teaching from Socrates to Francois Quesnay, the author of *Tableau Economique*,[1] and from Adam Smith back to the Bible. In the period before 1965, less than 10 percent of total World Bank lending went to agriculture. Of this quite meager amount, the bulk of the credit was used for land clearing or for the purchase of heavy duty agricultural equipment from the North.

Accordingly, during the first 25 years of World Bank activity, the bank's primary role consisted of investment in economic infrastructure, what the economist calls "public overhead": electric power, railways, port facilities, communications, roads, and like projects related largely to the mining of raw material, to industrial output, or to the production of exportable cash crops. In turn, these projects served to integrate further local production with a global marketplace.

The World Bank's mandate to "promote development" was circumscribed by three additional factors: First, the bank was designed not to compete with private sector finance. At its origins and at the urging of the New York banking community, the U.S. Treasury actually opposed the creation of the bank itself. It was the Chicago banker, Edward E. Brown, then chairman of The First National Bank of Chicago, who worked with Lord Keynes and Harry Dexter White in establishing the modalities of World Bank operations.

As a compromise to various interest groups, the World Bank concentrated, especially at its start-up, on long-term project finance in which the commercial banking community had no interest. Within the context of the models being pursued, this meant the large engineering projects already mentioned, the results of which the then established development indicators could easily capture. In keeping with prevailing development theory, the projects were defended as a "precondition to development." As it turned out, the projects—and the money—served as a precondition to development strategy . . . and to the debt trap that followed.

It was only at the start of the Second Development Decade that World Bank investment criteria shifted from public overhead and infrastructure to include other sectors of the economy, in this case, indigenous commerce and industry. The shift was accomplished through the creation of the International Development Association (IDA) and the International Finance Corporation (IFC). IDA was founded as a soft loan window of the World Bank. The organization provides long-term investment credits (over 50 years) to the world's poorest countries at subsidized rates. The IFC lends or invests in the private sector for directly productive enterprise. At the founding of IDA and the IFC, the World Bank became known as the World Bank Group. IDA now accounts for nearly a quarter of cumulative World Bank lending of $125 billion plus.

The second factor setting the measure for World Bank activities (again a compromise with existing lobbies) relates to the various components of World Bank project finance. The World Bank is prohibited from financing more than 10 percent of the local cost component of a given project. In practice, this makes the World Bank a sort of multilateral export agency, a cruel term indeed given the quality of World Bank management and its genuine desire to "promote development." Although information is not readily available, American business won slightly more than 25 percent of the internationally bidded World Bank contracts in 1982. While this speaks well for the competitiveness of U.S. exports, it also corresponds with the approximate size of U.S. government voting power within the World Bank Group. This parallelism is not circumstantial. As we shall argue, the development schema and export finance go hand in hand, or better, like a glove on an iron fist.

Because World Bank credit is concentrated on the foreign exchange component of a country's development program, it is not surprising that project identification and subsequent implementation take shape around imported talent, imported know-how, and imported equipment. This was especially true during the first 25 years of World Bank operations when the methodology for the reconstruction of Western Europe was not clearly delimited from the much more humble requirements of the average Third World country. Even today, with a slightly different set of development criteria, the World Bank finds itself, without the necessary charter amendments, obligated to finance foreign components and, by extension, foreign know-how.

In the meanwhile, it is the distance between know-how and know-why that has triggered the development of "bottlenecks" that we are witnessing today. These "bottlenecks" affect not only individual project performance, or worse, overall program planning, but, more fundamentally, they threaten economic and political stability across the better part of the Third World. This, in turn, impacts on our global trading and financial system. On the material side, the bottlenecks now include a lack of foreign parts, talent, equipment, and the money to pay for them. Inversely, this means a lack of foreign markets, or even worse, the lack of appropriate domestic food and industrial production. Related to this last item, we should note the lack of domestic incentives. On the normative side, the bottlenecks include a lack of self-identity, which turns political leadership into an alien force and which ends in a loss of liberty. This loss of liberty is both cultural and civic for the two go together. Curiously, the best examples consist precisely of those Third World countries with some of the largest foreign debt obligations, for example, Algeria, Brazil, Chile, Korea, Indonesia, the Philippines, Turkey, and, of course, Zaire. For a slightly different set of reasons, we might add to this list Peru, Taiwan, and Mexico. In nearly every instance, global economic integration and debt have surpassed self-identity and financial solvency.

More recently, the World Bank has attempted to confront the material and normative problems mentioned above with an openness and flexibility not always manifest at other development agencies and even less so at the commercial banks or at the export credit arms of the major powers. The World Bank, however, can only operate within the restrictions of its existing charter. The charter, as we have shown, reflects our prevailing notion of order. Accordingly, like traffic jams in the North, bottlenecks in the South have become part of our modern landscape. Naturally, the bottlenecks related to economic modernization have posed a more severe set of problems in the South than in the North. For in the South, economic expansion has been based on trade-led growth, according to the law of the fittest, that is, as a function of Northern market needs. As a result, modernization has had no roots in local culture, in local history, and, by extension, in local reality. Perhaps even more so than in the North, man has become separated from himself, from others, and from nature, particularly those men who have participated actively in the development process itself.

As we shall see in Part II it is this break that Hobbes invented, Hegel confirmed, Marx and Nietzsche predicted, and the modern world has accepted. Development policy has been founded on conflict rather than cooperation, on force rather than thought, and on the parts rather than on the whole. Indeed, for modern man, hazard accounts for proportion, and violence for organization. This arrogance, *homo deus homini* (Feurerbach), finds its place in various formula for Third World Development. Neither the World Bank nor its sister organizations—the IFC and IDA—can escape the formula. And the formula has fixed the future, both for the commercial banks and for their massively indebted Third World clients.[2]

SIZE VERSUS PURPOSE

The third constraining factor on World Bank project identification relates to the World Bank's size and concentration. Individual projects must be large enough to attract a global agency. Anyone working within a large organization will understand the internal pressures to advance by economies of scale, despite the diseconomies involved in such practice. For a number of Third World countries, World Bank project selection automatically overwhelms local network facilities, whether mental or material. Based on our limited notion of causal reality, size and concentration of force go along with current Western concepts of efficiency and reason. The diseconomies not calculated in such policy relate mostly to long-term costs, especially to those that have to do with style of life or choice, with ecological balance, or, in the long run, with the development process itself. In this context, it should not come as a complete surprise that historically most World Bank project lending has gone to the biggest Third World countries, India and Pakistan. While a goodly number of the poor live in this region, neither country is the most poor nor the most helpless.

Based on a historical review of project performance, the World Bank has attempted, at least in the recent past, to bring its bigness down to size. Despite these efforts, of the more than 2,500 experts now working for the World Bank Group, about 90 percent of the task force live and work at headquarters in Washington, D.C. This concentration of power and talent reflects political covetousness as practiced in Washington, bureaucratic inertia, and, one might argue, a certain lack of foresight. Indeed, how can the World Bank Group respond sensitively and in a timely fashion to regional, let alone local, development needs from a window dominating the Potomac River? Making an abstraction of our one-sided notion of order, decentralization or regionalization does not mean, in every instance, lack of harmony. In the case of the World Bank, decentralization might possibly mean a more reasonable relationship between method, model, ends, and expectations. The world remains sufficiently diverse that a centralized World Development Bank represents almost a contradiction in terms. In fact, the very concept denotes a certain parochialism or a naivete of thought.

To pursue this idea one step further, Herbert Kahn maintains, not without reason, that centralized planning for development has become the "intellectual matrix" of what he calls "modernized ideology."[3] Planning for development, of course, is of great interest to politicians, government officials, and academic advisers as it provides a pseudo-scientific facade for their actions. Yet, in the end, the larger the plan the greater the distance between facade and fact.

Likewise, the plan risks to suppress human liberty, initiative, and action, more or less in direct proportion to its size. This suppression of liberty has become an accepted reality, part of our intellectual matrix. The matrix has precise history and a specific cause. The cause resides in our changing definition of man, and its history runs in a direct line from Hobbes to Hume to Smith to Darwin to Marx to Skinner. In each instance, man has been taken as greedy, self-interested, and purely sensate, without virtue nor absolute value. Unfortunately, the only possible exception is Marx, who gave man an absolute value only in socioeconomic terms. In each case, man has become a factor of production and virtue defined in terms of one's ability to play a part in the apparatus of the state. Centralized planning, particularly on a global basis, only adds to the apparatus and maintains the facade.

At the same time, empirical evidence tells us that in those countries where power and authority are diffuse, the society as a whole seems to be managed within the context of some reasonable harmony and prosperity. The United States is made up of some 51 poles of authority and decision making. It is when Washington attempts to preempt all initiative that not only the center but the parts are weakened.

The same is even more valid on a global basis. Even the economists and academics at the World Bank have admitted substantial failure and waste at the level of pan-global organizations, in some instances, including their own. Yet our "modernized ideology" justifies without hesitation the central role of the plan and of the technocrat. The central role of the technocrat is to centralize. Centralization has become the principal leitmotif of the development process itself. As a result, development increasingly resembles a lentic monster about to turn on its tail.

What needs to be done if we are to approach the problem in a serious manner is, firstly, to agree on a more dynamic, more complete definition of man and, secondly, to act on this definition by pushing responsibility out to the regions. Likewise, in order to establish the necessary authenticity in development design, then the obvious should be recognized, even cherished, as a political imperative, namely, that the center, over time, cannot pretend to *control* the parts just as the parts cannot always and systematically ignore the center. On a global basis, this problem, this imperative, is neither self-evident nor prosaic. For in order to establish within reason the appropriate synergism or reciprocity between the parts and the whole, it will be necessary to admit that man is:

1. living within a one-planet system,
2. responsible for the whole, collectively; and,
3. capable of acting humanely, that is, on the basis of care, of liberty, and not just on the basis of self-interest.

This turnabout will require a change in conceptual framework. For we will need to tell ourselves that man is pluralistic, not just selfish, or backward, or passive, or underdeveloped. Resolution of this question will determine the future of the community of man in the twenty-first century. Ironically, advances in technology, communications, and weaponry only render, as we have seen recently, the problem less self-evident, less prosaic, and more urgent. The rise of Pan-Arab fundamentalism is but one manifestation of the center overwhelming the periphery—with reaction in kind.

On a more practical level, it could prove appropriate (even necessary) to break up our global organizations into more flexible, interlinking parts. This means organizations such as the World Bank, the FAO, and even the United Nations. Each organization should have at least three global centers where needs and interests can be identified and protected on a regional, if not on a country by country basis. This thought is not too far from Western ideas on public order. *E pluribus unum.* Would it be too much to ask that we believe in our money?

Herbert Kahn noted that "an ounce of an interesting or proper perspective is often worth many pounds of brains or analysis in gaining insight."[4] One does not need too many pounds of brains nor elaborate computer analysis to recognize that centralization, in conformity with our notion of causal reality, has become a global fetish. This fetish is nowhere more manifest than at the United Nations or at its various agencies, including the World Bank.

Despite its relative independence from political and from commercial influence, the World Bank has established itself as the principal temple of worship for the propagation of Kahn's "modernized ideology." The World Bank has become the matrix and the mother of modern development policy. This matrix was consolidated under Robert McNamara despite his genuine efforts to help the poor and the destitute.

FROM PROJECT FINANCE TO PROPHECY

When Robert McNamara was recruited to head the World Bank Group in 1968, not only had the World Bank found a decidedly competent manager—ex-chairman of Ford Motor Company, ex-secretary of defense—but McNamara himself found that he had walked into a political power vacuum in Washington. This power vacuum allowed McNamara to undertake major policy changes at the World Bank, changes that were to leave their definitive mark on subsequent development thinking and action. We should note in anticipation of the next chapter that both the thinking and the action have been largely ignored by the major multinational banks.

By tradition, the president of the World Bank is always an American citizen. In the past, this had meant political allegiance (sometimes blind) to U.S. government foreign policy objectives as well as careful coordination with Treasury Department guidelines. McNamara, however, arrived at the summit of the World Bank in the very year that the Vietnam War and student revolts had shaken the Johnson administration to its foundation. McNamara himself was nominated to the presidency of the World Bank because he could no longer be counted upon to support unequivocally American military action in Vietnam. For the Johnson administration, the appointment meant a lateral move—into limbo. Indeed, U.S. development policy had taken a back seat to closing the Ho Chi Minh trail.

For Robert McNamara, the appointment represented an occasion to marry his own management capabilities with his long-standing, even passionate, concern for Third World poverty. Already known for his stoic virtues of self-discipline and self-sufficiency, McNamara lost no time in changing the direction and the scope of World Bank lending activities. He later was to argue with his critics that his policy changes were not anti-American but rather pro-development.

The McNamara policy initiatives have been understood by some observers as a response to the mistakes that he had made in Vietnam and to the lessons that he had learned from that unhappy experience. The mistakes and the lessons were both of a practical and of a moral order. Practical in the sense that for McNamara development policy should make use of appropriate technology or know-how, something that the people being developed can understand and relate to. Moral in the sense that development strategy should address human needs first and economic performance second. By 1970, McNamara was to argue openly: "We believe economic progress remains precarious and sterile without corresponding social improvement."[5] This dual concern for product and people earned McNamara the ambiguous title of "Prophet" and "Crusader."

Under Robert McNamara, the practical and the moral came together. For example, World Bank development indicators and subsequent project design were changed in such a way as to recognize, indeed promote, the synthesis between caring and cost. Project implementation attempted to blend human needs and human resource development with economic growth. Gradually, the World Bank was to lose what had become known as its "edifice complex." Increasingly, emphasis was placed on social and human infrastructure that is, training, nutrition, sanitation, and rural development in addition to the more classical concern for airports, bridges, and steel mills. The development indicators themselves, which previously related only to quantitatively measurable economic magnitudes, were expanded to include distribution, public participation, shelter, employment, and demographic change. In other words, development with growth; growth with distribution. "Social justice is not simply an abstract ideal," McNamara argued. "It is a sensible way of making life more livable for everyone."[6] But social justice is not simply practical or sensible. For McNamara, it is productive, rational, ethical, and, in the long run, the *sine qua non* condition for economic progress and development. Thus, social harmony was taken to be a precondition rather than the result of economic growth.

Accepting this as a premise, McNamara proposed sectorial shifts in the World Bank investment programs. These shifts were to change the lending officers of the World Bank from bankers to developers. In his first full year as president at the World Bank, lending for education tripled, and it quadrupled for agriculture. By his departure from office in 1981, lending for agriculture would total nearly 25 percent of cumulative World Bank Group investment and nearly 50 percent of the current lending program.[7] In the meanwhile, the World

Bank's yearly financial package to the Third World increased to more than $12 billion by 1981 compared to an annual investment program of about $1 billion in 1968. Hence, McNamara's tenure changed the quality and the quantity of World Bank development finance.

Unfortunately, while McNamara's goals shifted, and with them his orientation, the means, from a structural point of view, remained the same. And this for three reasons: First, while McNamara was able to expand the type of projects that the World Bank might be willing to finance, he was unable to reduce the foreign exchange or import component of World Bank Group credit. Second, it was not in McNamara's nature to decentralize bank activities. Third, and even more importantly, McNamara, like his successor A. W. Clausen, did not question the overall option by which post-World War II development theory and policy have been determined. We shall need to look briefly at each of these shortcomings in order to appreciate the precise role that the World Bank presently occupies in Third World development.

In terms of the World Bank's first constraint, both McNamara and Clausen have attempted without success to obtain from the World Bank's principal shareholders the right to finance more than 10 percent of the local costs of a given investment project. In the Third World, supply follows available finance like the moon follows the earth. Hence, the objective of an increased local cost component would be to expand local employment as well as local technical expertise. In turn, the objective would be to expand the development process itself.

In the face of sustained First World opposition to this idea, World Bank management has sought, as an alternative, approval to increase program or nonproject lending above an existing cap of 10 percent of total group credit. Program lending, like the IMF's Extended Fund Facility, is intended to allow for structural adjustment to changing global economic conditions and is not tied to foreign imports. Subsequent U.S. administrations have argued that the World Bank should stay out of the welfare business. This theme was particularly cherished by Bill Simon during the Nixon administration and, recently, by the more snappy Beryl Sprinkel, the current undersecretary of the Treasury for international affairs. McNamara and Clausen, however, would both agree that something structural must be done, as Clausen argues, "for alleviating pain and poverty." Before leaving office, McNamara simply noted: " 'Too little too late' is history's most universal epitaph for political regimes which have lost their mandate to the demands of landless, jobless, disenfranchised and desperate men."[8] For the moment, more program lending, as well as an increase in the local cost component, have been denied.

The second and third shortcomings to World Bank lending activity, that is, centralization and free trade, fit both the style and the principle on which World Bank management operates. For example, Robert McNamara's leadership style was one of a modern manager (not captain) of industry and government: clipped, efficient, controlled, and disciplined. These were the intellectual virtues by which McNamara was known and respected. In turn, the implementation of development policy was reduced to a matrix system: the bureaucracy increased and the bank centralized. Shortly after coming to office, McNamara announced a vastly expanded program of country economic missions: "These will be regularly scheduled, thoroughly staffed, comprehensive missions whose mandate will be to assist the member government to draw up an overall development strategy which will include every major sector of the economy, and every relevant aspect of the nation's social framework."[9]

In practice, these missions come from and return to Washington, D.C., leaving behind their perceptions, their life-style, their tastes, and their methods, models, and predilections. While World Bank lending has been expanded and now cuts across many more national and sectorial frontiers, the missions unfortunately tend to remain just that— a mission rather than an integrated participant in the long-term development process. In fact, inevitably the mission becomes a sort of crusade, manipulated in this case by the soft arm of centrally planned World Bank development models. Like a crusade, the models remain an alien force, subject to foreign influence and sponsored by foreign money. Like a crusade, the models tend to leave in their wake a goodly amount of indurate hostility and waste. If this is not true of individually sponsored World Bank projects, it is true of the overall development model into which the projects fit.

And this brings us to the third related constraint on World Bank operations. The third constraint is the most weighty for it inspires the first and the second. Both Robert McNamara and A. W. Clausen have believed in the efficiency of (and have supported) a global and centralizing development model based on Ricardian economic theory. Like Clausen today, Robert McNamara was to argue before his board of governors in 1976: "A serious and sustained effort to reduce trade barriers in the industrialized countries could mean more than $30

billion a year in increased export earnings for developing countries."[10]
The argument assumes that exports automatically aid development.
Ero in principio magnus est in fine.

In keeping with World Bank strategy, McNamara believed that
economic growth and development could be furthered by "broadening the scope of true comparative advantage."[11] This means, of
course, the wide-open shift, both North and South, "of capital and
labor away from marginal industries into more competitive and productive sectors."[12] Once again, we are face to face with our worldview:
competition determines choice. Likewise, the full play of self-interest
promotes progress. Both McNamara and Clausen have found themselves, perhaps unwittingly, working out of our prevailing Western
paradigm. They are convinced that the moral case for development
assistance is coincident with national interest, that the low road and
the high road lead to the same place. Self-interest, social justice, and
common sense all go together in making, according to McNamara, the
"poor more productive" and by establishing, according to World Bank
strategy, "a more rational framework of international trade."[13]

Both presidents of the World Bank, like many of our best inten-
tioned public leaders and international civil servants, would agree with
John Maynard Keynes when near the end of his life he wrote: "For
at least another hundred years we must pretend to ourselves and to
everyone that fair is foul and foul is fair; for foul is useful and fair is
not. Avarice and usury and precaution must be our Gods for a little
while longer." Lord Keynes wrote these sentences in the essay entitled
"Economic Possibilities for Our Grandchildren."[14] Unfortunately,
based on our defense calculations in terms of megatons, our Third
World lending in terms of megadollars, and based on World Bank
poverty figures, we might not enjoy another 100 years "to pretend."
In fact, the "Debt Bomb" and the real bomb would seem to argue
otherwise.

FREE TRADE VERSUS HUMAN NEEDS

From shared experience and common commitment, Robert Mc-
Namara and A. W. Clausen both have made the moral leap from machinery to purpose, from production to helping the poor. Yet they
have not stepped back to make a judgment of the whole. McNamara,
with more on-line experience in the shantytowns and bidonvilles of
the Third World has perhaps come closer than most of his colleagues
to questioning the model. He certainly decided that something was

not working and that this something was more than a simple problem of money, men, and machines.

For Robert McNamara, the key consideration was of a logical order and related to establishing goals ahead of the means. "The first requirement of management," McNamara often explained, "is to determine your objectives."[15] Did this clarity in reasoning process come from McNamara's experience at Ford Motor Company or from the more sobering lessons learned by the nation as a whole in Vietnam? In any case, after two or three years at the World Bank, Robert McNamara attempted to turn prevailing development programming on its head. With the assistance of some of his closest advisers, notable among them Barbara Ward and Hollis Chenery, McNamara reoriented development policy around what became known as "basic human needs."[16] According to the theory, or better the logic, human needs direct efforts back to the appropriate means and then forward to the ends. The human needs that the World Bank initially identified were material rather than normative. Nonetheless, the concern with people, not just with economic growth, represented a significant shift in development theory after more than 25 years of trial, error, and in some instances, enduring human tragedy.

Human need-oriented development strategy is based on the following observations: Firstly, sustained economic growth can only be achieved once the worst physical aspects of poverty are dealt with. Human needs later were expanded to include liberty and identity.

Secondly, it was recognized that where income distribution is severely distorted, market demand mechanism does not provide the only reliable basis on which to allocate scarce resources, including essential public services. The logical response, then, would be to bring production down to the level of demand possibility and to spread delivery systems of essential public services out to the poor. In its pure form, the theory would argue that consumption planning should precede production and that productivity can be improved through the heavy investment in social overhead, for example, schools, clinics, training centers, hospitals, and the like. Consumption planning, of course, might well contradict the more basic assumptions about free market forces. Likewise, investment in social overhead has been criticized as a statist solution to Third World development.

Thirdly, production models, in this case World Bank project selection, should take into consideration likely long-term social costs oftentimes ignored in microeconomic planning, for example, shifting land values, labor displacement, environmental change, effects on food production, and domestic terms of trade, as well as such *nonmaterial* factors as self-reliance, self-confidence, or, in a word, personal dignity. In order to achieve these various objectives, production might best be spread across a wider range of activity and be consistent with local manpower, aptitude, and technology. As was the case during the Marshall Plan, special arrangements could be made for what was called "participatory monitoring." In practice, nearly all of these objectives run at crosscurrents with the more fundamental organizing principle of comparative advantage.

Fourthly, World Bank planning theory attempts, however faintly, to focus policy action on the well-known political nettles, i.e., social injustice, land tenure and title, political abuse, and corruption. Since Robert McNamara, World Bank development policy has had the intellectual honesty to recognize that a direct attack on absolute poverty must rest fundamentally on political and not on economic decision making. This innovation won McNamara few friends and not a few enemies.

The donor member countries, for their part, were quick to pull back from McNamara's argument. The assertion personalizes responsibility and threatens the existing political relationship North-South. Consequently, long-term objectives are jeopardized in the name of temporary convenience and stability, what we might call the "status quo." Under pressure from the Nixon administration, McNamara was prepared to leave the World Bank. At Nixon's own hasty departure from government, McNamara was convinced to stay on for another term. The World Bank's concern for human needs coincided with President Jimmy Carter's concern for human rights.

In order to defend need-oriented development policy against rising criticism in the North and in the South, the World Bank has not ceased to explain (and believes) that by meeting essential human needs, its development efforts will improve the long-term productivity of the poor and likewise their competitiveness. Thus, the World Bank still operates within its traditional worldview. Attempts have been made simply to humanize the structure of our modernized ideology. As McNamara himself argued: "Just as the developing countries have begun to demonstrate their natural comparative advantage in certain labor-intensive manufactures, a new threat of protectionism is gathering momentum in the developed world. This is both inequitable and shortsighted since it denies the developing countries the only long-range economic strategy that can ultimately decrease their dependence on foreign assistance."[17]

World Bank management seems to have one foot in and one foot out of our prevailing Western paradigm. Trade-led growth according to comparative advantage remains at the heart of World Bank development theory. Thus, management should not be surprised to see certain of their poorer member countries crippled on international markets even when these same countries have played by rules of the game. For, as we have argued, the free trade growth model springs from a darker and more deadly vision of nature: from the law of the survival of the fittest. This law finds its origins at the dawn of the Age of Reason. "The Matter, Form, and Power of a Common-Wealth," as Thomas Hobbes instructed, "resembles a LEVIATHAN." The logic of the Leviathan continues to inspire global economic development planning and this despite the more genuine, more felt, and more reasonable moral instincts of those people primarily responsible for the design and for the implementation of policy.

To paraphrase the ancients, a small *crack* in the construction of one's logic leads to a mighty *fissure* at the accomplishment of one's task. The small crack in development logic originates with the almost benign confidence in the universality, the necessity, and the automaticity of free trade as the most viable path to Third World development. The fissure has taken on of late a more widespread, erratic, and manifold dimension.

In financial terms, the fissure can be seen in the Third World's recent attempts to export its way out of an economic crisis. These attempts manifestly are failing. The resultant debt crisis has led to a disguised rupture in our banking system. For example, most of the top ten U.S. banks have lent more than 50 percent of their capital base to Brazil alone. In the case of Citibank, the biggest bank of them all, credit exposure exceeds 75 percent of shareholders equity. In a negative sense, Brazil owns the bank, if ownership has anything to do with determining one's option. And Brazil is effectively broke.

In social, or more precisely, in human terms, the fissure translates into what the normally judicious World Bank has described as the "appalling deprivation" of growing and of grinding Third World poverty. When taken in context, the term itself is not adequate, but, is judicious. For as Willy Brandt describes in *Common Crisis*: "Every two seconds of this year a child will die of hunger or disease. And no statistic can express what it is to see even one child die . . . to see the uncomprehending panic in eyes which are still the clear and lucid eyes of a child."[18]

Robert McNamara has called this appalling deprivation "obscene." Accepting the term in its context, we might argue further that the situation is *morally obscene* because the event itself, this historical fact, finds its explanation, its roots, in a philosophy, in a worldview, and, finally, in a specific economic theory that can be changed. The question remains: Will the worldview, and the socioeconomic theory that follows, be changed (perhaps definitively) by the now terrifying force of its own internal logic, or will our paradigm be carefully disembodied by the intervention of *Homo sapiens*? In the nuclear age, the choice, not only for the Third World but for the First World as well, presents itself as fairly self-evident.

For its part, the World Bank under Robert McNamara and A. W. Clausen has gone half the distance, the most obvious half, in the right direction. The World Bank's concern for basic human needs clearly serves to bring process down to purpose. Unfortunately, the process itself remains wedded to the increasingly fragile and overworked free trade growth model. As a result, World Bank project design operates at cross-purposes: on the one hand, for individual people and communities, and, on the other hand, for global product. Both objectives are worthy, but the second, if the whole is to hold together, must clearly remain subordinate to the first. Our development model argues differently. Our model argues that the needs of the whole will be served by the interplay of comparative advantage even between the strong and the weak. In this context, the inherent conflict between human needs and global product turns the development process into a paradox. To work its way out of this paradox, the World Bank eventually will need to choose between paradigm and purpose, between global product and people, between a fissure or a change in premise. For the moment, the World Bank thinks that it can serve two gods at once.

Thus, the conflict between human needs and unlimited free trade, between poverty and advantage, has not been resolved. Yet it can be maintained that need-oriented development theory does put emphasis (even if distorted by process) on what development is all about, that is, the human person. As a function of these needs, the World Bank has pulled back from its one-dimensional concern for industry at the expense of agriculture and for purely economic growth at the expense of meaning. When the World Bank shifted emphasis from construction to collaboration and from product to promoting development, the bilateral lenders and the commercial banks rushed in to fill the void. In this way, the chasm between the rich and the poor, between the weak and the strong, has continued to expand. The same holds true for Third World debt and for the Third World's growing incapacity to service same.

By the mid-1970s, the primary responsibility for financing the development process moved from the multilateral aid agencies to the more aggressive export credit programs of individual governments and to the private sector commercial banks. Exports meant additional jobs in the North and what the commercial banks originally construed as "no risk" lending.

When a given multimillion dollar investment project no longer fit World Bank investment criteria, Third World governments would address themselves to their Northern allies and to their friendly foreign banker. Subsequent negotiations inevitably led, with rare exception, to a successful contract signing, whether for a billion dollar presidential palace in downtown Libreville, for an equally expensive OAU conference in Liberia, or for a useless pipeline in Ecuador. The results, we are contending with today both in the boardrooms of our major multinational banks and in every Third World bidonville.

Development has been hopelessly confused with foreign markets and foreign markets with easy money. How did this confusion penetrate from government to private sector banking, and where does the comity of nations go from here?

9
From Third World Project Finance to Government Export Promotion: The Origins of the "Debt Trap"

Until quite recently, a number of our leading multinational bankers have considered Third World sovereign borrowers to be risk free. "But a country does not go bankrupt," Walter Wriston explained to the *New York Times* in September 1982, just prior to the Mexican debt crisis.[1]

Some 30 years earlier, Walter Wriston's bank, Citicorp, now the largest bank in the world, set out "to make the whole world bankable." In turn, the big banks of the whole world followed, some would say, "like lemmings into the sea." They did so based on a lending logic corrosive to international economic order and to global political stability.[2]

By 1975, multinational banks had replaced multilateral development agencies as the single most important source of Third World credit. By 1980, commercial banks were providing nearly two-thirds of the foreign financing needs of the world's poorest nations, up from 15 percent in 1970. The result of this structural change in the complexion of capital flows to the Third World was immediate. Since the start of the Third Development Decade of the 1980s, about 40 countries have agreed to or applied for rescheduling or have had de facto substantial payment arrears on bank credit. Total official and private foreign debt of these countries at year-end 1984 exceeded $500 billion (more than 60 percent of the total Third World term debt.)

The numbers themselves confront politicians and international civil servants with the very real possibility of serious financial disorder moving from the Third World to our major financial centers. Indeed, the bankruptcy of single, heavily indebted Third World nations, for example, Brazil, Mexico, South Korea, and even Chile or Nigeria, could well spread to the community of nations. In the eyes of some well-placed observers, the disruption would surface as an extension into the international arena of the IMF riots mentioned earlier. That is, the riots would cause an implosion of international credit generally. The big banks are already making loans to a number of sovereign Third World governments to cover creditor interest only. We might call this the "finger-in-the-dike" approach to global economic order.

Yet not a few senior bankers continue to agree with the biggest of them all, Citibank, when its recent chairman, Walter Wriston, argues blandly that countries don't disappear, they just roll over.[3] That is, they simply renew their loans. Since the start of 1982, demand for rescheduling has quadrupled to include an additional 30 countries for an amount of payment arrears exceeding $150 billion. Coincidentally, this $150 billion corresponds to about 375 percent of *Fortune* magazine's estimate of the capital base of the largest 100 U.S. banks.[4] Thus, the debt trap has come to resemble for management a trapdoor leading to an endless encounter with the possibility of overnight insolvency.

THE START OF THE DEBT CRISIS

At the beginning, the reasoning process behind international lending to the Third World was neither as original nor as arrogant nor as vacuous as today's defense of commercial bank credit to the World's poorest nations. In fact, at the start of the First Development Decade, the big banks merely stepped into the development paradigm proposed by development theoreticians, their governments, and export lobbies. Or rather, the banks *were bought* in with attractive government incentives.

The development paradigm itself gave birth, as we have noted, to a series of decidedly mechanistic growth models based on free trade according to comparative advantage. The principal *advantage* turns out to be *finance*. The banks, for their part, have been drawn into the growth models by virtue primarily of bilateral aid programs and, more importantly, in connection with First World export credit guarantee schemes.

In addition to attractive commission business, both the aid programs and the guarantee schemes provided the banks, at least initially, with substantial risk free protection against Third World loan losses. These government insurance and guarantee programs eventually were extended to include participatory lending with banks at subsidized interest rates, buy back arrangements, discount facilities, and the blending of aid with bank credit. Thus, the banking system came to fit the economic model with the fee structure leading the way. In the process, private sector banks lost their proper identity as a storehouse of wealth and as a catalyst for sound economic growth. Instead, the big multinational banks have become an extension of public sector finance to a limited number of export industries in the North and to a less select group of sovereign government borrowers in the South. In sum, the export credit programs have reinforced the growth models, and the growth models have shaped bank-lending methodology in the Third World.

Hence, from the start, the application of the development paradigm itself served as the original "sweetener" activating the banks to enter the Third World "market." Lest we doubt the continued validity of this argument, interest rate subsidies have cost the Western taxpayer nearly $15 billion in the two calendar years of 1980-82 alone. These subsidies do not include the costs associated with the balance of the government-sponsored export credit schemes, including loan charge-offs, the funding of payment arrears, inflation and exchange rate guarantees, tax rebates, and the like.

In keeping with the growth model, government development theorists are tempted to argue that export subsidies represent a form of development transfer from the First World to the Third. However, the proliferation of export credits, like tied-aid, has been co-opted by export lobbies in the North and by their banks. This is entirely natural for the credit programs are designed to stimulate First World domestic production and to support positive trade flows. Thus, the development program operates on a horizontal line as a function of its one-dimensional nature. The argument is without nuance at the U.S. Export-Import Bank (Eximbank). We are told by government authorities:

> The recognition that export credit availability is as important a competitive tool as price, quality, or service has resulted in programs designed to meet specific exporter needs and to broaden significantly the horizon of export opportunity to American industry.[5]

Starting in the early 1960s, the export horizon was broadened to include the Third World as a bloc. The administrator of the U.S. Agency for International Development (AID) program, M. Peter McPherson, is yet more to the point. In 1981, he told Congress: "Private U.S. investment in developing countries has been encouraged and the system of international trade strengthened in recognition of the opportunities trade can offer as an engine of growth, especially for the market oriented economies."[6]

Progress becomes the expected by-product of Northern export programs. Leaving aside for a moment the broader developmental issues, even on economic grounds, the logic collapses at two points simultaneously.

Firstly, as every international businessman, civil servant, and banker knows, government-sponsored export credits tie high prices to limited choice on only nominally attractive financial terms. In the case of Pakistan, for instance, the weighted average price for 20 projects analyzed by the Ministry of Plan came out to be 151 percent higher from tied sources compared to international bidding. None of the big OECD countries were exempted from the findings. The projects surveyed included a sulphuric acid plant exported from France, a nylon twine plant from the United States, wheel and axle assemblies from Japan (plus 204 percent), a hardboard manufacturing plant from Germany, and engineering works from the United Kingdom.[7] Pakistan's experience, of course, is typical and probably on the low side given that country's relatively strong civil service. In the long run, export credits are excessively costly for the buyer, for the banks, and for their respective governments. Handsome markups have become the rule and rescheduling the result.

Second, export credits do not serve to expand markets but rather to "buy them"—especially in capital-deficit countries, where most of the credits go. This "buying" aspect further distorts the development process itself. The case of Korea provides ample testimony.

In 1965, U.S. aid and tied-credits accounted for about 75 percent of commercial exports to South Korea. In that same year, Japan signed a Normalization Treaty with the Seoul government. Under the terms of the treaty, Japan *gave* South Korea $300 million in grant aid and $500 million in loans. In five years, (1965-70), Japan's exports to Korea expanded fivefold to $754 million. By 1970, Japan had replaced the United States as South Korea's principal foreign supplier. During the same period, the multinational banks had followed their governments and their customer base into South Korea on the assumption that governments in the Third World do not disappear, nor would they be allowed to by their allies. Korea's commercial bank debt rose from $120 million in 1965 to $2.2 billion in 1970. The country's ratio of debt service to exports increase to 25 percent, or more than double the World Bank's recommended levels.[8]

By the early 1970s, a full-scale supplier credit war broke out between the United States and Japan over exports to South Korea. As a result, the Seoul government continued its shopping spree: synthetic textile plants with privileged trade agreements for supply into already depressed U.S. markets (the boomerang effect), gigantic steel complexes, three nuclear power stations, a shipyard complex, and a host of other industrial projects, all of which rely not only on foreign capital and machines but on Northern markets for the expected payout. The credit war over South Korea subsequently expanded to include French, German, and English suppliers. The final paradox within the paradigm has been nicely summarized by a senior executive of Westinghouse Electric Company, Gordon Hurlbert, when he told Congress:

> We were offered an opportunity by the Korean Electric Co. to be awarded two nuclear turbine generator units last year, and all we had to do was have financing that was equal to what the French were offering.[9]

The same witness testified earlier that a nuclear power plant cost about $1 billion and that its export to South Korea would provide "25 thousand man-years worth of employment for American workers."[10]

After Brazil and Mexico, South Korea remains by far one of the world's most heavily indebted Third World nations. The World Bank has severely criticized the sale of nuclear power stations to South Korea on financial, economic, and domestic security grounds. The sophistication of the equipment has been judged incompatible with locally available technical skills and training. Nonetheless, the sales continued in keeping with our worldwide growth model, not only to Korea but to Brazil, Argentina, the Philippines, Taiwan, and to other heavily indebted Third World countries, including oil exporters such as Iraq, none of whom can now afford to pay for the purchases.

Because of its expense and danger, nuclear power provides a particularly hallucinating example of the built-in momentum behind bank lending and exports to the Third World. The same logic, however, applies to other big-ticket items such as jet aircraft, refineries, shipbuilding works, and the like.

In the case of Korea, some of these projects—shipbuilding, synthetic fibers, and steel—have come back to haunt Northern industrialists. For South Korea enjoys, at the cost of an extreme form of economic extroversion, the factors that have allowed high-priced export credits "to work for development." The factors include a disciplined labor force, a highly centralized government, a relatively homogeneous society, and, most importantly, favored access to Northern markets, mostly American. The combination of these factors seldom exist among the poorest members of the world community, that is, among the vast majority of Third World countries. And even Korea, Eximbank's favorite and favored client, has asked commercial banks for a debt stretch-out.

Meanwhile, had Westinghouse won the sale of the two nuclear generator units to South Korea, the company could have counted on Eximbank support for up to 85 percent of the sale. Of this amount, commercial banks would participate in the financing of the credit against partial Eximbank guarantees covering both commercial and political risks. Put differently, the commercial banks would be buying risk on the U.S. government at considerably higher yields than U.S. Treasury bills of similar maturity in return for its participation in the credit. For its part, Eximbank would attempt when possible to sell to the banks some share of straight Korean risk in order to "keep the banks honest" and to conserve its own resources for further exports. In addition, the commercial banks would be requested by their customer, the exporter, to finance the 15 percent down payment, plus local costs not covered in the Eximbank credit, plus cost overruns, working capital, and, in some instances, even early debt repayment and interest charges on the Eximbank loan. The precise details would be worked out between the buyer, the Eximbank, the seller, and the banks. In turn, the seller would offer its banks a special domestic relationship against participation in the "deal." Westinghouse Corporation, like other major exporters, Boeing, GE, Caterpillar Tractor, Bechtel, GM, and Rockwell International to name but a few, are much sought after corporate relationships. Thus, participation is consistent with development North-South. The trap is set—for the buyer, the seller and the banks.

Meanwhile, the buyer, if he is sharp enough, can finance more than 100 percent of the purchased equipment for his own development. In the end, the development process has become synonymous not even with growth for its own sake but with excess industrial capacity in the North and/or with unemployment. The growth model is neither invented nor constructed in participation with Third World development requirements but rather sold on a "turnkey" basis. The terms of the sale ultimately are detrimental to the North as well as to the South. Growth, according to unlimited comparative advantage, has turned into a multifaceted Hydra representing not orderly development but the Python with which the world community is struggling in today's financial markets.

The borrower arrives on stage at the end of the play as a minor character to recite his own epilogue. What he has to tell us—namely, that there are people in the cities rioting and people in the country-side starving—surprisingly takes us off guard. The banks have been looking the other way. They have been banking the exporter. The borrower, that is, the client, remains of secondary importance in the decision-making process. As the chairman of Boeing, T. A. Wilson, told Congress in recent testimony: "Without the involvement of Ex-Im, commercial banks will not participate in loans to emerging nations."[11] To be more precise, he should have said that banks certainly would not participate in loans to emerging nations based on the way that those loans currently are conceived and executed. They have done so, however, based on the tacit assumption that the money lent to LDC governments eventually would be backed up by First World aid and guarantees. Accordingly, the free trade paradigm has been distorted to include the competitive, even predatory financing of First World exports, sometimes in the form of foreign aid and sometimes in the form of commercial bank loans.

Likewise, the assumption of a government takeout probably accounts for the analytic judgment and even for the personal conduct of a number of today's leading bankers. At Citicorp, Walter Wriston is reported to have advised his fellow lending officers: "Around here, it's Jakarta that pays the check."[12] And at Chase Manhattan, the chairman, Willard Butcher, asks rhetorically: "Is Mexico worth $85 billion? Of course, it is. It has oil . . . gold, silver, copper."[13] These reflections, and others, represent a singular lack of responsibility to depositors and to clients as well as a manifest parochialism in analytic ability. The problem perhaps stems firstly from blurred perceptions of what a bank is all about and secondly, from a lack of distinction between multi-national and domestic banking. Our banks have been taken as passive financial intermediaries. At the same time, what we call multinational, transnational, or international banks are in reality domestic banks with international networks. This latter distinction is important to recognize as it explains the inappropriate language being used to explain bank lending activities in the Third World. Both the perceptions of what a bank is all about and the distinctions between multinational and domestic banking have been greatly confused by our system of government-sponsored export credit guarantee programs and by the growth scheme within which they operate. In fact, the programs have connected our private banking system and our major corporations to a caricature of Third World development. Both the language and the caricature are not without political consequence.

For instance, while it still might be possible to argue with Walter Wriston that "countries don't disappear," the same cannot be said for people nor for their economies. Historically, the rescheduling of bank credit corresponds, in the case of sovereign Third World borrowers, to a particularly ugly form of bankruptcy at the national level: 26 people dead in Peru (1977), 79 people dead in Egypt (1979), two aborted revolutions in Zaire (1977 and 1978), harsh repression in Turkey (1975), followed by Pakistan, Indonesia, the Philippines, and South Korea, a military takeover in Brazil (1965), and a near total breakdown of social order in Ghana dating from that country's first rescheduling in 1966. In every case, with the exception of Zaire, a severe debt crisis (bankruptcy) has resulted in a change of government. While countries do not literally disappear, their governments, a number of desperately poor civilians, and the bank's money sometimes do.

To disguise the loss of money, the big banks simply lent more. In fact, a lot more. Between 1975 and 1980, commercial bank lending to the Third World net of repayments accelerated from $15 billion to $50 billion on an annual basis. Net disbursements reached about $55 billion in 1981. In 1982, the music slowed down, to come to a near halt in 1983. The cumulative scare from the debt rescheduling of the big borrowers—Poland, then Mexico, Brazil, Argentina, and the Philippines—reduced net private bank flows to less than $15 billion per year. Nonetheless, the disguise, what has been called "the money allusion," continues. By 1982, approximately four out of every five dollars of new Third World bank credit had been committed by the banks for purposes of repaying interest and principal on previous loans. By year-end 1984, virtually all new LDC loans represented refinancing of existing debt and interest payments only. The gaps between previous and current capital flows, that is, the minimum necessary to keep the Third World and the banks afloat, has been provided in the form of emergency relief from the IMF, from the Bank for International Settlements, and from individual taxpayers in the North and South alike.

For example, in the first round of debt renegotiations for Mexico, the overall financial package totaled $19.7 billion. Of this amount, the IMF provided $4.5 billion, the U.S. government $2.9 billion, and foreign governments $1.2 billion. The balance (approximately $11 billion) came from over 600 commercial banks with existing exposure in Mexico. Of this $11 billion in question, $10 billion represented postponement of debt repayment. In other words, of the $19.7 billion rescue package, foreign governments provided $9.7 billion in net new monies, while the banks disbursed not more than $1 billion in additional credit.

Not by coincidence, this $1 billion represented about one year's interest payments on the $10 billion in bank debt that was rescheduled. In addition, the banks walked away with a 1 percent flat restructuring fee.

As Paul Volcker explained to a congressional joint economic committee: "When you get these strong adjustment programs, what you will find in every one of these cases is that the amount of new credit that is necessary is sharply reduced from what the banks had been providing in recent years."[14] With more urgency, we might argue that the adjustment program has become an extremely expensive bandage, a bandage applied by the IMF and the Fed but paid for by the taxpayer.

What is sometimes called "Mexico's bailout" resembles the overall pattern of sovereign risk debt reschedulings that the commercial banks want strengthened. Morgan Guaranty's chief economist, Rimmer de Vries is quite specific on the subject. In a question-and-answer memorandum sent out to all corporate officers at Morgan Guaranty, de Vries puts the First World governments themselves on the carpet:

> Most . . . loans to LDC's that are on the books of banks today were made sometime during the past ten years. Well before then developing countries had turned to banks for loans as the financing needed to sustain their economic growth and development outstripped the willingness of industrial-country governments and international institutions to provide assistance.[15]

Morgan Guaranty's senior economist then goes from *banking* to *begging*.

Mr. Rimmer de Vries wants the assistance now, valued at about $10 billion. He asks: "Why should the U.S. contribute additional money to the IMF to bail out the banks, especially when the taxpayer's money could be put to better use creating jobs and stimulating the economy?"[16] The answer for de Vries is simple: There is no alternative choice. "In the absence of IMF support, LDC's could be forced to cut back their economic growth and imports even more severely than under IMF programs. Such cutbacks could be a serious drag on U.S. economic recovery, and could also have destabilizing effects on developing countries."[17]

The argument at Citibank rings yet louder, and, typically, it is expressed in more self-righteous fashion. When questioned publicly by Congress about the Third World bailout, a bank spokesman, George J. Clarke, said that "to my knowledge, no banker has asked the government for help."[18] Taken at face value, this statement would indicate that some banks either are decidedly ungrateful or, alternatively, unconscious of their own financial weakness. A third explanation might be that certain bankers are in the process of acting out a big bluff in the face of an increasingly fragile financial system. As Barry Sullivan, chairman of First Chicago Corporation, told the American Bankers Association in Washington on September 21, 1981: ". . . as human beings we are all capable of responding to bad news with 'denial.' "

"What countries with liquidity problems will do," says Hans H. Angermuller, a Citibank vice-chairman, "is what . . . they historically have done. They will slow down . . . less essential imports, even at the political cost of curtailing popular internal programs. They will adopt internal austerity measures that will reduce deficits, subsidies and inflation, all designed to enhance exports which will start to pay off old, and support new, debt."[19] The eternal return.

Notwithstanding Citibank's optimism, the financial gaps mentioned earlier most certainly will continue into the late 1980s. For the banks themselves no longer enjoy the capital base, the liquidity, nor the income stream necessary to carry the system. Under the best of circumstances, the most that the banks might be able to do would be to change direction, or rather, Third World lending methodology, before, as one banker put it, "the whole world comes due." This change in direction can only be achieved through a revision in Third World development strategy and related First World export incentive programs.

THE DEPTH OF THE PROBLEM

At the start of 1984, the top ten commercial banks in the United States were reporting $43.7 billion at risk to financially troubled developing countries. These figures were contained in the annual reports of the banks themselves and represent more than half again the value of their equity. By order of asset size, three out of the four largest banks had more than 200 percent of equity capital tied up or frozen in problem loans to Third World sovereign states: Citibank (203 percent), Chase Manhattan (220 percent), and Manufacturers Hanover (245 percent). These figures inevitably are "massaged" in keeping with decidedly lenient reporting requirements. For example, the numbers do not include local currency loans made in the foreign countries by branches and subsidiaries. These amounts are substantial, especially for those banks with large overseas branch networks—Citibank, Chase Manhattan, and Bank of America. In addition, successfully rescheduled loans for a number of developing countries are considered current as long as interest payments remain no longer than 90 days past due. These loans now total $200 billion plus.

In 1977, the Financial Accounting Standards Board backed down on a proposal with respect to troubled credits that would have compelled the banks to disclose and perhaps write-down loans in cases of rescheduling or "stretch-outs."[20] Instead, the definition of what constitutes a troubled credit was left largely where it belongs, to the discretion of the banks themselves. Since countries, it is argued, neither vanish nor die, a number of troubled credits simply have been rolled over on a nonstop basis—including interest payments and front-end renegotiation fees. In the process, bankers have shifted from lending for investment to brokering export credits and balance of payment loans. Unfortunately, this is consistent with the program. The deterioration in a bank's credibility seems to grow with the expansion of export credit to clients in whom the banks have neither taken an interest nor in whom they believe. Thus, the banks are connected to the model. The model has created but the illusion of Third World development, what we have earlier called a "caricature." A few examples.

In the case of the Republic of the Ivory Coast, not only was one project (a $60 million sugar plantation and mill) discouraged by the World Bank Group, but five additional complexes were built and financed under bilateral export credit guarantee programs from OECD member states: one from Belgium, one from Canada, one from Holland, one from the United States, and two from France, the country's principal trading partner. The Canadians shared the market with the British through subcontracts; the Belgians with the Austrians; the Dutch with the Germans; and the United States with no one. The French supported two agro-industrial exporting groups, the first in the French private sector and the second in the competing public sector, one for the right and one for the left. The overall cost of the Ivory Coast sugar program (a country of eight million people) exceeded $1 billion. At start-up in the late 1970s, production costs for a pound of sugar averaged nearly 300 percent of world market prices. In every case, investment expenditures surpassed original estimates by more than 200 percent to 300 percent. The entire sugar program, including original feasibility studies, down payments, front-end fees, and early interest payments were funded on borrowed money, that is, through a combination of export credits and associated commercial bank loans.

The vignette ends with the picture of an Ivory Coast farmhand spraying unwanted molasses on a dirt road in order to keep the dust down.

The image repeats itself throughout Africa and the rest of the Third World in direct proportion to the absorption capacity of the borrowing government. In Guinea, a missionary arrives to find a field full of bidets for which no one has any use parked next to the airport —express from France. In Togo, West Germany finances an important steel complex near Lome, Togo's capital. On completion, the Togolese government realizes that no iron ore nor scrap metals are available for start-up. The credibility of Togo's head of state is in jeopardy. German technicians quickly dismantle an iron pier located at the port. Ironically, the pier had been constructed by Germany prior to World War I and was still functional and functioning. The steel mill closed down its operations when pig iron from the pier was exhausted. Simultaneously, the British were completing an oil refinery about three miles from Lome with export credit from Britain. Although subsequently completed, the lights have yet to go on at the refinery. Only the debt remains as testimony to Togo's ambitious development program. The country's foreign debt was first renegotiated in Paris in the spring of 1979. While negotiations were taking place, the borrowing government was moving toward completion in downtown Lome of what has been estimated by an officer of the West African Development Bank as the world's most expensive hotel per square foot. The hotel had been financed on guaranteed supplier credits from Europe and through the local French-controlled banking system.

Geopolitically, neither the Ivory Coast, Guinea, nor Togo represent the most strategic of Third World nations, notwithstanding the fact that the Ivory Coast is the world's largest single producer of cocoa and the world's third largest producer of coffee, Guinea the free world's largest supplier of bauxite, and Togo a relatively cheap source of phosphate. For Western Europe the really strategic powers in this area of the world are Nigeria and Zaire. Nigeria has surpassed Venezuela as the second largest supplier of crude oil to the United States. Zaire enjoys a quasi-monopoly on the Free World's supply of imported cobalt and is the world's largest producer of industrial diamonds. Cobalt serves as a vital component for the U.S. aerospace, aircraft, and computer industries.

In the case both of Nigeria and Zaire, the ill-advised use of foreign credit has served but to push each country toward bankruptcy and beyond.

In the industrial sector, Nigeria has set out to become one of the Third World's principal producers of steel, both for domestic consumption and for export. Despite important revenues from oil exports, the Republic of Nigeria purchased on a turnkey basis an integrated steel complex from Germany under a combination of export credits and through a $350 million term loan syndicated by German commercial banks. The steel plant was originally conceived to utilize on-site, relatively low grade iron ore deposits. But Nigeria typically was sold—and bought—at the top of the line. With subsequent add-ons, the steel plant became increasingly sophisticated. In fact, so sophisticated that the Nigerian government has since attempted to enter into long-term supplier contracts with Brazil and Liberia for the purchase of higher quality ore. The cost of the steel complex alone will exceed $1 billion, or more than 50 percent the original estimates. This price tag does not include the future expenses of replacing Nigeria's relative comparative advantage in low grade iron ore deposits. Nor does the price tag of $1 billion pay for the higher operating costs, additional technical services, and the purchase of vessels to transport the ore. In relative terms, the $1 billion loan can be equated to about *one-tenth of the per capita income of every person* within Nigeria's vast population of some 85 million people. And this amount covers only the loan principal—not interest, commissions, nor front-end fees, nor the cost of refinancing now that the country is insolvent.

In the agricultural sector, Nigeria holds the record as the world's highest cost producer of sugar. At last count, a $750 million sugar program financed from the United Kingdom has resulted in cane output equivalent to an investment program in the industry of some $85 million maximum.[21] This represents an overcost or mismanagement factor of nearly ten to one. The sugar program has taken place within Nigeria's Five-Year Agricultural Plan. Since independence, Nigeria has become a net importer of foodstuffs, and this, not because of population growth nor natural impediments but rather because of urban migration. The sugar program has been designed to help develop the interior. In 1982, Nigeria had requested and obtained from the IMF and the banks a rescheduling of its foreign debts. In 1983 a military government replaced an elected government while the powers-to-be were negotiating under pressure an IMF Extended Fund Facility.

The case of Zaire is yet more illustrative, if not by quantity of debt then by quality, or rather, lack thereof. In the early 1970s, the banks banked on Zaire's rich copper-cobalt deposits, and the country's head of state, Joseph Mobutu, banked on the banks. By 1975, the country could no longer service its foreign bank debt nor maintain its interior transport system, nor pay for its children's schoolbooks. Between 1975 and 1978, copper and cobalt production had fallen by some 25 percent, the production of tin and strategically important columbium and tantalum ran below capacity, and the mining of manganese stopped altogether due to collapsing transport systems, lack of supplies, parts, and technicians. Meanwhile, the bank's money had been spent on a world trade center in downtown Kinshasa, an underground parking lot, a fleet of jet aircraft, an elaborate airport next to the head of state's native village, and for the importation of growing quantities of food, automobiles, and arms, with the arms partially guaranteed by the U.S. Department of Defense and the food subsidized by the Department of Agriculture. A report to Congress entitled, *Sub-Sahara Africa: Its Role in Critical Mineral Needs of the Western World*, discretely notes that during the period 1971-74, "President Mobutu embarked upon an expensive expansion program for projects of uncertain economic benefit which were financed largely by heavy borrowing from foreign banks."[22]

One of the most heavy borrowings was for construction of the Inga-Shaba hydroelectric project and power transmission line, the longest in the world. The project was financed through a combination of Eximbank loans and guarantees in collaboration with commercial banks. The original feasibility studies (1973) estimated that the project would cost about $450 million for delivery in 1976. By 1981, and some $500 million in cost overruns funded by the banks, the power line originating at the Inga Dam on the Zaire River near Kinshasa reached the site of the Shaba copper-cobalt mines near Kolwezi. In the interim, the Belgians, who were running the mines for the Zaire government, had tapped their own sources of external finance as well as locally available hydroelectric power. At a total cost of nearly $1 billion, the Inga-Shaba transmission line was connected when it was no longer needed at the mining site. In terms of maintenance, the line passes 1,800 kilometers across impressive natural obstacles and through a decidedly hostile political terrain. The high-voltage power line to Kolwezi represents not only the world's longest but the world's most expensive and useless.

While Zaire under Mobutu clearly represents one of the most artificial of Third World governments, the economic evolution of Zaire is not atypical among mineral rich developing countries. In addition to Zaire and Nigeria we need but cite the examples of Indonesia, Iran, Mexico, Peru, Venezuela, Brazil, Cameroon, and others. While most of the socioeconomic problems experienced in these countries undoubtedly are homegrown, the balance are imported. Our growth model reinforces not only the payments predicament but, more importantly, global political imbalances. Meanwhile, each of the countries mentioned above has rescheduled its foreign debt in the recent past and borrowed more money in the process.

We must ask ourselves to whose comparative advantage have export loans and attendant bank credit been used? For in the end, the most relevant question is not how much—but why? In fact, the debt trap as we shall observe turns on this key issue.

CAVEAT EMPTOR: LET THE BUYER BEWARE

At the end of the First Development Decade, the World Bank appointed Lester B. Pearson, the retired Canadian prime minister, to head up an independent research team on Third World development. Like the Brandt Commission ten years later, the Pearson Commission started out by studying the tragic effects of Third World poverty and wound up focusing on finance. "As things now stand," the Pearson Commission argued, "the problem is that suppliers of export credits are less concerned about the borrowing country's creditworthiness because of the facility of export credit insurance."[23] The commission continued, "The excessive use of export credits has created serious balance of payments problems" and is "a major reason for the need to reschedule the debts of a number of countries, notably Argentina, Brazil, Chile, Ghana, Indonesia, and Turkey. This rescheduling will be more difficult if export credits are imprudently used." Well, they were.

In fact, by halfway into the Second Development Decade, industrial and agricultural policy in the North was being merged with the system of export credits. In turn, liberal trade credits to Northern exporters favored, in the South, capital-intensive growth strategies that deny, in flagrant manner, the very concept of the Third World's comparative advantage in cheap land and labor. Meanwhile, the Pearson Commission was receiving unidentified reports of serious overpricing under export credits and had warned:

> More than one project rejected for financing by the World Bank Group on economic grounds has been promptly financed by an export credit agency. This is the most unfortunate aspect of export credit finance; it provides a temporarily painless way of financing projects conceived by overoptimistic civil servants, by politicians more concerned with im-

mediate political advantage than with potential future economic problems, and by unscrupulous salesmen for the manufacturers of capital
equipment in developed countries.[24]

The term "unscrupulous" is perhaps not a fitting adjective for
the salesmen of our major multinational companies and their bankers.
Rather, the companies and the banks have chosen (at great cost to
the community of nations) simply to perform within the context of
the development model proposed for them, the fundamentals of which
the Pearson Commission, like the Brandt Commission ten years later,
did not question. The model argues that development takes place automatically as a collateral effect of growing trade volumes. Even if one
accepted the logic at face value, the very principle itself of comparative advantage has been distorted to hinge on credit. Both the program
and the distortion have led to a paralysis of orderly growth in trade
and finance on a worldwide basis. This was inevitable.

Between 1970 and 1976, export credit programs among the OECD
nations expanded on a massive scale. By 1980, the U.S. Export-Import
Bank alone had assisted in the sale of over $100 billion worth of equip-
ment to Third World purchasers. Of this amount, $18 billion was
committed in the last year of the decade. Today, Third World debt,
or rather, the *structure* and *purpose* of this debt, has become not only
a stumbling block to economic recovery but one of the single most
important obstacles to Third World development.

First, the structure. Over the five-year period from 1978 to 1982,
Third World debt increased from $350 billion to $626 billion. Of this
amount, nonconcessional loans increased from $259 billion to $495
billion. Within the category of nonconcessional loans, export credits
and commercial bank exposure grew at approximately the same
rhythm. Export credit outstanding went from $85 billion to $148
billion, while associated bank loans expanded from $105 billion in
1978 to $210 billion in 1982. In the so-called low income LDCs, the
correlation is even greater. In other words, Third World lending during the period followed First World export credit programs rather
than simply reacting to the overall size of international liquidity available to banks on the Eurodollar or international money markets.[25]

For their part, the bankers, along with their government export
credit agencies, were not unscrupulous. Instead, they conveniently
operated on the naive assumption that tied-credits automatically
stimulate development or at least represent a competitive form of
investment. In other words, the big banks and their major exporting
clients entered a trapdoor lined, on the outside, with gold.

In terms of the purpose of these subsidized loans, let us put ourselves in the chair of a U.S. congressman and listen to Boeing Aircraft
Company when its president, Malcolm T. Stamper, explains:

> My understanding of the Ex-Im Bank is that it was created to help pro-
> mote exports. But in addition, it was created to help foreign firms and
> their nations to buy big-ticket goods that would be of social and eco-
> nomic benefit. Airplanes certainly meet this description. Air travel and
> air cargo have significantly contributed to the good of this planet, par-
> ticularly among the smaller and less developed nations. Thus, the Export-
> Import Bank's assistance to the airlines of the world has been in keeping
> with America's vision of itself as a facilitator and motivator of world
> development and commerce. Airplane exports are also very good business
> for this country's own economy, by the way.[26]

In the trade, Eximbank has come to be known as "Boeing's
Bank."[27] Some of the "smaller and less developed nations" that have
bought large, commercial aircraft (by the way) with export credit include, in Africa alone, the Central African Republic, Liberia, Gabon,
Mali, the Sudan, Mauritius, and, of course, Nigeria, Zaire, Cameroon,
and other bankrupt big borrowers. In the case of Liberia, a conditionality clause in the first IMF Extended Fund Facility stipulates that
the government must sell its state-owned jet aircraft as maintenance
costs alone were putting undue pressure on quite limited Treasury resources. The conditionality clause might appear harsh were it not for
the fact that the aircraft itself became a local symbol of government
abuse. In Gabon, President Omar Bongo not only purchased with U.S.
buyer credits his own presidential jet (a 747) but a small fleet, with
regular service programmed between Paris, Geneva, Rome, and Libreville. In consortia with Boeing's commercial banks, Eximbank funded
the purchase of the airplanes while the French government export
credit agency, COFACE, assured financing of subsequent ground
maintenance and in-flight operations. Gabon is a nation of fewer than
500,000 inhabitants, of whom about 100,000 participate in the
moneyed economy. Mr. Stamper ended his statement with the following remark: "Over the long run exporting countries will be required
to maintain export credits like Eximbank in order to sell Lesser Developed Countries in any significant volume."[28]

At Boeing Aircraft some two-thirds of the company's sales of
commercial jets sold abroad are guaranteed under Eximbank financing
programs, mostly to the Third World. Similar statistics are applicable
to Eximbank's other big clients: Westinghouse, Caterpillar Tractor,
GE, and a number of large U.S. construction companies. The problem

is yet more acute for many foreign multinationals, especially in France and Japan, where export credit schemes are the most ambitious and self-serving.

In France, 65 percent of all exports are purported to enjoy some form of guarantee protection. By 1978, the discounting of export paper by the banks had become so widespread that the Banque de France complained that it was unable to properly control the domestic money supply. And, in Japan, Third World export promotion is such an important part of the Japanese way of doing business that the credit program winds up being funded not only by commercial banks but through the postal savings deposits and the social security premiums of individual Japanese workers.

By virtue of expanding export credit programs, the concept of free trade has come to reveal itself, in reality, as a form of international escapism rather than a vehicle for international development. In Britain, for example, by the late 1970s 42 percent of that country's construction equipment, 33 percent of new aircraft, and 32 percent of British textile machinery went to Third World markets.[29] In the United States, by 1980, the Third World market accounted for one-third of U.S. corporate profit, 20 percent of U.S. industrial product, and about one-quarter of gross farm income. "I think that we have been very successful," reports an aid official from the Department of Agriculture. "We can document the countries that have had concessional sales, and they have become some of our very best commercial clients."[30] These "best commercial clients" include Egypt, Indonesia, Nigeria, Mexico, South Korea, Zaire, and a host of smaller, less well-endowed developing countries that have accepted financial subsidies for the purchase of food rather than grow their own.

To pursue the export dilemma one step further, it has been estimated that four-fifths (80 percent) of new jobs created in the United States from 1977 through 1980 were associated with the growth of exports during that period. Not by coincidence, these growth figures seem proportionate to the growth of Third World debt. Likewise, when bank credit to Mexico stopped in 1982, more jobs were lost in the following six months in the United States than in three previous years of a depressed U.S. auto industry. According to President Ronald Reagan's U.S. trade representative, William E. Brock, 240,000 U.S. jobs were lost as a result of the Mexican debt crisis.[31]

In brief, our development program seems to demand more and more capital and even wider markets, while the solvent market shrinks. "We are reaching a point," insists the French banker and development theorist, Francois Partant, "where the system is beginning to strangle itself." "The problem," he adds, "is not so much trade qua trade, but the terms under which it is concluded. When we trade with a country we must not condemn it to poverty."[3][2] Whether we like it or not, our growth models are doing just that. To paraphrase Partant, most Third World countries should, in theory, have dropped out of the system by now since they are, after all, bankrupt. Highly liberal export credits and bank loans have contributed to this bankruptcy. Additional loans from the First World are now being used to maintain the appearance of solvency.

Our financial system has turned the theory of comparative advantage inside out. Thanks to the system, what we are now confronted with is an unintended case of nineteenth-century mercantilism, operative North-South. Meanwhile, feigned competition among the industrial powers based on credit has sent Western man not only on an expensive but on a quite dangerous adventure. Our development model, or better, the trading system that backs it up, might possibly (again to cite Partant) have caused the economic and financial difficulties that have broken free of political and social control. This breaking away provides us with a concrete definition of what the Third World debt crisis is really all about.

In the end, development strategy and concomitant finance has become outward looking, extroverted, or schizophrenic not only for the Third World (an endemic sign of economic and social fragility) but for the First as well. The banks have participated in this schizophrenia, this escapism, and have profited from its ambiguities. In some instances, they have led it.

A Salomon Brothers financial study shows that between 1970 and 1975, earnings of the 13 largest U.S. banks had risen from $177 million to $836 million.[33] This spectacular increase in earnings was due, in no small part, to a rapid run-up in foreign lending and/or deposit taking. The most profitable part of the business related to Third World markets. By 1976, Chase Manhattan Bank was earning 78 percent of its income abroad, Citibank 72 percent, Bank of America 40 percent, First Boston 68 percent, Morgan Guaranty 53 percent, and Manufacturers Hanover 56 percent. To cite an unreported example from abroad, the Banque Nationale de Paris (BNP), one of the world's largest banking houses, was rumored to be generating more net income through its affiliates in Africa than through its branch network in France, which was operating at about break-even. In absolute terms, Nigeria alone came to account for up to 20 percent of BNP's after-tax earnings in the late 1970s.

Liquidity or Insolvency

Most official observers would argue that the larger Third World countries—Brazil, Mexico, Nigeria, and Indonesia—have been forced to renegotiate foreign debt due to a combination of falling world market prices for most commodities and for light manufacturers, redoubled by tight monetary policies in the North. At the start of the banking crisis, a confidential U.S. government study leaked to the press by the Treasury Department concluded that an economic recovery by the major industrial countries would be sufficient to solve the emergency.[34] The report was released in the fall of 1982 as Treasury officials were struggling with the simultaneous payment defaults of Poland, Mexico, Brazil, Peru, Argentina, Nigeria, and Venezuela. Consistent with development logic, the debt problem was viewed as a liquidity crisis rather than as a crisis of Third World solvency. Put differently, the debt problem should merely go away through lower interest rates or higher growth in the North and through additional capital flows southward. In other words, more of the same.

Economists at the OECD agreed that the aggregate debt figures "merely reflect the amount of external loan resources which have not yet been repaid and are therefore still 'at work' for development in the borrowing countries."[35] Here we find a lovely *non sequitur* couched in the normally guarded language of the international reporting process. For its part, the World Bank, at least officially, continues to stand behind the theme of its president, A. W. Clausen, when he notes that there is no generalized debt problem but rather a "growth problem."[36]

The confusion originates in the difference between the *structure* and the *purpose* of Third World debt. This confusion has been reinforced by current methods of compiling debt statistics. Since the mid-1970s, the computer printouts at the World Bank, the IMF, and the OECD have shown aggregate term debt by country on a reasonably accurate basis. These figures are compared with GNP, export earnings, terms of trade, and projected economic growth rates. While the debt ratios have never ceased to deteriorate, it is estimated that a growth rate in the North of 4 percent per year should be enough to permit a second takeoff in the Third World. Every 1 percent increase in the GNP of the Northern economies is said to account for $12 billion in Third World export receipts. According to most official economists, a hyping of the growth rate to 4 percent would reduce economic strain in the South and allow a number of Third World countries to resume servicing foreign debt without borrowing more. The same theme was invoked at a recent International Monetary Conference by guest speaker Jeffrey E. Garten, an investment banker and former State Department official. Garten told the bankers assembled at the meeting: "Without faster growth, we're buying not only economic and political chaos, in my view, but de facto defaults on the order not yet seen."[37] In other words, a 4 percent growth rate should bring the community of nations back from the brink.

A Look at the Numbers

The computerized data base on LDC debt is shared by the World Bank, the IMF, and the UN. The numbers themselves originate from a data reporting system completed by debtor countries. On the other side, the Bank for International Settlements compiles corresponding information gathered from commercial banks by the central banks of the major OECD nations. In order to collate the information, the data flow runs heavy at times both among and between multilateral agencies and their respective member governments. The major multinational banks have recently established their own information clearinghouse in Washington, D.C., while the OECD prepares a separate set of numbers from all of these sources.

The creditor nations and their banks act as if better information on Third World debt aggregates, plus a big push in the growth rate to 4 percent will make the liquidity and thereby the debt crisis go away. In point of fact, however, the debt information collection method itself and its comparison with macroeconomic growth indicators serve only to disguise a solvency crisis by insisting that it is a liquidity crisis. The survey process resembles the empirical method practiced in *Snow White and the Seven Dwarfs*: "Mirror, mirror, ever fair?"

Our debt surveys never ask the essential question. For to do so would be to question the program itself. On what has the money been spent? What has been the purpose of Third World lending? It is not by coincidence perhaps that the only debtor country said to have a solvency crisis is Poland. As a U.S. Treasury official told *Business Week*: "Mexico is not Poland. They face an illiquidity problem, but they will be able to resume payment on their debt."[38] This lack of intellectual honesty (the self-flattery) fails, even in the short run, to be self-serving. The questioning process and the endless empirical data that flow from it not only obscures the debt problem but relegates its solution to obscurity. As Auden quipped: "The wrong question initiates nothing."

THE EMPIRICAL METHOD

When asked straightaway about the anomaly of routine price mark-ups and other omissions, one of the senior officials at the OECD responsible for coordinating export credit programs among the Western powers responded in blank fashion: "We don't want to know." The West perhaps can still afford this mental hide-and-seek, without crossing any domestic, financial thresholds. The same is no longer true in the Third World. In the final analysis, the numbers charade itself might help to explain why the Third World market has stagnated and why political disruption has become increasingly frequent.

On what specifically has the money been spent? Not to ask this question and to establish a monitoring system accordingly is a bit like looking at the balance sheet of a billion dollar company and presuming that the company will prosper if only the economy grows. No domestic banker worth the price of his travel bags would undertake such a risk. The confusion between means and ends, between numbers and results, between structure and purpose in Third World lending represents a form of intellectual blackout. The blackout is both self-serving and deliberated.

Method or Myopia

To pursue the dilemma in reporting methodology to its end, the World Bank and the International Monetary Fund in 1981 organized a Joint Ministerial Development Committee task force to confront head-on the issue of nonconcessional money flows to developing countries. The topics highlighted were capital adequacy ratios within the banking system, in-house country limits or the concentration of bank assets, the size of Third World debt, the elasticity of the Eurodollar market, and projected Third World borrowing needs.

The joint task force was headed by the deputy director of the Bank of Mexico, Alfredo Phillips. Private sector participants included the then vice-chairman of Citibank, G. A. Costanzo; the head of the international banking department of Credit Lyonnais, Jean Deflassieux; and the president of Morgan Stanley International, Richard Debs. In conjunction with the report's preparation, 27 background and research papers were completed by IMF and World Bank staffs or by outside economists. The findings concluded that the banking system as currently operating was quite capable of protecting orderly economic growth for the balance of the decade. A final optimistic report[39] was released at the IMF in March 1982, that is, about six months prior to the Latin American debt crisis. Ironically, the crisis began with Mexico's own inability to service short-term foreign bank debt. The chairman of the committee, a Mexican national, was caught hands down, playing intellectual gamesmanship with the important subject of the Third World debt—as were the distinguished panel, their economists, and government sponsors.

The joint IMF/World Bank development task force addressed only the topics of banking mechanism and ratios. The central issue was left aside. The key issue deals with the purpose of export credit and of multinational bank lending to the Third World. When depositors, stock analysts, and concerned politicians ask themselves why the big banks have overcommitted in certain LDC countries, the response is not simply the profit motive "that age-old motivator—greed", nor inflation, nor keeping up with the needs of existing corporate clients. These answers are the most obvious. Intuitively, the public is asking a more basic question. As it turns out, the question has not been clearly posed by the banks, nor by bank regulators, nor by those institutions responsible for protecting the development process. The question has nothing to do with the mere size of Third World debt but with its finality, its purpose, its telos. Looked at from this point of view, we are back to the *raison d'être* of the program. Not how much—but why?

At the end of the First Development Decade, the Pearson Commission had already suggested that the World Bank monitor more carefully potential abuses in bank lending and export credit programs. This was not done. Likewise, the U.S. government has attempted to control the periodic export "credit wars" that have broken out among OECD member states. To this end, the U.S. government regularly has set the example by maintaining the least aggressive subsidy programs. The root problem, however, stems not from the credit programs themselves but rather from the development model that backs them up. The model not only promotes specialization on a worldwide basis or the concomitant need for ever larger markets. More importantly, the growth models are confrontational by nature, not merely competitive. As a function of this confrontation between the OECD nations one with the other and between the North-South trading blocs, the reporting methodology has become myopic. The statistics have hidden the real crisis while reinforcing careless bank lending. This careless bank lending defines the real nature of the debt crisis. The disassociation between bank loans and purpose eventually will cost the international community about one thousand *billion* dollars in lost time and money.

This one thousand billion dollars has gone to pay for the bidets that the French missionary stumbled upon outside the airport in Guinea, for the nuclear power plant that the Israelis bombed near Bagdad, and for the megamillion dollar shipping scandals in Indonesia—funded largely by the banks. Insolvency or illiquidity? Size or purpose?

As we move toward the close of the twentieth century, the so-called mountain of Third World debt cannot be reduced nor simply inflated away. The resources are not available to undertake such a task without risking serious political repercussions for a large majority of mankind, including the minority in the West. What is most important is that the direction and nature of Third World debt, over time, change. This, of course, will require a change in development logic.

In the meanwhile, it is the nature of bank lending that has added to rather than stabilized the Third World development crisis. The same lending strategy has destabilized the balance sheets of the majority of our big multinational banks. For example, of the top ten U.S. banks, Morgan Guaranty alone has protected its Triple AAA bond rating. This encouraged a feisty Treasury official at the World Bank to note privately that our principal multinational banks are not as creditworthy as Campbells Soup. One might wonder how this bodes for the U.S. economy itself and for its capacity to promote healthy growth. In a more serious vein, Felix Rohatyn, a senior partner and public spokesman at Lazard Freres and Company, comments that "our banking system is one of the more precious assets of our economy and of free society itself."[40] He should have added that it also is one of the most precarious.

The quite delicate situation in which the Western world finds itself did not occur abruptly nor by forces unknown but rather by forces ignored, both material and intellectual. As we shall explain in Part II, the confusion between means and ends, between method and purpose, between liquidity and solvency is consistent with the Western World's limited notion of cause and, by extension, with our worldview. This confusion accounts for the behavior of our multinational banks vis-à-vis the world community. The worldview has obscured both the banker's analytic ability and his sense of identity or of purpose. A chronic loss of identity has guided the impact of multinational banking in the Third World and has led us to what some have called, irreverently, the Third World "debt bomb."[41] The defusing of this debt bomb has the broadest implications for the future of modern society. The debt bomb, like the bomb itself, certainly is a symbol of modern man's loss of purpose and of measure. In the West, this loss of purpose and of measure translates as a loss of identity. The banks have not been spared this loss, and, by extension, neither has the World community. The loss is now felt by the taxpayer in the North and by the destitute in the South. The banks have only begun to feel its impact.

10
The Impact of Multinational Banking in the Third World

The word "crack", designating a fissure in our global financial system, has found its way into the normally conservative financial press in the United States and Europe. A headline in *The Economist* reads: "Bankers Feel the Earth Move Under Their Feet."[1] Understandably, bankers are apprehensive of the term "crack." Indeed, when the alarm button is pushed, the financiers are forced back to the realization that banking is faith, not money, confidence not ratios. The very term "credit" comes from the latin word "credere" meaning "to believe." In a primordial sense, the banks live on and dispense *credere*.

Clamorous language, then, strikes at the very heart of what banking is all about. The language questions the bank's credibility. Yet the numbers themselves have forced the Third World debt issue and the associated human drama into the headlines. In turn, the language used to describe the problem might motivate the banks and the bankers to reassess their identity, that is, their purpose and their place within the world community. Certainly, the bank regulators have failed to do this for them.

A bank is a temple and a temple guards the grain. Here is the origin of commercial banking as first practiced in antiquity nearly 4,000 years ago. To the extent that banks divert from their purpose, from their primary responsibility of safeguarding value, a vital component of the economy and of society is subtracted out of the system. This is what occurred in the 1960s. In fact, the crisis in bank identity began in New York City in 1967. In that year, the First National City Bank became a one-bank holding company known as Citicorp. The object of the exercise was to permit the bank to expand its operations outside of its traditional business—i.e., of lending money. During the late 1960s and throughout the 1970s, pacemaker Citibank was to expand its business into leasing, credit cards, management advisory services, even insurance and travel. In the process, lending operations were to distance the bank's deposit base. By 1970, bank management was to refer to the corporation no longer as a bank but rather as a "world financial enterprise." Citibank was becoming a nonbank and opening the way for nonbanks to become deposit takers.

In keeping with the corporation's new identity, the complexion of bank assets and liabilities shifted dramatically, as did customer allegiance. By the end of 1982, demand deposits represented 6 percent of Citibank's liabilities, down from 50 percent two decades earlier. The decrease was intentional. Citicorp had become what is now known as a "money center bank." In fact, Citicorp had invented the notion. The notion was consistent with Citibank's new identity as a financial intermediary or money changer rather than banker. Today, most big banks no longer finance their loan portfolio from their client deposit base or from shareholders equity but largely through purchased money. The money is bought either on the stateless Eurodollar market or from other domestic money center banks. Both markets are anonymous in the sense that the crucial link between the community and the bank, between bank depositors and borrowers has been severed. In the process, the big money center banks have become little more than financial brokers. One of the more spectacular results to date: the Continental Illinois Bank bankruptcy.

Between 1970 and 1980, the much advertised "Citicorp Concept" was adopted by the majority of the world's top 50 or so banks, that is, by those banks that "make the market." To cite the degree of mimesis, David Rockefeller, the chairman of Chase Manhattan Bank, then Citicorp's chief rival, described his own bank just before retirement as a "multinational financial services corporation." More recently, Thomas C. Theobald, a one-time aide to Walter Wriston at Citibank explains: "Citicorp is committed to broadening its franchise and enhancing its services. While much more remains to be done, we have already broken free of the shackles of the lending function traditionally ascribed to our industry, and we can fairly claim to be a diversified financial services enterprise."[2] Nothing about banking. Nothing about investment. Nothing about guarding the grain and then sowing it under the right conditions. Not by coincidence, the contagion of the Citicorp Concept precisely parallels the rapid buildup in Third World export credits and syndicated Eurocurrency lending.

The heavy reliance on purchased funds, or rather, the concept that backs it up, has enabled the banks to increase substantially loan volume, money market transactions, and, by extension, aggregate income. In the process, average return on assets among the biggest banks has decreased by more than half. Foreign exchange speculation and deposit trading have skyrocketed. Meanwhile, the capital ratios—borrowed money against shareholder investment and reserves—have more than doubled over the last 30 years from about 10 to 1 to in excess of 20 to 1. These exceedingly high-leverage ratios combined with heavy reliance on purchased funds go hand in hand with the concept of financial brokering as opposed to banking. This brokering element not only has weakened the balance sheets, but it has changed the corporate culture at most of the major multinational banks. In turn, the changed corporate culture promotes faulty credit judgment, a weakened lending methodology, and a loss of fixed purpose.

On the domestic side, the general public witnessed first the commercial real estate speculation of the mid-1970s funded with bank money, then the collapse of silver prices inflated through bank borrowing, then the bankruptcy of such speculative ventures as Drome Petroleum, Drysdale Securities, and the Penn Square Bank. By the third quarter of 1984 some 797 U.S. banks required special supervisory attention while, the P/E ratios of the average money center bank had dropped from about 22 to 1 in 1973 to less than 6 to 1 in 1983—a more than 300 percent decline in future earnings expectations. The Continental Illinois bankruptcy fulfilled an accurate prophecy.

On the international side, the excessive number of countries currently in payment default would indicate that, even in the Third World, bankers have not been lending money; they have been brokering money. The very service of recycling for which so many bankers flatter themselves while defending credit policy in the Third World speaks of money changing, not of investment. "If the commercial banks had not financed the LDC's," explained Walter Wriston at the time of the second OPEC oil price increase, then "the world would have blown up."[3] This clever remark studiously misses a central verity of post-war international finance.

Indeed, the World Bank was founded at the end of World War II for the very purpose of shifting excess investment flows from capital surplus to capital deficit countries. Instead of the banks, the bulk of the petrodollar overhang could have been sanitized through the World Bank or the IMF. The Western powers, however, were unwilling to open the equity base of either institution to additional Third World capital or to further OPEC participation in the development process itself. Alternatively, the OPEC countries might have been more aggressive in establishing their own multilateral development banks. Instead, they played the money markets (as they continue to do) and, like the First World, left the recycling process to the banks.

The banks, in turn, could have used the additional OPEC deposits to shore up their own liquidity problems by purchasing the readily salable and safe treasury bills of their own governments. Between 1970 and 1980, the treasury portfolios of the major U.S. banks (rainy day reserves) fell on average from 30 percent to 10 percent of bank assets. When the now retired chairman of The First National Bank of Chicago, Gaylord Freeman, was asked in 1974 about his bank's weakened capital and liquidity ratios, the very capable Mr. Freeman responded in characteristically direct fashion. He said in effect (1) that the analyst asking the question should "go to the head of the class" and (2) that he, Mr. Freeman, was required to keep the bank's ratios in line with those of the other top ten U.S. banks. The pressure came from shareholders, from the board of directors, and of all places, even from bank regulators. Citibank was setting the pace. The regulators went for a ride with all but a few seemingly flattered to act as spectators in the charmed world of international finance.

HERE COMES THE FED

After the collapse of the REITs (Real Estate Investment Trusts) in the U.S. market, then chairman of the Federal Reserve, Arthur Burns, called a group of leading bankers to Washington to discuss informally their rapidly growing Third World credit exposure. The bankers informed Mr. Burns politely that they knew more about foreign banking than he did. As Chairman Burns was an economist and not a banker by training, they were probably right. The bankers themselves, however, had lost their own sense of identity. The top ten U.S. banks were striving as a group to obtain the 15 percent quarterly earnings increase set by the leader, Citibank. The objective itself reflects the seriousness of the identity crisis. The method to obtain this ill-considered objective was via foreign exchange trading, export credits, deposit trading, and commercial bank loans to Third World governments. The most lucrative business could be had by tying all four together in the form of jumbo loans to the "richer" LDC nations. The key to the lending dynamic became size, volume, and turnover, not purpose.

In short order, the element of money changing influenced marketing strategies and the division of labor within the largest international banks. For instance, by the mid-1970s, the function of loan identification and sales was separated from that of credit analysis or lending in its proper sense. This division of labor, this shift in emphasis—and responsibility—accounts for a number of the more spectacular abuses that have occurred in the lending patterns of the major multinational banks. The shift likewise explains Lord Harold Lever's exasperation when the outspoken retired cabinet minister and financial adviser to the British government observed that Third World countries were "being sold steel plants and textile factories the same way that a discount store sells refrigerators."[4]

Ironically, the specialization of labor within the banks occurred, or rather was justified, post facto on the advice of outside management consultants such as McKinsey and Company or Arthur D. Little. The frame of reference for the consultants was industry and commerce, not banking. The consultants simply intellectualized the metamorphosis that was going on in the banking industry itself—not to the displeasure of bank management.

THE CITICORP CONCEPT: MONEY AND METHOD

Citibank's public relations department gets to the heart of the matter in a high-powered brochure entitled "The Citicorp Concept." In the brochure, the bank's recent chairman, Walter Wriston, explains: "Our strategy is not one of making loans; our strategy is one of making money."[5] The signals sent to aspiring loan officers make up in precision and emphasis what they lack in ambiguity. "Our competition," Wriston observes, "is not really Chemical and Morgan but . . . Sears, IBM, and American Express."[6] Curiously, Mr. Wriston left out the names of Prudential Life Insurance Company, Hartford Fire and Casualty, and Blue Cross. For at Citibank, Third World country limit exposure has been established on a global actuarial basis. Since countries do not disappear, it has been assumed that the Third World would not merely go under as a bloc. Like the rest of the industry, Citibank now finds itself explaining Third World credit exposure much like a life insurance company justifies its own risk taking. Capital ratios, it is argued, should depend on a bank's size. The bigger the bank, the higher (more careless) the ratio because the bigger banks enjoy economies of scale in risk taking and in diversification of borrower and of deposit base. In other words, the biggest banks need the least equity, or said differently, the least internal protection.

Not surprisingly, the actuarial or insurance concept has nothing to do with sound banking. The confusion of concepts is mutiple when applied to entire Third World economies. For a bank loan to be more than sheer speculation (even if the risks are low), it must have a purpose, not just a risk that can be defended. This confusion of a logical order—and of identity—started at Citibank.

Given this bank's chimerical success on the stock market, the Citibank Concept quickly spread to other banks, while the regulators could not understand its consequences. As a result, risk spreading rather than risk taking has marked the rhythm of Third World lending. Consistent with the confusion of purpose, the responsibility for setting country limits has shifted at most big banks from the lending divisions to the economic research departments. The economists set country limits. The blanks are then filled in by bankers who have become traveling salesmen. This lending methodology explains Anthony Sampson's bewilderment when he describes in his book, *The Money Lenders*, "those young men with their alligator briefcases who sold money to places like Ghana."[7]

The method resembles the real estate developer who constructs a building without consulting an architect. The developer (in this case the economist) decides how much the vacant lot is worth and the bankers arrive not to design a building but to sell bricks and mortar on irresistible credit terms. As long as the borrower signs the contract, the material is delivered. Indeed, not only have the banks financed the bulk of the Third World credit program, they likewise have financed their changing definition of themselves. As a symbol of this change, on-line lending officers have been renamed "business development" or "marketing" officers. The name change is revealing for it depicts a fundamental mistake in Third World lending strategies—a mistake that started with the crisis in self-identity and ended in the debt trap.

REPORTING REVISITED

The regulators subsequently reinforced the confusion between banking, insurance, and marketing by virtue of the international reporting requirements and methodology noted above. The reporting requirements for U.S. banks at home reflect those designed by the multilateral regulatory agencies. When the Third World debt crisis began to surface in the United States in the mid-1970s, the comptroller of the currency requested the U.S. banks to report foreign exposure by country according to a means and purpose test. The only purpose, however, that was identified was the difference between direct government, government agency, and private sector debt. In the Third World, these distinctions are often blurred and sometimes nonexistent. For instance, agricultural and commodity sales generally are controlled by a government-owned marketing board. Capital-intensive projects are often guaranteed by government authorities so as to reduce, for outside investors, local political and economic risks. Even the retail sector of most Third World economies functions in keeping with elaborate foreign exchange controls and letter of credit licenses. Given the extroverted nature of these economies, the principal source of government revenue is not personal income tax nor sales tax but revenue generated from taxes on imports and exports. Thus, foreign borrowing becomes synonymous with state borrowing and/or with government guarantees. Even in the private sector, local borrowers are required, in nearly every case, to obtain foreign exchange guarantees from a local bank, oftentimes nationalized, or from the central bank itself. Hence, the problem of means and purposes *as presently defined* becomes, in terms of development and in terms of statistical value, almost a nonissue for external creditors lending to countries with nonconvertible currencies. The numbers can identify *when* a country is bankrupt but not *why*. The distinction of purpose by government borrower versus agency versus the private sector only has meaning if use of proceeds is judged on its specific merits. The categories themselves are interchangeable.

In keeping with the Citibank Concept, this simple fact has been overlooked by the bank examiners. As Henry C. Wallich, the Federal Reserve's chief spokesman on matters concerning international banking, proclaimed to a group of social scientists assembled at New Year's 1983 in San Francisco: "The underlying principle of this [regulatory reporting] system has been a good one—to reduce as far as possible the need to rate credit quality of particular countries and to focus instead on risk diversification."[8]

It is clear from a statement like this that the reporting system itself does not track the long-term viability of individual loans even the biggest. Only the macroeconomic aggregates are important. Accordingly, the financing of a post office building or of a soccer stadium enjoys the same statistical profile as the investment in a copper mine or health clinic. Diversity by country rather than by purpose has become the single most important guage for measuring the severity of the debt crisis: $100 billion in Brazil, $80 billion in Mexico, $45 billion in South Korea, bankruptcy in Senegal.

The debt figures of course mean almost nothing without a better definition of the end for which these monies have been invested. Surely, a reporting system could be devised, at least for the larger impact loans, to account for their likely benefit to both the borrower and the lender. In other words, the reporting criteria might attempt to measure lending in keeping with the bank's means and the country's ends. Similar reporting requirements already exist for corporate banking within the U.S. economy. It would suffice to add a developmental index to the existing measuring techniques. For example, instead of classifying a bank credit in accordance with its likely impact on the net cash flow of a company's operations, the reporting procedure would attempt to capture the impact on a country's foreign exchange receipts. Does the foreign bank credit add to the borrower's capacity to generate foreign exchange in the form of import substitution or export earnings? Is supporting loan documentation, including feasibility studies, comparable to international standards? Are short-term credits being extended to finance essential imports? Are the size of balance of payment loans consistent with local political stability, economic management, and current international reserves—not minerals in the ground? The questioning process itself would put the bankers on notice that they are bankers not brokers, nor insurance agents, nor salesmen, nor international marketeers.

UPSTAGING THE BOSS

For the moment, the macroeconomic concept of risk spreading by country hides a series of microeconomic problems that have come to overwhelm the system both internally and externally. For instance, when two well-known French and U.S. banks opened branches in Gabon in the mid-1970s, the local managers were under pressure to show a profit within 12 months from start-up. Like a number of other countries, Gabon was benefiting from higher oil revenue. Meanwhile, the one-year turnaround period at the branch was consistent with systems-wide expectations—especially in a growth market. At a hardship assignment like Gabon, branch management changes about every 18 to 24 months, with successive management motivated to improve on the earnings stream of its predecessors. The result in the case of Gabon? About $600 million in officially guaranteed export credits and $679 million in syndicated loans and other bank credit to government. Over a three-year period 1974 to 1977, direct bank credit increased by more than 300 percent, while export guaranteed credits doubled. The purpose? A triumphal highway connecting the airport to the Presidential Palace (a highway that began to break up at completion), a hotel sector with excessively low occupancy rates (constructed by private entrepreneurs with government guarantees), one of the world's least economic railroad lines (built in opposition to World

Bank planning advice), and, of course, the small fleet of commercial jet aircraft mentioned earlier, plus a number of elaborate government office buildings to lodge an enlarged government bureaucracy.

Throughout the period, the minister of finance could not keep the bankers at bay. At the signing ceremony of a $100 million syndicated credit, the minister kept his bankers waiting for about six hours in an unairconditioned antechamber while he sneaked away from the ministry to preside at the opening ceremonies of his own laundromat. The anecdote became known to a small coterie of international bankers both in and out of the credit.

In a figurative sense, the Minister and his government not only took the banks and their lawyers to the laundry but the Gabonese people as well. The buildup in foreign debt had occurred so rapidly that neither the minister nor the banks knew how much money the government had borrowed or guaranteed. The figures were tallied in June 1978 when Gabon could no longer repay the foreign creditors. The payment shortfalls of some $250 million were then refinanced by the banks in conjunction with an IMF stabilization program. The refinancing only covered current interest and principal amounts due the banks and their clients. Net new monies for development had dried up.

The macro- and the microeconomic problems just cited started with the identity crisis prevalent in the banking industry itself. If even one-half of the world's top 50 banks establish country limits on an actuarial basis and proportionate to overall asset size, then they must automatically find themselves competing in a Third World buyer's market. Naturally, this is what has occurred, not only in Gabon, but even more so in the big second tier countries, Algeria, Argentina, Brazil, Iran, Iraq, Mexico, Nigeria, and others. At times, interest rates for all of these countries have been barely different from yields on U.K. treasury bills. Supply had overwhelmed demand. Meanwhile, the supply was senseless.

To bring the issue yet closer to the surface, the cumulative size of our major banks represents an economic unit considerably larger than the GNP of even the largest Third World economies. If the banks are vying for risks or market share rather than making directly productive loans in an otherwise fragile, impoverished economy, should it come as a surprise that the house of cards has fallen, for the moment, on the heads of some of the world's poorest citizens—not a few of whom are starving?

Money center banking has turned into a sort of Third World insurance lottery. Funds intermediation, recycling, loan syndications with banks competing in the league tables for volume, are all part of the identity crisis that started with the Citibank Concept. The identity crisis was contagious and extended to bank regulators who, instead of regulating, became unawares captive of the industry's own faulty logic.

From Process to Protection

In the late 1970s, the central banks of the major Western trading nations established an ad hoc intergovernmental committee, the Cooke Committee, charged with coordinating central bank regulatory controls. Under the auspices of the Bank for International Settlements (BIS), an informal program of information and policy proposals led to what became known as the Bale Concordat. Under the terms of the concordat, the central banks agreed to move toward regulatory asymmetry in efforts to modulate, or rather, to rationalize international money flows. Arthur Burns later complained that the Western Europeans suspected the American delegation of attempting to protect its overseas banking and export market share. The suspicion probably worked in the opposite direction as well, if not at the Fed then certainly with Bill Simon at the U.S. Treasury. Accordingly, Third World money flows continued their rapid pace into the 1980s. In the interim, the Bank for International Settlements has produced an authoritative manual on money flows and on international lending by country—but next to nothing on the finality of these transactions. For its part, the U.S. Comptroller of the Currency introduced the above mentioned means-and-purpose test. Thus, in the end, purpose was determined largely by the competitive rush into foreign markets and by the availability of adequate finance.

Although export credits provided the original "sweetener" for the commercial banks to enter an otherwise difficult Third World Market, actuarial accounting became the principal leitmotiv for justifying the larger, untied, syndicated credit or Jumbo Loans, to countries like Brazil, Mexico, Nigeria, South Korea, and others. In the case of export credits, the purpose, as we have seen, oftentimes is dictated by export lobbies and by easy money on apparently favorable terms. Exclusive of routine price markups, the transactions nonetheless are at least tangible. In other words, a product is sold. This is not the case with the average syndicated Eurodollar loan. Rather, the terms of the transaction come to be fixed as a function of bank funding rather than bank lending. The world's principal source for bank funding has become the Eurodollar market and its role, the funding of general purpose loans to Third World governments.

Without describing at length the technical aspects of bank borrowing, suffice it to note that the Eurodollar market represents a pool of funds available to commercial banks, which pool is outside the control of any single central bank. The market itself was created in the 1950s when the Russian government placed its dollar deposits in banks in London to avoid possible seizure in New York. Since that time, the size of the Eurodollar market has not ceased to grow, geometrically. Funds poured into this offshore market, first from sustained U.S. balance of payment deficits in the 1960s, then from the huge expenditures in Vietnam that were not repatriated back to America, and, subsequently, from OPEC capital surpluses. Throughout this period, bank lending added tremendous momentum to the size of this pool of funds by virtue of the well-known multiplier effect. Over the period from 1972 to 1980, an average of 66 new banks entered the international loan syndication market each year. International bank lending expanded at an annual rate of some 20 percent per year compounded or in almost direct proportion to the growth of the Eurodollar market.

In a research volume recently published by the Atlantic Institute in Paris, a think tank sponsored by Western governments and multinational corporate subscribers, it is noted that after 1970, monetary reserve creation became privatized and uncontrolled. This was the result of a too rapid growth in the Eurodollar market and in interbank deposit trading. Fabio Basagni, the institute's banking specialist, makes the following observation—a chilling one based on the copious data provided in the report:

> The crucial question is whether international lending is developing in stable and manageable directions; or whether it could grow pathologically out of reach of national and international authorities, possibly destabilizing the world financial system.[9]

Since 1970, the Eurodollar market has become a Eurocurrency market, with the trading center shifting from London (still the capital) to Paris, Frankfurt, Bahrein, Hongkong, and tax havens such as Barbados and the Cayman Islands. The money center banks in keeping with their new vocation—or vocations—have funded their Third World "book" from these markets. In fact, the size of the book has been a function of the size of the market. The two have reinforced one another to bring us to the sorry state of affairs that we are witnessing today—i.e. what the Atlantic Institute dares to suggest could be "pathological."

Thus, the recycling process has been associated with spectacular growth in Third World lending, a sort of purposeless overflow from First World markets. The overflow can be nicely charted. In 1970, private and government guaranteed export credits made up about 15 percent of the external financial receipts of developing countries versus 16 percent for untied bank credit, often denominated under the rubric "balance of payment" loans. Some ten years later, these same figures had shifted from 15 percent and 16 percent respectively to 13 percent and 23 percent. While the percentage changes might not seem large in themselves, the aggregates are.

During the Second Development Decade, syndicated Eurodollar loans outstanding increased from about $9 billion to in excess of $140 billion. This latter figure does not include the growth in short-term interbank lines to Third World commercial banks, which probably exceeded $50 billion by 1980. In the meanwhile, by 1973, it had become so easy for multinational bank marketing officers to buy and sell Third World loans that one bank was able to syndicate a Eurodollar term loan to a small Central American government (Costa Rico) based on a news clipping from *Time* magazine. While *Time* magazine maintains a very competent staff of economic and financial journalists, the investment decision of the banks themselves would indicate a somewhat faulty lending methodology, not to mention a costly one.

By 1975, the major banks attempted to improve their procedures for sovereign risk credit analysis. They did this by maintaining their marketing staffs and by hiring additional economists. The economists were thought to add a certain scientific validity to Third World banking. Eventually, a system of checks and balances was installed between the economists and the bankers. The checks were put into place at the request of central bank authorities instead of groom lending officers in the art—and responsibility—of lending money.

At the suggestion of bank regulators, the economic units within the largest banks were rearranged according to geographic regions and given the authority for establishing in-house country limits. Diversification by country served as the premise for future Third World lending. By virtue of the new country limit approval system, federal examiners found themselves endorsing (with Citibank, Chase Manhattan, and others) the idea that the biggest banks were the safest because of their ability to self-insure through the prudent (but purposeless) spread of risk. Thus, the regulators became caught in the same dinosaur-like logic as the regulated. For their part, not a few bankers lost all notion of their calling.

Diversity and size rather than purpose continued to determine money flows. As the country limit became "full up," the bank marketing and syndication officers moved elsewhere. In 1979, Citibank discovered Mauritius, and Chase Manhattan Bank, Malawi. Since neither country had yet come to the syndicated Eurodollar market, and since all the major banks had modest country limits available, both loans were heavily oversubscribed. Both countries borrowed more money than they needed—only to reschedule on more punitive terms slightly after the first principal payments were due. In the meanwhile, the loan proceeds had vanished into suddenly inflated government operating budgets, state office buildings, automobiles, and airplanes.

The Missing Money

Given the very nature of current lending methodology as practiced at our major banks, syndicated Eurodollar credits and balance of payment loans hide a multitude of omissions. In Mexico, President Jose Lopez Portillo's fast rise to power and his extravagant living precisely paralleled heavy government borrowing on the Eurodollar markets. His demise occurred when Mexico could no longer service its foreign bank debt.

The case of Nigeria provides yet a better example. Given that country's important oil and untapped natural gas reserves, each of the world's top 50 banks by 1978 had established country limits ranging from a base of no less than $100 million and up. At most banks, country limits are divided between short- and long-term exposure and between export versus untied cross-border sovereign risk.

In 1979, Nigeria decided to come to market for a $1 billion, ten-year term loan, the second in as many years. Despite the fact that payments for imports were slow and that the purpose for the first billion dollar loan was unclear, the banks fought among themselves for a management position in the loan syndicate. Interest rates were bid downward to a split margin of 5/8 and 7/8 over the cost of matching Eurodollar deposits on the London Interbank Market or over LIBOR, as the acronym appears in loan documentation. An in-house commentary among certain lead banks recounted that the loan proceeds once again would be used "for beer and baby carriages." The bankers were lending against the oil in the ground and the managers against a 1 percent front-end fee. To obtain the fee, the Nigerians required each of the lead managers to underwrite on a best-effort basis $100 million for their own book. Because Nigeria was having a difficult time rolling over foreign exchange contracts to service the first Jumbo, the banks closed the syndicate at $750 million. Of this amount, only a fraction was downstreamed to smaller banks. This brought some of the managing banks over their own internally established country limits. Nonetheless, the credit was closed just prior to Christmas, 1979 for two reasons: First, Nigeria desperately needed the foreign exchange to pay for imports let alone service the first Jumbo Loan. Second, and more importantly, individual bank profit centers wanted to accrue into income the front-end fees prior to year-end. For all of those readers who are not bankers, let us recall that 1 percent of $100 million is $1 million flat. Within 12 months of the signing of the second Nigerian Jumbo loan, it was reported in the financial press that accountants for the Nigerian National Petroleum Company had discovered a $1,000 million discrepancy in the company's financial statements. In tracking the discrepancy, it later was reported that the $1 billion in question had fled into numbered Swiss accounts. Meanwhile, the military regime in power had retired—with political immunity.[10]

The Nigerian case, and others, painfully establish several important lessons. Firstly, foreign borrowings are, to use an official phrase, "fungible." That is, they can be used to displace resources already available domestically for investment. They can also be used for a variety of other purposes, some legitimate, others less so. When our biggest lending institutions operate as financial intermediaries or as brokers rather than as bankers, the problem of funds displacement and of overlending generally can become chronic. This is what has happened in the case of Mexico, Nigeria, Indonesia, Zaire, and Brazil, to name but a few of the larger Third World economies. To add to the Atlantic Institute's analysis, not only have monetary reserves become privatized and uncontrollable but so has Third World lending and corresponding debt.

Second, actuarial accounting not only denies purpose in lending but inevitably adds to blurred credit judgment. Until the first big round of debt rescheduling in 1982, the world's major multinational banks thought that they enjoyed adequate self-insurance through the managed spread of risk. The only big countries to have defaulted simultaneously were Indonesia, Pakistan, and Turkey. To this list were added between 1982 and 1983, the so-called, "Gang of Four," that is, Argentina, Brazil, Mexico, and South Korea, plus 36 other Third

World states. Round-one debt reschedulings collectively represented the biggest, most costly rollover in the history of banking. Actuarial accounting had turned into an unambiguous case of creative accounting, with the Third World beneficiary and the First World taxpayer discreetly footing the bill. In the case of the beneficiary, the subsequent and rapid decompression of foreign bank credit has meant more than just belt-tightening. It has meant economic and social dislocation not known in the West since the bleakest days of the Industrial Revolution. For some, these bleakest days are their last.

Third, the pell-mell confusion between banking, brokering, and the insurance business has propelled a number of banks toward arbitrary bigness. As a result, not only have leverage ratios doubled, but average return on assets have dropped sharply at most of the large multinational banking houses. Worse, loan loss reserves have become woefully inadequate. In a trade journal, *The Banker*, of April 1983, it is noted that "although banks have all reported a sharp increase in nonperforming loans (where servicing is behindhand) actual additions to loan loss reserves have been modest."[11] The only major charge-offs in the recent past have taken place at Chase Manhattan and at Continental Illinois. These loan losses were related to the collapse of Drysdale Securities in New York and Penn Square Bank in Kansas City. At Manufacturers Hanover, the bank with the largest LDC debt ($6.8 billion) as a percentage of equity (245 percent), bank management chose to add only $47 million to loan loss reserves for the entire bank, both domestic and international. This $47 million charge to current earnings brought total loan loss reserves at the nation's fourth largest bank to a modest $376 million versus total assets in excess of $40 billion. The use of discretionary authority at Manufacturers Hanover is typical of our major banks. It is permitted in lieu of a possible banking collapse. For example, of $140 billion in Third World debt payable in 1982, $80 million was renegotiated and thereby made current. Had even a portion of these loans been given a true market value, then a number of banks would in fact be bankrupt. For the moment, only Poland, North Korea, and Zaire are considered by central bank authorities to be insolvent. The other countries, according to bank examiners, are suffering from what are mythically called "liquidity" problems. As Henry C. Wallich, a member of the board of governors of the Federal Reserve System argues: "I believe that the debts of the major borrowing countries are manageable, in the sense that recent debt-service difficulties represent liquidity rather than solvency problems."[12] Following the logic of this argument, one assumes that the big banks simply should lend more—and, in the process, become yet bigger.

The bigness syndrome has contributed to another persuasive, structural problem in addition to the deterioration in bank ratios coincident with purposeless lending. The syndrome has reinforced, in its turn, the original identity problem. For instance, at First Chicago in the early 1970s, by the time an assistant-to-an-officer (ATO) was promoted to an on-line lending position, he would have known every other lending officer on the staff, at least by name. In the process of his election to bank officer, the candidate would have been evaluated by a cross-section of banking professionals, all of whom understood the corporate culture and the values that this culture represented. The chairman's home telephone number was clearly marked in the bank telephone directory. The system was personalized. Some ten years later, bank staff had grown from about 3,000 people to 15,000, while the bank telephone directory now looks like that of a medium-size city.

Banks are people intensive. In fact, that is all there is in a bank—people and money. No machines, no fields. Bigness in a bank automatically breeds either bureaucracy or disorganization. Neither is healthy for the economy since the most valuable element that a bank sells is value judgment. Fundamentally, a bank is judged on this issue only. For a bank is not known *a priori* for its ratios but rather by its capacity to live with these ratios. Judgment both precedes and succeeds the numbers. In a bank, excessive bigness automatically suppresses judgment, let alone meaningful communication.

For example, when Walter Wriston was asked by CBS's "60 Minutes" to explain his bank's participation in the financing of Zaire's Inga-Shaba transmission line, he replied, in essence that he did not know enough about the credit to discuss it. Regrettably, Mr. Wriston's ignorance is not feigned, and this despite the fact that Citibank has either raised or lent more than half a billion dollars into Zaire's now impoverished economy. Citibank went on a hunting expedition (for a quick profit)—without a guide. Both the hunter and the hunted fell into the same trap.

WHAT CAN BE DONE AND WHY?

The conclusion to be drawn from Zaire, from Nigeria, from Mexico and Brazil incorporates in ascending order the problem of bank size, of bank purpose, and of bank identity. The first conclusion is fairly obvious. Our legislators should set out to break down our biggest banks into separate units of no larger than $20 billion. A reasonable and corresponding capital base should be set at $2 billion. Instead, our *non-regulators* are pushing the giant banks to reach an asset size of $150 billion. Even at $50 billion, the judgment factor inevitably yields to the teletype machine, to the computer, and to the fragmentation of lending responsibilities.

Were the banks reduced to a more manageable size of $20 billion in assets and were capital ratios strengthened to their pre-inflationary levels of 10 to 1, several positive results could be expected. As a start, the judgment factor—and accountability—would be restored at the major multinational banking houses. Second, more healthy competition between the giant money center banks and regional U.S. banks would help to skew investment funds more evenly throughout the economy and help restore more equilibrium to the corporate client/ bank relationship. Third, the measure would encourage the banks to emphasize quality over quantity in marketing domestic and international loans. For the moment, our banks, the so-called "conscience of the free market system," have come to resemble what the French call a "hypermarche," a mammoth discount department store. Margins are thin and the risk of bankruptcy—on a grand scale—ever present.

Fourth, a cap on leverage ratios would orient bank management to compete for higher real earnings, not just asset growth. In turn, the curtailed limits on asset growth would correspond with more balanced development and with the absorption capacity of both the First and Third World economies.

Finally, the undue concentration of risk within the banking system itself would be reduced. The government regulators would not find themselves in the uncomfortable position of letting some poorly managed small banks go under while saving the largest money center banks for lack of an alternative. In other words, market forces once again would be permitted to operate evenly across the system. The rules of the market simply would be adjusted, by conscious political choice, to assure that all the participants enjoy comparable advantage. Thus, the system would be rendered intelligible, or measure and purpose restored.

A reduction in the asset size of our largest international banks would need to be undertaken with important but temporary government intervention. In order to strengthen the capital base of each of the new banks, the federal authorities could create, for a second time, as suggested by Felix Rohatyn, a government-funded Reconstruction Finance Corporation (RFC) similar to the one founded in the 1930s.

The corporation would purchase equity in each of the new banks necessary to respect the capital ratio of 10 to 1 as bank assets are divided up into parts of $20 billion. A $2 billion capital base would permit a legal lending limit of $200 million to any one customer according to current banking practice. This $200 million lending capability certainly is sufficient to match the borrowing needs of the largest corporate clients while respecting a reasonable economy of scale. Government equity might be represented in the form of convertible debentures but repurchased at the earliest possible occasion out of earnings or resold through the equity markets once investor confidence was restored. Like bigness, a bank becomes a bureaucracy with too much government participation, protection, or regulation. Judgment withers and the banking system becomes but an extension of state administration. This is what has happened in a number of European countries—France, Italy, Sweden, and Austria. When the government takes over the banks permanently, not only are individual liberties sacrificed, but normal checks and balances on economic management are lost. The conscience of the private sector disappears leaving Big Brother with the biggest chip in every game in town. Thus, the government bailout should be both temporary and selective. Not all big banks need the same amount of help.

In order to maintain stock market acceptability and depositor confidence, a number of Third World loans would need to be revalued (downward), purchased by government, and/or cross-guaranteed by multilateral development agencies. The reevaluation process should take place *by purpose* of the loan *not simply by country*. For instance, bank loans to the bauxite mines in Guinea are being serviced while those to the government are not. The receipt of the bauxite sales are secured through payment assignments in New York. Accordingly, the purpose of the loan and the assurance of repayment are consistent with productive bank lending. These loans should be encouraged not discouraged in any realignment of Third World debt.

By way of protecting bank market visibility, or rather, credibility, Lord Harold Lever has proposed that First World governments swap their own treasury bills against stale Third World loans. That is, the governments would step up to match defaults or payment delays by Third World borrowers with an infusion of new liquidity. As a *quid pro quo*, the banks would absorb the eventual loss of income that the purchasing government might sustain but over a longer period of time and "without calling their own liquidity or insolvency into question."

As Lord Lever explains: "The banking system would thereby be protected while the governments avoid the charge that they were themselves meeting the cost of misjudgments."[13]

Felix Rohatyn has proposed the creation of a Big Mac similar to the scheme that he worked out for New York City. Instead of a New York State cross-guarantee of municipal bonds, the IMF, or a like institution, would cross-guarantee some of the Third World debt owing the banks. The idea of a planetary Big Mac could certainly be considered as a negotiating piece in bringing bank management and their banks down to size—i.e., $20 billion maximum. For his part, Rohatyn observes that "It took 6 years for New York City to back away from bankruptcy."[14] How long will it take the world economy? Rohatyn demonstrates the intellectual honesty of admitting that the world economy is courting bankruptcy and not confronting a mere, temporary, Third World liquidity crisis. For Rohatyn, the debt trap is real and much more complicated than most bankers and bank examiners are prepared to admit.

The proposals just outlined and others deserve serious consideration by legislators, regulators, international civil servants, and the bankers themselves. More-of-the-same or business-as-usual could well lead to what *The Economist* has described as the "big bang theory" on how the banking world, as we presently know it, ends: "One gloomy morning, Argentina, or some similar disaster area, will abandon the struggle to keep up with repaying its debts and declare itself in default. By lunch time in New York, bank share prices will have fallen through the floor. By tea time, the other debtor countries will have followed the Argentine example."[15] To some extent, this has already happened. Banks have simply rolled over the debt while their p/e ratios, in comparison with the Standard & Poor's 500 index, stands at the lowest level ever. The bankruptcy itself has simply been diffracted southward and now envelops the better part of the Third World economy.

LENDING METHODOLOGY AND MULTINATIONAL BANKING

A deteriorating world economic order has created the conditions for a more fertile dialogue between central bank regulators, multilateral creditors, borrowing governments and private sector banks. It can be hoped that this dialogue will result in a more viable lending environment for all parties concerned. In the meantime, the banks might do more on an institutional basis to prepare themselves for a place at the table. They might start by looking carefully at their size, purpose, identity and overall commitment to the Third World market. Without a more viable approach to the market, the banks will undoubtedly find themselves in the vortex of important loan losses compounded by an even more hostile regulatory environment, both at home and abroad. The banks know this.

In searching for a more suitable lending methodology, some of the more important questions to be posed can be conveniently summarized under three general categories.

First, what are the practical limits of cooperation between private multinational banks and multilateral creditors, particularly the World Bank and the International Monetary Fund? Only in the very recent past have official lenders recognized that the problems of development finance require a partnership with private sector banks. This is a function of the sheer size of commercial bank loans to LDC borrowers.

It has been more generally assumed that multilateral lending agencies were concerned with "development" and the commercial banks with "profit." Neither party has been particularly sensitive to the possible compatibility—and long-term inevitability—of these two goals.

Thus, the first question to be posed relates to the place to be appriated the larger multinational banks in the overall scheme of Third World lending. Without a clearer definition, it is not surprising that the activities of certain large multinational banks have had a decidedly negative impact on the development—social, economic, and political —of not a few Third World countries.

The banks might best participate in the development process by tying the bulk of future credit to project-oriented finance or, in the case of short-term loans, to essential trade items. As we have remarked, this allows the lender to identify a specific economic, if not financial, payout in the form of export receipts or import substitution.

In most instances, long-term infrastructure or general budgetary finance is best left in the hands of the bilateral and the multilateral lenders. Official government creditors generally have more leverage in dealing with government borrowers and in controlling, through peer pressure and otherwise, spendthrift heads of state.

For their part, the IMF and the World Bank will need to be made responsible not only for safeguarding the development process but for changing it. This implies a radical alteration of the growth models in which our banks and export agencies participate, that is, a shift from worldwide competition to regional development and from free trade to North-South cooperation. This important change to our development paradigm should not be understood as a theoretical luxury but rather as a formal necessity if our banking and trading systems are not to fragment and the comity of nations with them. The IMF and the World Bank not only need more money, which they will get. Much more importantly, they need a different mandate. With this new mandate, the IMF might better control the dead-end reasoning process of export credit programs, their associated investment criteria, and the abuses therein. In this way, the next development decade, the fourth, which carries us into the twenty-first century might actually represent a new beginning rather than a sort of evolutionary cul de sac. The world community, North-South, would move beyond the age of high mass consumption, which Walter Rostow himself has come to question, and advance toward a period of real exchange, growth, and development.

The second most urgent question that needs to be posed relates to the internal organization of the multinational banking houses themselves. The boards of directors of most large international banks are exclusively composed of local nationals from corporate and community affairs. The structure of the boards of directors of certain banks will need to be broadened to reflect more accurately the changed complexion of their loan portfolios and the communities that they are now serving. Some big banks already have established international advisory committees made up of well-known members of the world community. Yet these committees have no voting power at the level of the board of directors. As an interim solution, the international advisory committees might vote one member to the boards of our major banks. Alternatively, the IMF could name an observer in exchange for the cross-guarantees proposed under the Big Mac formula.

Changes at the board level certainly would lead to a more institutionalized approach to LDC lending. For the time being, practitioners, that is, on-line branch managers and lending officers, seldom make a distinction between the nature of their lending activities in Monrovia from those in Manhattan or Manchester. This is because the policy issues at hand have not been clearly defined at the top.

The third important question that needs to be posed has to do with the precise mandate of our regulators. As the much respected George Champion, chairman of Chase Manhattan from 1961 to 1969, argued in the January 10, 1984 Forum Section of the *New York Times*: "The dismal failure of our examining forces to carry out their responsibility clearly shows that new leadership and greatly strengthened organizations are needed."

New leadership and organization can only come through the workings of the political process, that is, through the U.S. Congress. More specifically, legislation originates in the House and Senate Banking Committees headed respectively by Representative Fernand J. St Germain (D-RI) and by Senator Jake Garn (R-UT). Both committees currently are fashioning new bank legislation which will have an enduring impact on the U.S. and the world economy. The principal trade associations (lobbies) involved in the legislative process are the American Bankers Association (ABA) and the Independent Bankers Association of America (IBAA). Both are located in Washington, D.C.

For its part, the IBAA is fighting a rear guard action in an attempt to close the so-called non-bank loophole. The loophole allows for private companies that are not licensed as banks to set up deposit-taking offices to compete with the nation's fiduciary banking system. The IBAA rightfully argues that the new powers given to nonbanks by the Comptroller of the Currency threatens to destroy the existing banking structure of the United States to the detriment of all but a handful of major corporations and some multinational banks that want to become nonbanks.

The American Bankers Association (ABA), which represents not only independent banks but the country's major regional and money center banks, likewise wants the nonbank loophole closed but with nuance. The ABA supports bank deregulation allowing in effect the largest banks with holding companies to engage in so-called non-bank activities. A partial listing consists of insurance underwriting, real estate brokerage, ownership of thrift institutions, sponsorship and sale of mutual funds, travel promotion, information services and the like. In large measure, Senator Garn supports the ABA and the Administration's misguided contention that new legislation should seek to achieve regulatory parity between banks, bank holding companies and nonbanks. The thrust of the same argument logically would lead to nationwide banking, especially for those banks (the biggest) that have been assured by the Federal Deposit Insurance Company (FDIC) that they will not be allowed to fail. What we stand witness to is a rescue operation disguised as horizontal and vertical expansion. The net, global result is a weakened economy.

Instead of allowing nonbanks to become quasi banks and banks to become nonbanks, what Congress and the Administration should be striving for is a return to purposeful banking and bank lending. To clarify the issue, we best might envision a bank as the center of an economic wheel with the spokes emanating from this single point. If our legislators, and a few large banks that want to become nonbanks, succeed in voiding the pivotal center then the economy as a whole will be confronted with an enormous gap at the precise point in the system that needs the most stability. A dispersion of bank interest and purpose separates the bank from the community that it is serving and separates the banker from relevant accountability. Accordingly, ongoing legislation must seek to end the crazy-quilt banking/nonbanking-network that has sprung up in the past four years due to a loophole in the law and due to active encouragement by the regulatory authorities. If the loophole is not closed retroactively then the careless banking practices that we have seen in Third World lending, where the regulators were not present, will rebound in the First.

THE LOOPHOLE AND FOREIGN LENDING

On the international side once these issues, regulatory, financial, and developmental, have been defined and the senior managements of the banks made aware of a slightly different set of expectations, then a wide range of planning and training criteria would be changed. The long-term results undoubtedly would make for a more consistent income stream netted against possible loan losses. Likewise, important benefits would accrue in geopolitical and in human terms. Not only would the taxpayer in the North be spared the ongoing cost of big bank bailouts, but equally important, his distant brethren in the South might start obtaining some value on his borrowed dollar.

One meaningful example of a structural change would be to halt the growing tendency at the large banks to set country limits at home and then assign marketing officers in the field to fill the book. As we have insisted, this specialization manifestly does not work in the Third World. The dichotomy between economic or political analysis and business development means a vast separation between theory and application. What is needed is the careful grooming of loan officers—not just salesmen—who have been trained to appreciate the conceptual differences between corporate business development and Third World sovereign risk lending. The methodology is not the same, nor should be the emphasis. To be sure, the responsibilities are of a different order. Meanwhile, some banks have gone so far as to request Third World branch and country lending officers to prepare their annual budgets based on projected loan volume, turnover, and commission business with no reference to market risk, that is, to the country's development goals and the available means to reach those goals. Hence, the local branch comes to resemble its head office as little more than a financial intermediary or broker instead of a bank. The Third World market comes to be but another measure—perhaps the most tragic—of bank mismanagement and of regulatory ignorance of what a bank is.

The fourth question to be examined relates to the first three and deals with the abstract issue of corporate citizenship. A bank cannot develop a meaningful lending program—particularly at an institutional level—without a corresponding morality. In their important book, *In Search of Excellence*, two experienced management consultants, Thomas J. Peterson and Robert H. Waterman, Jr., describe eight key variables that account for the success of what they identify as "America's best-run companies." The selection was based on operating performance and innovation over a long period of time. The key variables explaining the most excellent companies were gleaned from thousands of personal interviews and tapings. Not by surprise, the key variable turns out to be not a single-minded preoccupation with profit, with costs, nor with growth for its own sake but rather with a "corporate culture," a common ground of meaning and values shared by all the members. Although not a single bank ranked among the truly excellent or best-run American companies, nowhere is this common ground of value more important than in the banking industry. The need for common values is especially critical in the Third World where by definition the banks are dealing with a quite delicate web of political economic and social issues, not the least of which is abject poverty and hunger. When big banks are working in small economies with these sorts of realities, one can appreciate the need for an appropriate moral imperative.

In establishing at the institutional level the right corporate culture and the lending program to match it, it would serve little purpose to detail a specific code of conduct. What the banks and regulators must focus on is not an internal code per se but rather a certain attitudinal bias on the part of bank management. In the Third World, the banks will need to modify their profile, their orientation, and their planning procedures to meet a decidedly different set of lending variables.

For instance, budget periods and performance ratings (particularly for management at new installations) should be changed to account for a 24- or 36-month reporting period rather than a 12-month period. This would allow for a more strategic approach to new markets. Central banks already garnish biographical information on new branch managers. The right moral persuasion should encourage the banks to set a longer time horizon when judging branch performance.

On the lending side, large syndicated credits should be rated not only on the immediate risk/reward relationship but, equally important, on the less obvious issues of longer-term economic impact. The same is true for export credits. The World Bank as the world's largest independent development agency should be given some overlord authority to rank new commercial bank loans according to their economic and/or developmental value. A scale of 1 to 5 would be sufficient to keep the banks and the export credit agencies honest. In the meantime, borrowed money, even for those countries endowed with important mineral wealth, is and will remain a limited resource. The offshore financing of inflated domestic operating budgets, imperial highways, and unused hotels clearly should be recognized as a thing of the past—even in the richest Third World countries—Brazil, Mexico, South Korea, Nigeria, and the like. Likewise, bank examiners should be made aware of the fact by legislators that the lending parameters have changed.

Thus, what is at issue is a slightly different set of value judgments and measuring devices. A future methodology on Third World bank lending should encourage this. These observations take on particular relevance at big institutions, where norms are set and where lending patterns incorporate a large percentage of the financial market in question.

Meanwhile, beggar-thy-neighbor justifications for lending strategies will only seem reasonable in the short run. Going forward, the big banks will need to measure their conduct and their vocation against the sheer weight of their presence in the Third World, a Third World where sovereign borrowers often do not enjoy the institutional stability of the banks themselves.

A fifth consideration should be added to the first four. In today's financial system, there is no lender of last resort with sufficient financial muscle to provide even implicit guarantees against additional abusive lending. A few large banks will continue to be in and out of the Third World market on the theory that over time they will be able to modulate their sovereign risks in an acceptable manner. As we have seen, the profit incentives, at times, are not negligible. Such a policy represents a nonstrategy. The problem is not one of timing but one of overall corporate culture and the lending methodology that flows from it.[16]

Meanwhile, the major LDC defaults that have occurred to date have not been primarily triggered by deteriorating terms of trade, nor by climactic conditions, nor by high interest rates. These are but surrogate issues protecting borrowers, bankers, and examiners. For barring exceptional circumstances, the variables can normally be supported by the system. In almost every case, the most serious defaults on the international capital markets have been caused ultimately by extraordinary mismanagement of foreign debt. Normally, there are a host of local political reasons for this not to mention sheer greed. Nonetheless, a lending ethic understood and commonly accepted by lender and borrower alike might provide the institutional support necessary to avoid in the future the very costly financial excesses that the world community has witnessed thus far and for which it is paying dearly.

In the future, multinational banks will need to position themselves to play the same role in the Third World markets that they traditionally have played at home, that is, as regulators in a free but not predatory, nor extroverted, nor pathological market economy. In order for the banks to play this role effectively, they will need to review some of the common premises on which they are now operating. This is particularly true if, in the long run, the banks want to service properly their depositors, their clients, and, ultimately, their shareholders. Meanwhile, if this is no longer the case, then bank management should be changed as a *quid pro quo* for a bailout.

In the end, the Third World, like the First, needs bankers, not money changers. To the extent that the transition does not take place, then the current language being employed to describe the state of Third World debt, while not entirely helpful, would seem prophetic. The term "crack," mentioned at the beginning of this chapter, is a way that depositors have of describing in negative fashion what a bank should be. Perhaps the simplicity of the term will help bankers focus on their own *raison d'être*. Without a more fixed sense of identity, the very meaning of a bank evaporates in a profusion of numbers and of ratios that have very little to do with the real world of poverty, of profit, and of financial performance. In fact, performance itself becomes meaningless and unmeasurable, which might account for the recent poor value of bank stock in general.

The lack of definition certainly accounts for the increasingly strident language being used to describe our global financial system. The violence of the language and of the queries will not go away until the bankers themselves can decide who they are. This accomplished, appropriate methodology, training, and ratios will fall into place in such a way as to provide hope for a solution to the much discussed *crack* in our system. In the meanwhile, without a revision in definition, in purpose, and even in worldview, the veiled *crack* will surely become a *fissure* affecting not only our banking system but our existing political orders.

Thus, we have come full circle. Our worldview—as best exemplified in modern development theory by the Law of Comparative Advantage—sets the internal and external conditions in which our major multinational banks are operating. Internally, our vision tells management that competition is a more positive organizing principle than cohesion. As a result, banks have been broken down into limitless profit centers or separate businesses with individual operating units spending more time in-fighting over income or cost allocations than in servicing customers. Consequently, administration outpaces advances in computer application, while communication and corporate culture suffer. A lack of coherence in lending, à la the Nigerian case study, inevitably follows.

Externally, the worldview argues that force (in this case size or self-insurance) is more important than purpose or finality.

Both internal competition inflated by management philosophy, and size have rendered our banking system unresponsive to real market needs, especially in the Third World where most of the profits have been coming from. The external and internal environment have been further, and perhaps fatefully, confused by inadequate regulation and by a trading system based on comparative advantage between the rich and the poor. Thus, the individual parts fit together into a larger picture. The larger picture is the product of our worldview.

A PARADIGM, DISCOVERY, AND THE DOMAINS OF KNOWLEDGE

Historically, *Homo sapiens* has been sensitive to the need of adapting his analytic skills to the specific nature of the problem with which he is dealing. On this basis, viable objectives can be determined. The World community has entered halfway into the Third Development Decade. During the first two and a half decades, modern man seems to have forgotten the importance of an appropriate First World/Third World development philosophy. As a result, objectives have changed as if bankers, economists, and regulators were looking at a moving target. Perhaps this blind spot developed because hopes were too obvious, perhaps because the community of man recognized neither the danger nor the complexity of the issues at hand. In any case, our current models appear not to be working and our superstructures, both financial and ideological, need significant revamping. Hopefully, by the end of the Third Development Decade, new models and structures will have been proposed and accepted by the international development community. Suggestions have been made on how our banks and international aid institutions might contribute to a more sound, less dangerous world order. Nonetheless, the banks and other financiers need a model or game plan within which to conduct business. A more relevant model can only be invented once our notion of order has shifted. Accordingly, the following chapters set out to detail not only another growth model, but, perhaps more importantly, an alternative intellectual foundation for future model building. Our emphasis shall shift from money to method, from the real world of international finance to its conceptual framework.

We shall question our common paradigm, even our epistemology in order to determine if the World community cannot bring a more suitable logic to the seemingly intractable problem posed by the First World: Third World question. In questioning the paradigm, we shall propose a new one.

To do this, we shall need to start our analysis with a discussion of the intellectual tools currently being brought to bear to save our planet from the potential risk of financial, economic, and political chaos, a chaos that is already manifest in what we have referred to as the second holocaust of wide-scale famine. As we shall see, the analytic tools are, in the end, more important than our technology. Method shapes not only content but action as well. In turn, method is based on a worldview. Our worldview determines discovery.

For example, in development planning and related financial analysis, it is generally thought that economics is a predictive science. Most bankers and certainly the regulators operate on this premise. Economics, however, is not a science but a value system that cannot be separated from its social and political moorings. In the Third World, economics when considered as a science for policy purposes oftentimes obscures rather than clarifies the appropriate development path. Economics as science also closes options. Nonetheless, economic model building continues to take on the air of empirical verity, and the modern sector of most Third World economies seems to grow out of separate soil. Unfortunately, the separate soil all too often possesses the quality of sand.

Economic laws, it can be shown, are by no means neutral. Nor are they, even in a remote sense, scientific. The laws are man-made. They reflect a specific worldview. Thus, the model cannot be transplanted unless the ideological—even ontological—support systems exist to give the model nourishment.

Accordingly, in order to understand the model, we shall need to analyze the building blocks or seminal ideas that make up the current logic of our development strategies. Only on this basis can we test the feasibility of Northern models in a Southern setting, of Western finance in the Third World market.

Our concern going forward shall be with reason and method in Third World development, not just with development per se. We will argue that the common paradigm that underscores our growth models—whether East or West—is linked inextricably to a defined break in the Western World's philosophic traditions. Before exporting either growth model or variations thereof to the Third World, we should understand their common premise, both by origin and by content. We should also understand their limitations.

Both systems grew out of a hiatus in our intellectual heritage that started with the collapse of Renaissance culture but was made manifest in the abuses of the Industrial Revolution and the two world wars which followed.

The break can be most clearly defined in nineteenth century concepts of economic determinism. Our ideas about nature as being "red in tooth and claw" found similar voice in the earlier economic treatises of Adam Smith, and later in the political and economic writings of Karl Marx. Both Smith and Marx were outspoken materialists. Both thinkers were convinced that economic and social progress depended on conflict.

We live in a world today where economic, political and financial strategies in the West, as in the East Bloc Countries, are based fundamentally on nineteenth century concepts of "survival of the fittest." In our dealings with the South, we in the North should recognize this concept as part of our recent intellectual heritage. We also should recognize this heritage as part of our current world profile.

The "law of the jungle" is a relatively modern western concept not appreciated by our forefathers nor understood by our poorer, vastly more numerous neighbors to the South. This is particularly true in the poorest countries where cooperation rather than conflict within society means the difference between survival or disappearance of entire civilizations.

It can be argued likewise that Western civilization also was founded on quite different, less fateful principles of nature and of man. The dichotomy between the "law of the jungle" and a more instrinsically harmonious view of the cosmos might be at the origin of the identity crisis that has prevailed in the West in recent times. It also gives us a split image of ourselves vis-à-vis the Third World.

At the founding of our civilization, Aristotle noted that human thinking started from the astonishment that "things are as they are." He meant by this that there is a fundamental harmony in nature that needs to be "discovered." Chaos is the antipode of the cosmos.

This fundamental worldview has inspired Western thought for two millenia and continues to lend impetus to much of our basic scientific research. On social, political and economic fronts this sort of thinking largely has gone to the wind.

As we have shown, foreign aid programs and Third World multinational bank lending strategies are premised all too often on theories of economic determinism rather than on the goals of economic development. In Part II, we will discuss the intellectual origin of these theories, their validity, and their inevitable result if nothing is done to change them.

Most businessmen think that they know something about banking. Most bankers think that they know something about business. Most economists think that they know something about both. Most lawyers, of course, think that they know something about all three—that is, banking, business, and economics.

The fact of the matter is that everyone participates in someone else' special domain of knowledge. Paradoxically, the domains of knowledge have been obscured by the facility, if not intellectual lassitude, of modern man's definition of himself. This definition has led not only to the insolvency of our banking systems but, likewise, it has committed a goodly portion of mankind to a contingent future. In the North, this contingency is measured in terms of a hyperinflated financial system and in terms of thermonuclear weaponry. In the South, the contingency is equally real, although less spectacular to the average reader. For the contingency relates to today's "daily bread."

Part II
The Western Question

Listen, Box,
And keep quiet. Listen courteously to us
Four reformers who have founded—why not?—
The Gung-Ho Group, the Ganymede Club
For homesick young angels, the Arctic League
Of Tropical Fish, the Tomboy Fund
For Blushing Brides and the Bide-a-wees
Of Sans-Souci, assembled again
For a Think-Fest: our theme tonight is

HOMO ABYSSUS OCCIDENTALIS

or

A CURIOUS CASE OF COLD FEET

or

SEVEN SELFISH SUPPERLESS AGES

And now, at Rosetta's suggestion, they left their bar-stools and moved to the quieter intimacy of a booth. Drinks were ordered and the discussion began.

W. H. Auden, *The Age of Anxiety*

11
First Analytic to the Western Question: Economics as Science

It is man's natural tendency to straighten what is crooked, to define what is undefined, to make beautiful what is ugly. This tendency is manifest in the domain of philosophy, in the domain of pure mathematics, and in the domain of physics. The tendency is not always manifest in the domain of economics. We might ask ourselves why? For economics, as an intellectual discipline, theoretically tells us how to allocate our resources, that is, how we live from day to day. Economics also provides the models through which we measure investment decisions, aid policy, and international lending generally. Thus, the simple, perhaps radical, question to be posed reads as follows: Can we rely on economics for this sort of information? The answer is by no means obvious.

The effort to straighten out what is crooked, to define what is undefined, to make beautiful what is ugly is spoken of traditionally as either an art or as a science. Most intellectual disciplines in the West fall within either of these two quite distinct categories of human knowledge.

Mathematics, for instance gives us our notions of time and of space. Biology defines for us our knowledge of living organism. The arts render the cosmos beautiful; First philosophy or metaphysics rationalizes the whole.

The issues at hand do not represent idle dialectic. In fact, our position on what constitutes knowledge, and why, determines how we in the West define our universe. The position subsequently explains our conduct in the organization of domestic and of international affairs. Moreover, this division of knowledge distinguishes, in large measure, a particular Western profile via-à-vis that of the rest of the world, including the Third World. This intellectual profile, this vision of ourselves is vital to understand if we are to conduct human affairs with those on the planet who do not share our particular cultural heritage.

The problematic comes into better focus to the extent that we are able to define our key terms. What is an art? What is a science? Where do the recently invented social sciences fit into the overall scheme of Western thought? For the moment, suffice it to note simply that the arts are tentative and that the sciences are definitive.

Not only are these two issues important to grasp for an appropriate analysis of our thought process and of our identity, but they also are important for two reasons as regards an analysis of Third World political and economic reality.

First, in any analytic method, we need to know the range and the applicability of our knowledge. "For it is part of the educated man," writes Aristotle, "to require exactness in each class of subject, only so far as the nature of the subject allows."[1] Without this basic understanding about the nature of knowing, knowledge itself has no foundation. Knowledge becomes mired in magic or prejudice, and facts stand isolated without real meaning. This concern for the nature of knowledge is a specifically Western preoccupation. The West cannot afford to forget the issue when interfacing with the Third World. This is especially true for bankers and international civil servants or for those directly responsible for the development process itself.

Second, in Third World Development strategies as presently conceived, the social sciences stand at the core of our analytic process. The social sciences serve to measure the reality that we are attempting to understand. Accordingly, we would do well to have a firm definition of the terms and of their relevance to the analytic process.

This is particularly true of economies. For at the core of our development strategies, we discover, more often than not, that the social sciences are reduced to a set of economic laws. The science of economics not only inspires but, in most instances, determines the development process. Sociology, political science, history, even psychology and anthropology are distilled into economic models. In turn, the economic models shape the subsequent ordering of our societies. In discussing a specific political order, we cite a given economic system. Increasingly, the system is refined so that the political facts fit neatly into preconceived economic theory. As we shall see shortly, the economic theory or laws are based on a quite fixed definition of man, a definition that betrays a goodly part of the West's intellectual heritage and culture. This betrayal is at the source of the worldview that accounts for the Law of Comparative Advantage.

For the moment it is important to emphasize simply that economic laws serve as the base of a social science that the North—both East and West—brandishes before the South as a source of power and of material well-being.

Indeed, it has become deceptively easy to equate progress with the success of a specific economic model. This is particularly true when the model is said to be based on scientific fact, or rather, on a scientific method. As such, the facts, the indicators, the model are devoid of prejudice. They are devoid of what Adam Smith called "superstition" and Karl Marx "metaphysics."

In other words, what we are dealing with is a world that is real because it is rendered obvious. This world is obvious because it is measurable in economic and, finally, in sociological terms. The terms, of course, are thought to be objective. In fact, it is this objectivity that gives the terms their presumed scientific value. In the process, what we are leaving out (and it is deliberate) is value judgment.

The Third World abounds with development and financial programs designed to fit in modular form a specific scientific or economic theory. The current size of these programs will soon represent about $1,000 billion in Third World debt. This does not include a growing volume of military credits. Thus, the North has invested heavily and deeply in its own social and economic theory. The South is struggling desperately to apply this science to its quite specific human needs.

With only few exceptions, everyone's faith in the magic of scientifically discovered economic theory of late has taken the trappings of religious conviction. A similar logic prevails in geopolitical and for bankers in sovereign risk credit analysis. Our bankers, aid people, and their economists attempt to isolate predetermined changes in the evolution of a given society by citing underlying economic reality. It is thought that economic reality ultimately determines political and social options rather than vice versa. A change in the economic structure of a society represents, it is argued, a corresponding change in the social, even mental construct of a people. In turn, these changes are said to be predictable, at least on a statistically reliable basis.

Economics can be thought of as the king of the social sciences. We in the North place considerable trust in the capacity of economics as science to dictate a given development path. The underlying assumption serves as a premise for countless recommendations on world economic integration, on banking and investment policy, on relief programs, and on geopolitical strategy generally. Economics as science is expected to yield predictable and verifiable results. Hence, economic theory serves increasingly as the premise of our political thinking. Economic theory also functions as the almost exclusive premise of the North-South dialogue.

We would do well, however, to be more careful with our terms. For a careful definition of our terms will tell us something about the nature and the applicability of Third World development strategies. For if the social sciences—particularly economics—are truly scientific, then we should posture ourselves according to their laws. This would be a relatively simple thing to do if we truly believed in our logic.

Indeed, if economics were a science, reasonably thoughtful men with adequate technical skills should be able to embark on economic development programs that provide for basic human needs, at least in those instances where political power is firmly in hand. Most of our ideologies today are infused with this conviction. The same can be said of our expectations.

A brief review of what our forefathers had to say about the categories of knowledge should shed some light on the problematic at hand. The review might also tell us something about the tools currently being employed in efforts to pull approximately two-thirds of the world's population out of relative, if not, abject poverty. This latter task, as we have noted, is a complex but necessary one if we are to enter the twenty-first century whole.

Let us ask ourselves what measures of a logical order might be adopted to promote a development process consistent with Third World and with First World needs. For the time being, the answers are coming from our bankers, our economists, and our international civil servants. When our politicians approach the problem, they rely on the advice of these experts. Our experts are calling for more money and for more people. Thus, the circle is expanding. The same holds true as regards the distance between the rich and the poor, the creditor and his client.

When we try to theorize the issues of bank debt, aid, absorption capacity, and related poverty at the institutional level, our thought process and our models are based on economics as a predictive science. The two models are communism and capitalism. These models serve as the polar forces in most Third World development schemes. The schemes themselves, however, are not providing the empirical results anticipated. In fact, what the experts call "systemic" problems in international trade and financial flows are, in a deeper sense, reflective of a logic that has failed.

THE ARTS AND THE SCIENCES

When we in the West look to our own heritage for what constitutes knowledge, and why, our first important source of reference is found in the person of Xenocrates. We need to go back to Greece in the fifth century B.C. not for rhetorical purposes, as readily thought, but rather in order to understand the specificity and the practicality of our thought process.

According to Xenocrates, all human learning can be broken into three intellectual disciplines: physics, ethics, and logic.[2] Physics deals with the material world and its contents. Ethics deals with personal conduct and political order. Logic includes all methods of expression and gives to the other orders of knowledge the ability to verify their underlying intuitions. While the system is not conclusive, the effort to provide order to our knowing marks an important step in the evolution of man's thought process and in the development of his analytic skills.

Aristotle subsequently provided a more detailed division of human learnings. Aristotle's schema is infused with the cumulative weight of earlier Greek thought. It also provides form and substance to our own.

The Stagirite's division of learning is important to visualize because it distinguishes a specific intellectual profile. It also provides a more reasonable situs for the study of economics and for its appropriate application in Third World development, in banking, and in aid policy.

The Order of Knowing

For Aristotle, the various disciplines of learning can be divided into the theoretic, the practical, and the poetic. These three categories of knowledge later became known more simply as the sciences and the arts.

Theoretic knowledge is scientific knowledge. The definition is strict. Science deals with what is *necessary*, with what is *universal*, and with what is *unchanging* in the realm of human experience. The terms "necessary," "universal," and "unchanging," are key to our understanding of what constitutes science, and why.[3] Without these distinctions, our order of knowing becomes blurred.

For instance, the fact that two plus two equals four is necessary because it could not be otherwise as a function of the internal order of its logic. The formula also is universal in its application and unchanging in time. Most importantly, the formula is based on a first principle or premise that inspires subsequent discovery. In mathematics, the first principle is the number one as the composite figure for unity. Without this first principle, subsequent arithmetic knowledge would not be conceivable in its current form.

The same sort of reasoning holds true in the applied sciences. In biology, we anticipate the birth of certain viruses because we know their causes. When we know their causes, we know that they are necessary because they could not be otherwise. We also know that the causes are universal and unchanging. Aristotle would say "eternal."

A robin cannot give birth to a blackbird. For this to be more than a simple observation, we must know the cause. Knowledge of a fact without knowledge of a cause is opinion, according to our forefathers.

Thus, theoretic or scientific knowledge is certain. There is no science of particulars. "For unless a man knows the principles," writes Aristotle, "even better than the conclusion, he will only possess science accidentally."[4]

The ancients were looking for stability in scientific knowledge as opposed to the instability of human opinion. In fact, this represents their particular genius.

For the school of Athens, science presumes a first principle that is incorruptible. While some will argue with this premise, what is most interesting for our purposes in the fact that Greek thought insisted that we distinguish between *what* we know (the *sciences*) from *how* we apply our knowledge (the *arts*).

This invention or rhetorical device is perhaps more critical to the evolution of Western man than the development of all of our technological equipment put together. For without an underlying logic, scientific invention would not have been possible, at least on the order that we know it today.

We can conclude by saying that science explains our knowledge of reality; art applies, in a practical sense, this knowledge to man's needs. Science discovers nature; art extends it. Science is certain; art is problematic. These distinctions are important to remember in any analysis of First and Third World development. Indeed, the distinctions serve to define our approach. And this approach determines the outcome of our thought process.

It is only when we forget the proper limits of scientific knowledge that our understanding and, by extension, our actions on a societal level become blurred. It was in the fifth century B.C. that Democritus hypothesized the atom. It was in the twentieth century A.D. that the atom was split over Hiroshima. The discovery and subsequent harnessing of the atom was theoretic, or scientific. The application of the atom in the realm of human activity is of a different order.

These distinctions are important to remember. Without them, our analysis of any society, whether economic, political, or social becomes lost in the quicksand of false premises or in the never-never land of false expectations. In brief, our expectations relate to our method. If our methods are inadequate then our expectations are likely to be groundless. As we have shown, our expectations have been groundless in attempting to solve the complex problem of global poverty.

This brings us to our definition of the arts—what our forefathers referred to as the "practical sciences." The practical sciences do not deal with demonstrable truths emanating from a necessary, identifiable cause. Rather, their subject matter deals with value judgment, or the application of scientific knowledge to human affairs.

Unlike the speculative or theoretic sciences, the arts are not defined by their subject matter per se. The arts are defined by the *object* or goal of their activities. Ethics is the study of personal conduct as a means of obtaining individual happiness. Happiness was understood to mean the actualization of one's potential, not simply pleasure as described by modern utilitarians and on which modern economic theory is based. Politics extends the study of ethics to the state. The goal of politics is the realization of the common good in the context of the proper utilization of the *res publica*. Rhetoric measures the validity of our thought process in order to give to the sciences and to the arts their just hold on society. The goal of rhetoric is clear thinking and precise expression.

The distinctions between the sciences and the arts are critical to our understanding of both. Science considers its subject matter as necessary or universal and therefore suppresses the contingent. Art thinks of its object as possible and therefore suggests alternatives. Art incorporates scientific and technological knowledge into human society. Science serves art, not vice versa. In our Western tradition, art is practice; science is theory. Science discovers; art decides. We would do well to remember these principles when we attempt to apply the so-called "laws" of economic theory to the art of nation building. Without a clear definition between the arts and the sciences, no one knows who is in charge, and why. Responsibility becomes diffuse, while nature is taken as the cause of the human condition, whatever that condition might be.

THE LAWS OF SOCIETY

The hypothesis that man is not free is essential to the application of the scientific method to the study of human behavior.
B. F. Skinner in *Science and Human Behavior*, 1954.

Our distinctions between the sciences and the arts began to break down in the mid-eighteenth century, that is, at the collapse of Renaissance culture. It was at this time that modern Western thinkers started looking for and finding what they took to be demonstrable scientific laws in the conduct of human affairs. Charles-Louis de Secondat, the Count of Montesquieu, published in 1748 his very important political treatise entitled *De l'Esprit des Lois*. The treatise analyzes various societies according to the laws of nature. The laws that govern society were determined to be not unlike the physical or biological laws that govern the universe. This was the book's invention, and this explains its success. De Montesquieu writes in his preface: "I have examined men and find them guided, in the infinite diversity of their laws and customs, not simply by their fantasy."[5] For de Montesquieu, the term "fantasy" meant imagination, creativity, or worse, the arbitrary. His effort was to reduce man and society to a set quantitative laws or first principles that would allow for subsequent scientific investigation. The effort eventually resulted in the creation of those intellectual disciplines known today as the "social" or "behavioral" sciences, including economics.

De Montesquieu's ultimate goal was to reverse, on a rational basis, the political and economic abuses of the court of Louis XIV. His method was to adopt the mechanistic theories of eighteenth-century physical sciences to the study of man. For the logic to hold, however, it ultimately was necessary to change the definition of *Homo sapiens*.

As we shall see, the effort already was quite advanced in England in the writings of Thomas Hobbes and later in the epistemological speculations of David Hume. We should observe, in fact, that David Hume's *An Enquiry Concerning Human Understanding* was published in the same year as de Montesquieu's *De l'Esprit des Lois*. De Montesquieu was a lawyer; Hume a professional economist, essayist, diplomat, and philosopher. Both men were coming out of the same intellectual tradition known today, ironically, as the "Age of Reason."

For Hume, man could be defined as a complex of sensory perceptions, which perceptions were able to give at best a partial view of reality. "The most lively thought," he writes, "is still inferior to the dullest sensation."[6] On this basis, creativity becomes a question of wiring; conviction is reduced to a series of repetitive sense impressions. In other words, *Homo sapiens* now includes within its definition the fact that man can be conditioned. It suffices to understand the wiring, the impulses, the sense impressions. Hume continues: "All inferences from Experience, therefore, are Effects of Custom, not of Reasoning. Custom, then, is the great Guide of human life. 'Tis that Principle alone, which renders our Experience useful to us."[7]

What we are dealing with here is a radical departure in our definition of what constitutes man and his place in the universe. The definition of *Homo sapiens* now quite easily admits of scientific investigation.

Accordingly, when eighteenth-century secular culture became mass culture, the arts and the sciences were fused into a single whole. The cause for this confusion centered on Western man's changing definition of himself.

In the Judeo-Christian tradition, man is contingent. That is, he possesses by definition a moral choice in his personal conduct and, by extension, in the structure of his society.[8] The Greek Prometheus, the Jewish Adam, the Christian Saint George are three symbols of a broad cultural reality that defines man as distinct from, and superior to, his immediate physical environment.

With the introduction in the eighteenth century of the scientific method to the study of man, man himself was depicted as the product of his immediate habitat. This description inevitably followed from the logic of the method.

Mechanistic theories of eighteenth-century physical science gave way in the nineteenth century to biological theories of evolutionary determinism. In turn, these theories were applied to a range of mental disciplines now called the "social sciences." In fact, the social sciences had to be invented in order to make the method fit. The method has come to overwhelm not only our definition of man and his social habitat but also our expectations of man's potential.

In sum, the social sciences are said to have their own set of laws. These laws are thought to be consistent with scientific theory. At least, this is the underlying assumption in most quarters of modern society. The assumption, however, represents blind faith in the logic of the Age of Reason. The assumption currently inspires First World and Third World social, financial, and economic analysis. It also determines, as we have noted, our options. That is, our social theories are taken to be *necessary, universal,* and *unchanging.* Hence, the nature of today's global economic planning.

According to our forefathers, the study of man in society is not a science nor can it be. There is no science of contingents. "A science of contingents," writes Aristotle, "destroys the contingent." The contingent is defined as that which could be otherwise. Our modern methodology does not allow for this problematic. Hence, a purely technocratic, supposedly value neutral ethos has overwhelmed the planning process.

THE HEDONISTIC PRINCIPLE

Having reviewed the logical distinctions between the arts and the sciences, we now shall look at the recent historical path that bankers and Third World planners have taken to justify the art of development economics as a predictive science. In order to fix our argument at a specific point in time, we will review the two fundamental conceptual pillars historically used to underpin economics as a science. The first is demand theory, known in the economic world as the "hedonistic principle." The second is supply theory, known alternatively as "capital formation." In economics, capital starts the productive process. Capital is considered as the ultimate source of wealth. Capital creates production. Production means supply.

By exploring carefully the two theoretic pillars of economics as science, we should be able to decide once and for all if economic reality should be allowed to preempt our hopes. We should be able to decide likewise whether our decisions as regards political strategy, banking, business, and ultimately world development should depend on our current logic and on the measuring devices which operate as a function of this logic.

Both the hedonistic principle (demand) and our theories of capital formation (supply) are associated with the early formulation of economics as a science. Economics as a separate intellectual discipline was founded in Europe in the early seventeenth century, that is, at the beginning of the Age of Enlightenment. Prior to this time, economics simply meant, more modestly, the management of the household. The definition was expanded to become a *science* of the state when man was judged to learn, and to decide, by sense experience rather than by thought. At this moment, *homo rationalis* becomes *homo economicus*. In turn, a determinate Newtonian mechanism replaced morality. The art of managing the state gave way to a human science founded on an arithmetic of pleasure. Eventually, *homo economicus* becomes *homo abyssus*. The process started in earnest with Adam Smith.

It is worthwhile to remark that Adam Smith's *The Wealth of Nations* evolved out of a series of lectures on moral philosophy that he had given at Glasgow University between the years 1751 and 1764. Thus, the father of the value-free science of economics was a professionally trained moralist; that is, he was concerned above all with value judgment or with the way that men give value to objects. However, for Smith, as for his immediate peers, value is determined through sense impressions of pleasure and of pain. In his first book, *The Theory of Moral Sentiments*, Adam Smith writes: "These first perceptions . . . upon which any general rules are founded, cannot be the object of reason, but of immediate sense and feeling."[9] Accordingly, Smith, the moralist cum economist, helped to lay the methodological groundwork in political science for Jeremy Bentham's Felicific Calculus and, a century later, for B. F. Skinner's stimulus-response psychology. Feeling prevails over thought.

For Adam Smith, market demand or the price value of commodities is determined by the *instinct* of self-interest, what he called the "invisible hand." In turn, self-interest, like all knowledge, can be calculated by measures of pleasure and of pain. According to Adam Smith, the pursuit of pleasure and the avoidance of pain is the ultimate source of value, both economic and moral. Adam Smith pushed David Hume's theory of knowledge, his epistemology, from ethics and politics into the marketplace.

Adam Smith's theory of value became known on the Continent as the *principe edonistique*, or the hedonistic principle. Economists in France and in Germany, being yet more rigorously speculative than the Scotsman, Adam Smith, were looking to simplify further their subject matter. German economists, in particular, were searching to find the basic unit of economic activity; that is, they were searching for a first principle on which to base their science, a first principle that was at once universal, necessary, and unchanging. They discovered *homo economicus*. *Homo economicus* was moved solely by self-interest. This specific trait of man was considered valid for all times and for all circumstances.

Nearly seventy-five years later, when Karl Marx attacked Adam Smith's specific definition of capital and of its role in the creation of wealth, he did not attack the hedonistic principle of classical economics. This first principle can be summarized as follows: In every instance, man searches his own self-interest, which interest is determined ultimately by sense impression.

One must ask if this first principle is of an economic, psychological, or even anthropological nature. In any case, the theory serves as a primary means for explaining economics as a science. The theory likewise obscures for man what is already his very fragile vision of freedom. The motive force in the flow of economic life as first explained by the Physiocrats is *le desir de jouir*, the desire for pleasure. The measure of this desire for pleasure became known as the theory of cardinal utility. The theory underscores our modern calculations of economic value and, by extension, our current understanding of barter and exchange rates.

Joseph A. Schumpeter, one of the twentieth century's leading experts on economic method writes: "Let me repeat once more: in the beginning, utility, both total and marginal, was considered a psychic reality." He continues: "Though we cannot measure utility or 'motive' or pleasantness and unpleasantness of sensations *directly*, we can measure them indirectly by their observable effects, a pleasure for instance by the sum of money a man is prepared to give up in order to obtain it rather than go without it."[10]

The more primitive theory of cardinal utility, the hedonistic principle, was later refined by the introduction of a measurable scale of preference. These scales of preference can be plotted on indifference surfaces or, in the case of commodities, on curves of equal choice.

The "discoverer" as Schumpeter points out, of the modern theory of value was an Italian, Vilfredo Pareto. Pareto folded his indifference curves (curves of equal choice) into three-dimensional diagrams representing the total possible utility to be enjoyed between the choice of various commodities. The graph represented a succession of rising horizontal planes, which Pareto called "la colline du plaisir," the column of pleasure.

Recognizing the rather one-dimensional assumption at the heart of his logic, Pareto, at the end of his career, referred to the theory of cardinal utility as "ophelimity theory." "Ophelimity" apparently sounded less hedonistic or, at least, more clinical or scientific than cardinal utility. Parallel with Pareto, the influential English economist, Francis Edgeworth, while describing man as a "pleasure machine," proposed that utility (pleasure) could be measured mathematically once an appropriate "hedonimeter" could be invented.

While cardinal utility analysis serves as an important base for current foreign trade, distribution, and price theory, economists have come to disregard its heavy reliance on quantity as the principal measure of value. In the 1920s, utility theories of value were refined into more subtle theories of elasticity of demand to include *preference* as well as *utility*. There seemed to be partial recognition of the Roman proverb: *de gustibus non est disputandum* (taste cannot be argued).

In recognition of the dynamic relationship between quantity and quality in taste or desire, the mathematics of economic analysis has become decidedly more complicated. And here it rests today.

Utility or preference analysis finds its most important recent expression in Paul Samuelson's consistency postulate. To paraphrase Schumpeter:

> Faced with a given set of prices and a given "income," everybody chooses to buy (or sell) in a uniquely determined way. Everything else is idle decoration and justified, if at all, by such interest as we may attach to it *from the standpoint of other purposes.*[11] [my italics]

The phrase, "from the standpoint of other purposes," is revealing as it demonstrates that there could be a crack in the measurability of taste and in the mathematical analysis of preference. This is despite modern analytic methods of identifying, through the calculus of infinite number, stable difference systems and using matrix algebra in sensitivity analysis. Economists generally substitute for the phrase "from the standpoint of other purposes" the more simple Latin idiom "ceteris paribus," all things being equal.

In other words, what we are referring to in economic analysis are not facts emanating from a known and certain first principle but rather somewhat arbitrary units taken from reality to fit a particular theory or worldview. Economics, if not a handmaiden to the art of politics as understood by the ancients, is but observation and fact gathering, not science. We might note that Samuelson's formula just paraphrased is a postulate and not a scientific theory.

THE LAW OF SCARCITY AND CAPITAL FORMATION

To understand more clearly our economic and, thereby, our political options as currently defined in the North, we should have a clear idea of the second most important principle or preconcept that underscores economics as science. As we have shown, the first deals with desire, or expressed differently, self-interest as measured by sense experience. The second deals with scarcity and its presumed economic remedy, *capital.*

Without an adequate understanding of both issues, the layman cannot hope to understand what his government, let alone his banker, is doing or not doing as regards Third World development finance. What hangs in the balance, we might add, is the likely shape of our global political order as we approach the last development decade of this century.

Once we accept the fact that man's primary motive force resides in his desire to seek pleasure and to avoid pain (demand), we must then ask the question: How does man go about achieving this task (supply)?

The second most important (perhaps co-equal) law of economics as science has to do with capital formation. In today's world, one's specific definition of capital defines the subsequent shape of one's economic model building. Karl Marx understood this; hence, the title of his most seminal work, *Das Kapital*.

Some historic perspective might be important if we are to understand the significance of the capital formation debate and its current impact on Third World development. Capital formation combined with utility theory (the hedonistic principle) leads to a complementary explanation of our current approach to Third World development and of our financial strategies to promote same. That is, the two principles define the balance of our methodology. We need to understand both principles if we are to provide viable alternatives to our current and costly approach to the development process. This is particularly true for those who control the purse strings, that is, the bankers and aid donors.

In classical economic theory, the units of production typically are divided into land (natural resources), labor, and capital. Looked at from the point of view of national revenue rather than from the point of view of production, the basic units are rent which comes from land, wages which come from labor, and interest which comes from capital. These production/revenue relationships account for what is known as the "circular flow of economic life."[12]

The first two terms, "land" and "labor" are quite easy to understand as concepts, namely, because they exist in nature. This is not the case with the term "capital," at least as an economic unit of production.

Modern economics is described oftentimes as the "science of wealth." In this sense, capital does not mean the equity portion of a company's balance sheet, nor the principal of a loan, nor one's deposit in the bank. Capital is *the* source of wealth. In economic model building, capital is that portion of savings or net revenue that is available for productive reinvestment. The capital invested in an obsolete industry is not capital inasmuch as it is not a source of wealth. The same would hold true for savings hidden in a safe-deposit box or placed with a poorly managed bank.

The economists understand capital as that which causes wealth. And here we have walked into an enormous tautology. As a source of wealth, the term "capital" cannot be distinguished from the terms "land" and "labor." In fact, the further we push the issue, the more we realize that the term "capital" has no conceptual nor scientific value.

In the history of economic theory, the term "capital" has served at best as an artificial if not arbitrary concept, a concept that hides wider political, cultural, even metaphysical convictions.

Economists, as one might expect, are decidedly sensitive to the issue. In his important and monumental work, *Capital and Interest*, the influential academic economist, Eugen von Böhm-Bawerk pleaded among his colleagues for a common definition of capital. He writes:

> There is a manifest necessity of a settlement of the controversy. Economic Science cannot through all eternity guarantee to its devotees the liberty of calling ten or a dozen different things by one name. A science demands clear thoughts, and the prerequisites for those are clear concepts and clear language. Economists *must* agree. And they will, just as surely as did scholars of the descriptive natural sciences—of zoology, botany, mineralogy and geography.[13]

Böhm-Bawerk then offers a compromise: "Let us call capital, in general, an aggregate of products which serve as a means of acquiring goods." Or rather, "products that serve the purpose of acquisition."[14]

Böhm-Bawerk manifestly is searching for a compromise. The problem is that his definition of capital is not scientific. The description is sufficiently wide open that it defines nothing either qualitatively or quantitatively. This is despite the fact that "capital is the name of a category of goods possessing supreme scientific importance."[15]

Indeed, if economics is the science of wealth and if capital is the source of wealth, then we would do well to have a fixed definition of capital if our system is to hold together.

As we shall argue, a fixed definition of capital is impossible. Capital embodies, as it were, the fine threads of power and of knowledge that make up the political and social tissues of a given society. Thus, capital represents not only real value or wealth but, more importantly, value judgments about who should share in the wealth and to what degree. In other words, capital explains who should exploit what resources and why.

There is nothing fixed, universal, or necessary in anyone's definition of capital as the source of national revenue. To the extent that economists attempt to compress the term into scientific language, they are practicing a sort of falsified intellectual formalism that has very little to do with the real world. The issue is of particular importance for those experts—the politicians, the international bureaucrats, the diplomats, and bankers—who are involved in the economic development business generally or in the aid and finance business specifically.

If the international community, for instance, agrees with Adam Smith that the regenerative power of savings is the source of wealth, then savings rates in the poor countries will be pushed as a matter of policy guidelines. Investment flows will be augmented by foreign borrowing as a panacea for local poverty. At the same time, commercial banks will look to savings rates as an important determinant in their own willingness to step up with additional private credits. They also will assume naively—as they oftentimes have—that their own credits automatically create wealth.

To be sure, belt-tightening at home and private credits from abroad can be used as an effective vehicle for increasing productive capacity within a given society. The problem is that the panacea all too often assumes that there is a cause/effect relationship between savings, investment and growth. In point of fact, higher investment rates are relevant only in those instances where the economy in question enjoys the cohesive political or management capacity to utilize effectively the funds in question. All too often, higher investment flows only result in significantly higher debt levels, or alternatively, in distortions of savings into irrelevent sectors of the economy.

When we are talking about savings as a source of capital formation, we should remember that the central question is political, not economic. A definition of savings or investment as capital is a garden-grown economic theory that can serve to distort rather than clarify our approach to economic development problems in the Third World. The definition also encourages our popular belief that what the Third World needs more than anything else is money. In not a few cases, the very opposite is true.

The capital-scarcity problem is a misnomer unless capital can buy justice, a sense of proportion, or wisdom. In classical economics, capital "puts into motion an additional quantity of industry, which gives an additional value to annual produce."[16] This rather harmless definition of capital was given to us by Adam Smith in *The Wealth of Nations*. The definition is probably apparent to many Third World societies where higher production or output levels are needed to cope with basic human needs and where better organization would result in higher output. The definition, however, tells us nothing about the origin of wealth.

In fact, John Maynard Keynes showed that under certain circumstances, savings, or what the classical economists called "parsimony" could be the "cause of unemployment and destruction of capital." This is particularly true when a high savings rate takes demand for goods out of the economy. Keynes, in fact, seemed so uncomfortable with the very term "capital" that he proposed instead that in dealing with the economic system as a whole, concern be given to two units: money and labor. In one of the few instances wherein Keynes ventures a definition of capital, he writes: "Capital is brought into existence not by the propensity to save but in response to the demand resulting from actual and prospective consumption."[17] If demand, of course, is any measure of capital formation then the Third World should have no problem in creating capital.

In economic theory from Adam Smith to John Maynard Keynes to current policy at the multinational banks and aid agencies, the question of economic development is formulated in terms of net capital formation or capital/output ratios. However, before worrying about output ratios, we ought to have a better definition of capital. We ought to realize that it is government cohesiveness, the quality of political management, or, in the end, a given society's worldview that determines both the input and the output. Economics only records the effects of political decision making, although it is used in many instances as a mask to hide new political options. Meanwhile, the options, we are told, are necessary because they are scientific. Thus, the methodology obscures at once means, their meaning, and even the measuring devices themselves.

When we look elsewhere in the history of economic theory for a suitable explanation of capital, we find its source in land (the Physiocrats), or in labor (Karl Marx).

These definitions likewise establish the wrong premise on which to build a model, let alone a viable Third World development strategy. If *land* is the source of capital or of accumulated wealth, how does one explain such notable economic failures as Iran, Turkey, the Sudan, or Zaire? Alternatively, how does one explain such notable success stories as Switzerland, or, more recently, the Ivory Coast and Sri Lanka? In each instance, the natural resource base, particularly land, was limited in relative and absolute terms compared with less prosperous neighbors.

Alternatively, if labor, as defined in socialist terms, constitutes capital or the source of wealth, why are not the earth's most populous, authoritarian nations also the richest. For Karl Marx, capital is defined as "crystalized labor."[18] "Almost all the value of things," he writes, "is bestowed by labor." Hence, labor becomes the first principle or the premise on which communist economic systems rest.

Marx was perhaps correct in describing labor as the single most important source of wealth. The problem is that Marx was writing within the narrow limits of economics as science. Labor is understood not as a person in the totality of his or her human dimension, but rather, as wage labor, that is, as a commodity. "Since labor power is a commodity," Marx tells us, "it is necessary to determine its value."[19]

Not only is labor a commodity, but capital for Marx is accumulated work. Thus, labor has two definitions: it is defined by Marx as a commodity in the capitalist system and as capital in the communist system. The problem is that given Marx's definition of man as an economic unit, both definitions come to the same thing. The source of wealth (capital) is man, but man takes his identity as wage labor. In other words, we have turned the definition of society upside down. Man becomes the means rather than the end of the economic process. In the final analysis, the definition of man is gutted of its most relevant features.

The source of this abomination is in the original eighteenth-century description of man as a commodity and in Marx's subsequent definition of man as capital. In the end, Marx did not design an economic system permitting the dictatorship of the proletariat but rather a political system permitting its capitalization. Obviously, this was not his intention. He simply fell into a trap, a trap inscribed in the logic of the Age of Enlightenment. In *Salary, Price and Profit*, Marx quotes in flattering terms Thomas Hobbes, the father of the capitalist worldview: "The value of a man is, as for all other things, his price: this is to say exactly what we give for the use of his force."[20]

Karl Marx used this idea to explain in *Das Kapital* the relationship between work, value, and wealth. Accordingly, in both the capitalist and in the communist systems, labor is taken as an economic unit of account abstracted, as it were, from the broader understanding of our more basic humanistic tradition. The cost of this logic, this failure in our thought process, has yet to be adequately measured. In fact, the logic itself serves to obscure the measuring devices that we dearly need if we are to create a political climate necessary for future growth. When we measure man as an economic unit, we are extending our problem rather than solving it.

THE CAPITAL FORMATION DEBATE

In our development schemes, we are inclined to think of natural resources (the OPEC countries), land (the United States), or labor (the Far East) as the primary source of wealth. Depending on one's particular economic theory, these units are commonly defined as *capital*. Foreign investment proposals, bilateral aid programs, and geopolitical strategy are keyed on these respective definitions of capital. In the final analysis, the big money and the big guns hang on a definition.

In the end, development is driven by a concept. Unfortunately, these concepts of capital, that mysterious source of wealth, are wholly economic rather than political. In many instances, these concepts of capital are used as an excuse for aberrant political behavior, or rather, as a justification for terror. Worse yet, our justification is thought to be founded on a scientific principle.

The wealth that the OPEC states enjoy and the positive trade flows running toward certain Asian countries are, in fact, dependent on the West, and there is a concrete reason for this. The same is true of communist bloc countries where wage labor (capital) is well organized and theoretically indistinguishable from the state. COMECON countries need Western investment in order to increase productive capacity. In other words, we cannot look at our common definitions of capital as a source of wealth. This is very important in economic development planning where our solutions are cast in orthodox economic terminology and where the economist has the final word.

We need to step back for a moment and ask ourselves what capital really means. Can the term be used as a help rather than a hindrance to current economic development planning and to the financing of same?

Capital, we would argue, represents a given society's collective capacity to manage itself and its resources. Capital represents the measure of national cohesiveness. In analytic terms, capital might best be defined as a country's ability to agree on realistic goals and to choose appropriate means to obtain those goals.

Capital equates to proportion. Our efforts should be to rationalize our economic analysis, our investment decisions and our *approach* to both on these lines. By rationalize, we mean to humanize. That is, we mean to place man at the center of our universe. Put differently, man must be described as *Homo sapiens* rather than as a commodity of wage labor or as capital.

For the economic world to admit these definitions would be tantamount to denying the pretensions of the science. The concept of *Homo sapiens* is not measurable. In addition, our concept of capital as *Homo sapiens* clearly defines the source of wealth in political rather than in economic terms. We might also add that the definition clearly establishes economics as an art rather than as a science.

Economics, we would argue, is a handmaiden to the art of politics. Economics should be understood as descriptive but not, in the words of John Maynard Keynes, as "predictive."[21] As a predictive science, economics is required to define the basic *numeraire*, man, in a fashion that is contrary to his nature, that is, as wage labor, as a commodity, or as capital. When we participate in this logic our systems ultimately short-circuit. We already have the abuses of the Industrial Revolution, the two world wars, and the rise of communism to prove the point. We should be aware of the fact that the Third World will have an even more difficult time accepting the logic. In the Third World, systems are frailer than our own and cannot support faulty or artifical reasoning.

The causes for this fragility are varied. They can be catalogued (depending on one's bias) in climactic, demographic, economic, political, social, even anthropological terms. The catalogue, however, does not give us a solution. The solution will not even come into focus until we are able to agree globally on a more satisfactory method and on its intended reach.

For the time being, our method is cast in economic terms. We have attempted to show that our method is not scientific nor is it value free, as oftentimes stated. Economic method cannot be disengaged from its political, even metaphysical moorings. What is this mooring? What is the source of the hedonistic principle and of our pseudo-scientific definitions of capital? Our response to this single question will tell us a great deal about the adequacy of current Third World development strategies and the financing of same. The response will also tell us a great deal about our seeming inability to bridge, in even modest terms, the gap between the rich nations and the poor nations.

In economic theory, both the hedonistic principle and our definition of capital emanate from a quite recent intellectual conviction of Western man. Both concepts are grounded in the idea that man's actions can be quite systematically determined; that is, they are determined by the necessity of the outside world or by feeling. Freedom means a willingness to go along with necessity or with the dictates of sensate experience. Necessity is a function of perceived economic reality. In the end, economic reality, it is thought, defines man's position within the kingdom of life.

This type of thinking leads to either of two conclusions: firstly, man is not really free to define his future. Second, if he is free to follow necessity, then he must do so within the limits of perceived economic theory. In the modern world, economics determines our alternatives. As a result, our values inevitably become one-dimensional. The logic also leads either to a distinct pessimism or to an unrealistic optimism about what can and cannot be done as regards structural poverty both at home and abroad.

For the moment, our economic determinism sets the tone of development theory and the financial means through which this theory is executed. We need to question, then, the underlying premise of our current logic if we want to find viable alternatives to the current morass in Third World finance and development.

The premise itself is found in the writings of Thomas Hobbes as handed down to us by his spiritual heirs including David Hume, Adam Smith, Thomas Malthus, David Ricardo, Karl Marx, Lenin, and other erstwhile political economists.

We might add to this list the anthropologists, Charles Darwin and Herbert Spencer, who adopted the Hobbesian worldview to nature and supposedly reinforced post factum the scientic value of previous economic theory.

In following a single ideological thread, we shall see that the king of the social sciences, economics, currently is parading in a costume hardly adequate for its existing responsibilities. We want to show that the ideological support systems for both the hedonistic principle and our current definitions of capital are not appropriate to our current needs. In fact, their pseudoscientific assumptions block any real hope for economic, social, or cultural adjustment on a global basis. Our intellectual horizon does not stretch into the twenty-first century because our ideology directs us back to the so-called Age of Reason—an age where the dictates of reason are determined by fear and by the arithmetic of feeling.

12
Economic Development versus Economic Determinism

Since the eighteenth century, Western man has premised *self-interest* and *instinct* as the guiding principles of social order. These two principles find their origin in a specific political philosophy first laid down by Thomas Hobbes nearly a century earlier.

The philosophy of the eighteenth century, a philosophy of sentiment, today inspires our educational systems, our theory of government, our sociology, and our Third World development strategy.

Likewise, the philosophy of the so-called Age of Enlightenment fashions the two main pillars of modern economic theory. *Self-interest* explains our concepts of capital formation and *instinct* our theories of value. Both principles serve as the foundation for the Law of Comparative Advantage.

The manifest result is that our cities, both figuratively and in fact, are without limit. The same can be said for our systems of ethical value.

When we extend the logic on a global basis, it should come as no surprise that development, like banking, is distorted and, in not a few instances, pathological.

Conflict becomes the hallmark of our worldview, for our passions exclude the possibility of reasoned goals or of limited ambition. In East-West relations, our political systems are poised for instant annihilation. In the North-South dialogue, we presume instinctively that our global interests are mutually exclusive. We do this despite the fact that the numbers prove quite the opposite.

Our worldview is, in an obvious sense, as unreasonable as it is uneconomic. There is no ultimate good, no *summum bonum*, only what

Thomas Hobbes calls the *bonum sibi*, the good of oneself. In Adam Smith, the *bonum sibi* translates as the invisible hand. In David Ricardo, the *bonum sibi* is obtained through comparative advantage. In Karl Marx, the *bonum sibi* is extrapolated into the larger whole to enter history as the class struggle. In each instance, the basic units of self-interest and instinct remain the same. They serve as the first premise of the commonweal. Likewise, they erringly permit both economics and politics to parade as a science.

We assume that our instincts are unfailing and that the primordial instinct of self-interest is universally reliable. Accordingly, our future is condemned to a determinisn as mindless as it is unacceptable. Man determines value by sense impression. In turn, sense impressions determine man. In other words, value is valueless. We should be calling this self-inflicted moral "blackout," the *summum malum*.

In a world of shrinking global resources and growing atomic weaponry, the logic on which our passions are justified needs to be questioned. Thus, what we shall propose to do is to analyze the heart of the paradigm that shapes our current economic, financial, and political orders. For our existing paradigm prevents us from extricating ourselves from the present suicidal trap into which so carelessly we have fallen.

Our current models perpetuate what we have called the second holocaust of mass starvation. The second holocaust, inevitably primes us for the first, a holocaust of infinite dimension for man. Indeed, the two are correlative.

Our economic, financial, trading, and political orders simultaneously are headed in the same direction. Like lemmings, we are about to throw ourselves into the sea. Unlike lemmings, the potential crime of nuclear annihilation, like the actual crime of mass starvation, represents a crime of logic and not a crime of instinct.

For this reason, the outcome of both holocausts, the first and the second, the ultimate denouement, as it were, enjoys a terrifying completeness—a total universality of thought and of action. In sum, the ominous logic of Thomas Hobbes and his successors has us by the throat.

The logic leads 1) to a geopolitical system wherein mutually assured annihilation becomes the first and perhaps last impulse in strategic planning; 2) to an economic system based on feeling and advantage rather than on thought; and 3) to a financial system that is about to crack under the weight of its own amorality, its arbitrary bigness, and its loss of direction.

All three orders, the political, the economic, and the financial spring from an identical paradigm. The First World and the Third World are now caught in its vortex, that is, in the embrace of a beast created by man's imaginative powers. Fortunately, the beast can be controlled once we understand its anatomy.

THE HOBBESIAN WORLDVIEW

Most university students well remember, at least vaguely, the term that Thomas Hobbes gave to the commonweal or state. He called the Commonweal a "LEVIATHAN."

Thomas Hobbes seems to have argued convincingly for his own and for subsequent generations, "that it is men and arms not words and promises that make the force and power of laws." Words and promises were taken correctly by Hobbes' peers to mean ideas and reasoned goals.

In the Hobbesian worldview, power replaces purpose as the primary cause of movement in human history. By the end of the eighteenth century, the argument had been accepted by leading statesmen and intellectuals as a self-evident truth. The consequences are with us today.

Thomas Hobbes had constructed a new paradigm. The paradigm breathes life into the body of our geopolitical strategy as well as our current Third World development programs.

We might ask ourselves if the paradigm has run its course. Its logic is devastating when applied on a global basis. In politics, force becomes a substitute for reason and in economics, advantage for thought, or growth for development.

In a word, the author of Leviathan introduced the scientific method of his predecessors—Francis Bacon[2] and René Descartes—to the study of the human species. The method is based on a mechanistic worldview as shortsighted as it is simplistic, particularly when applied to *Homo sapiens*.

Étienne Gilson tells us that our notion of order is inseparable from that of causation.[3] For Thomas Hobbes, political order is based on fear and self-interest, while economic reality is shaped by man's instincts, by his search for pleasure, and by the avoidance of pain.

According to Hobbes, man is "nasty, brutish and short," living in a "state of nature and hostility." Man's political and economic identity can be measured in terms of his "power of coercion." When this power of coercion is submitted to the larger whole for purposes of "reciprocal benefit," the sale represents the famous Social Contract.

The larger whole is called alternatively the "body politic" or the Leviathan, that is to say, a sea monster representing the collective force and violence of society, a sort of modern day Phyton against which Apollo was pitted.

When Hobbes identifies man as living in a state of nature and hostility, he means by this that nature is hostile rather than whole, violent rather than vital, mechanical rather than alive. The Leviathan accepts this state of nature as a given fact and incorporates hostility or conflict as the first building block of political and economic order. In society, violence replaces design, and in man instinct, intelligence.

Bellum omnium contra omnes, war of one against all and all against one, is the Hobbesian theory of nature and society that has given life to political and economic speculation from Adam Smith to David Ricardo, and from Karl Marx to the current nuclear standoff. The Marxian theory of class struggle is but an extension of the political principles enunciated in the *Leviathan*. Marx took Thomas Hobbes, David Hume, Adam Smith, and David Ricardo at face value. He then simply switched allegiance to the masses. Marx's starting point, however, was the same.

Albert Camus writes: "Philosophy secularizes the ideal. But tyrants appear who soon secularize the philosophers that give them the right to do so."[4] In other words, fact follows formulation.

Since the Age of Reason, unlimited force has been plausible on moral grounds (even a necessity) because order in nature and in man is deemed as implausible. Everything that is, is by force, including man's culture, his history, and his future.

The Hobbesian logic also explains in coherent philosophic terms the origin of much modern economic theory, particularly value theory (the hedonistic principle), the Law of Comparative Advantage, and those concepts of capital formation that inspire our two leading political systems. "Nobility," argues Hobbes, "is power."[5] The logic forms the base of what today passes as realistic economic theory in the West and in the Eastern bloc countries. When either model is parachuted without resistance into the Third World, the model itself is seen for what it is, that is, as mindless.

Economic order is said to originate in greed rather than in creativity and in conflict rather than in coordination. This we teach as sound economic doctrine to students, to bankers, to diplomats, even to aid donors and their recipients. What we are describing, of course, is the decay of an economic system, not its origin. Our method is as mindless as our metaphysics.

Capital formation and growth consist of doing the other fellow down whether as an individual (capitalism) or as a class (communism). This we learned from Thomas Hobbes and from those who share the logic of the *Leviathan*.

Likewise, value is said to spring from sense impression. "Felicity" writes Hobbes, "is a continual progress of desire from one object to another."[6] And "anything that is pleasure to the sense the same also is pleasure to the imagination."[7]

In other words, there are no *reasoned* absolutes. Felicity is indefinite, without measure nor purpose. In short, felicity is without limit. Here is the source of our predatory economic systems, systems that increasingly manifest themselves as being out of control. Value lacks reason, or, expressed differently, meaning. In the seventeenth century, *homo rationalis* opts to become *homo abyssus*.

In order to apply an essentially mechanistic wordview to the study of man in society, just reasoning and economic motivation are determined by feeling. All else is "vain philosophy." Thomas Hobbes is but the inversion of our philosophic traditions, and so are his conclusions.

Man is no longer the measure, giving value and thereby design to his surroundings. Instead, he becomes the by-product, the result of the indeterminate forces of nature that play on his senses. He is moved *by* something rather than *for* something.

In short, the model stands on its head Western man's definition of himself and of his place in the universe. Economic and political strategy become synonymous with scientific, even organic necessity. Ultimately, matter replaces mind as the starting point in the development process. Unlimited advantage spurred by fear takes precedence over meaning and life.

Not only does the Hobbesian revolution represent a break from the past. From an economic and social point of view, it represents a foolhardy dive into the future, a fissure rather than an extension of Western thought processes and ideals. Hence, in more ways than one, modern man faces an abyss.

In purely abstract terms, movement remains exclusively outside of the object being moved. In the end, all that is, is alien. At the dawn of the Age of Reason, order is said to stop at the limits of force, of violence, and of greed.

On this basis, a much needed patriotism of the species becomes impossible. We are dealing with a mechanical worldview in a vital universe. This worldview, when left unchecked, threatens to cancel life itself.

The paradigm substitutes force for reason, power for good government, determinism for design, and, not infrequently, inertia for action. Liberty is defined as our ability to predict our fate. Fear replaces freedom; comparative advantage threshold cooperation.

The logic weighs down on political and economic theory with purely mechanistic interpretations of society. It simplifies our understanding of economic phenomena by strapping them to such manifestly inadequate theories as the hedonistic principle and our current definitions of capital. Both concepts obscure rather than clarify our understanding of our own societies. They make impossible a comprehensive (let alone rational) understanding of others. Our logic throws away the essential in order to explain the apparent. One example: our common measurements of capital formation, even in Third World countries, do not include expenditures for health, for food consumption, and for education. That is, our criteria fails to measure human development as factors affecting national growth. Our measuring rods are a function of our worldview.

Our logic is simplistic rather than simple, static rather than dynamic. In the end, our paradigm leaves much to be desired as a value system, namely, because it is so entirely one-dimensional.

We should not allow the Hobbesian worldview to inspire economic theory, let alone banking and foreign policy. For with it, we are blindsided to the potential of our future, not to mention that of the rest of the globe.

As a function of our current logic, our options are short term and our goals obscured in the smoke and fury of what is basically an alien method. Increasingly, we are living from hand to mouth, for we have lost our way intellectually. The leviathan is loose upon the city.

Our current world order is the antithesis of order in its proper sense. It is a closed universe where mechanical law rather than purpose establishes our choices and where man consequently resides in society as the victim rather than the builder of a "brave new world."

Hobbesian fatalism ignores at the same time the central issues of political and economic theory: that is, human creativity and our enormous capacity for human folly. The fatalism causes us to look at economic reality in fixed terms, with identical expectation. The leviathan turns in repetitive circles, driven by instinct rather than by reason. Our options are determined in advance, for our logic is entirely mechanical and therefore lifeless. In the end, our hedonism leads to unilateral growth according to the violence of the Law of Comparative Advantage. Uncontrolled, this violence results in the destruction of value.

Happily, the model is not necessary because it is not sufficiently human. The paradigm captures only a small portion of the human experience, that portion that ties man to his most primitive order of existence. The model posits self-interest as the origin of social order and competition as the sole source of motivation. Violence becomes a necessity, while anarchy is presumed to be a law of nature, the alpha and the omega of animal and of human society. In the process, personhood is lost, not to mention any real notion of statehood.

Despite its built-in contradition, the logic of the *Leviathan* is with us today. It forms part of our sub-conscious approach to development theory and determines our popular acceptance of wide-scale human misery. In the end, the Age of Reason and of Enlightenment turns out to be an age of feeling and darkness, that is, an age of structural, unlimited disorder. We are living in this age today. It remains to be seen whether or not modern man can free himself of his current worldview and thereby enter the next century reasonably intact, both financially and as a civilization.

The Heritage of Hobbes

Lest we think that the Hobbesian worldview does not have an immediate, sustaining influence on the nature and the form of our global systems, political, economic or financial, we would do well to look briefly at Hobbes' lineage.

Out of the Hobbesian worldview, David Hume conceived his "knave theory" of government. Thomas Hobbes was able to develop a science of the state; Hume concentrated on what he called "the Science of human Nature." He used Hobbes' epistemology to reduce man to a small h and nature to a capital N. "Political writers," Hume advises, "have established it as a maxim, that, in contriving any system of government . . . every man ought to be supposed a knave, and to have no other end, in all his actions, than private interest."[8]

In turn, Hume's literary executor and disciple, Adam Smith, applied Hume's epistemology, his ontology, and his knave theory of government, to economics. In fact, Smith did even less. David Hume already was a well-known economist in his own right. *The Wealth of Nations* provides a lucid, popular account of David Hume's definition of the dismal science.

Pursuing our recent intellectual heritage, the anatomy of our logic, a step further, we arrive directly to Thomas Malthus and his well-known work *An Essay on the Principle of Population*. We should recall that Thomas Malthus was not a professionally trained demographer but rather an economist, clergyman, and mathematician. He tell us in advance: "The most important argument that I shall adduce is certainly not new. The principles on which it depends have been explained in part by Hume, and more at large by Dr. Adam Smith."[9]

Malthus applied the reasoning powers of the Age of Reason to the problem of scarcity and growing destitution in Europe, destitution brought on by the Napoleonic wars and by the violence of the Industrial Revolution. In fact, both events fit perfectly, or, more ironically, were the natural by-product of the new Hobbesian paradigm.

In order to defend economic disequilibrium (that is, wide-scale destitution) as a necessary prelude to progress, Malthus reasons in parallel with the pseudoscientific morality of his times:

> Famine seems to be the last, the most dreadful resource of nature. The power of the population is so superior to the power in the earth to produce subsistence for man, that premature death must in some shape or other visit the human race.[10]

Premature death by starvation serves to sharpen man's instinct for survival and for the advancement of the species. Malthus states:

> Necessity, that imperious all pervading law of nature, restrains them [living things] within the prescribed bounds. The race of plants and the race of animals shrink under this great restrictive law. And the race of man *cannot, by any efforts of reason* [my italics] escape it. Among plants and animals its effects are waste of seed, sickness, and premature death. Among mankind, misery and vice.[11]

For Malthus, malnutrition acts synergistically, at once as a source of control and as a source of progress within the human family. This was the established economic given in post-Tudor England until the Poor Laws of 1832.

Order springs from chaos, a sort of literal kick in the pants endowed by nature. From Malthus, comes fully born David Ricardo's theory of comparative advantage. Malthus, in fact, was David Ricardo's friend, intellectual patron, and literary advocate. For Ricardo, the full play individual advantage equates to progress and efficiency.

The Law of the Survival of the Fittest

From Malthus and Ricardo, the Hobbesian logic (and confusion) is redoubled in the writings of Charles Darwin to be lodged firmly in today's social science but not, as we shall see, in today's life sciences.

The modern reader commonly thinks of Charles Darwin as a naturalist and as a scientist of impeccable rigor. In point of fact, Darwin's popularity originated with his ability to verify, in supposedly scientific fashion, a preexisting ideology. Not only did he borrow from Malthus a paradigm, he even borrowed, word for word, the now famous expressions, "stuggle for existence," "competition," as well as the term "famine and death." Put differently, Charles Darwin preempted a worldview. He simply applied, in his own words, Malthus' theory of nature "to the whole animal and vegetable kingdoms."

Every biologist knows that Charles Darwin did not discover evolution. Darwin admits this himself. Rather, he adopted a preexisting paradigm to explain the formation and the development of new species. Darwin's theory of Natural Selection can be described aptly as evolution by virtue of the "battle for life." In other words, the formation of species occurs in the same manner as was understood for the formation of political and economic order, that is, through the violence of unlimited competition. Darwin writes in his preface to *On the Origin of the Species*, "I happen to read for amusement Malthus on Population and . . . I had at last got a theory by which to work."[12] As we know from history, Darwin's book, while hardly amusing, was a success before anyone had read it. His thesis fit the prevailing worldview of his immediate peers—and sponsors.

For Darwin, the foundation of all movement, whether in plant life or in man, is conflict. He writes, again in imitation of Malthus, that "man tends to increase at so rapid a rate, as to lead to occasional severe struggles for existence; and consequently to beneficial variation, whether in body or mind, being preserved and injurious ones eliminated."[13]

In other words, evolution is powered by brute force, while progress originates in chaos. Some zoologists have come to the conclusion that what Darwin was describing might be the extinction of species rather than their evolution.[14] In any case, the theory turns out to be as unscientific as it is deadly, especially when applied to the organization of human society, let alone to development.

While Darwin was explaining natural selection by an appeal to violence, what he called "the war of nature," Gregor Johann Mendel (1822-1884), an Austrian monk and botanist, was busy discovering genes, or the channels of hereditary transmission, by investigating in his own backyard the harmony of a pea pod. Mendel was looking at a different cosmos. He was looking for order in nature and found it.

Darwin's explanation of the evolutionary process is but a theory; Mendel's discovery of the gene a proven scientific fact. Darwin saw the cosmos as fortuitous, with chance variation of species brought about by struggle and by conflict. For Mendel, all matter had design, hierarchy, and natural balance, which serves as the basis of all life.

Darwin was successful and remains so in the social sciences especially in economics, because he struck the right chord, not because his ideas were new nor unique in a scientific sense. In sum, Darwin's "facts" were explained in such a way as to be consistent with prevailing political and economic thought. While Darwin, by no means, invented evolution, he did give a unique explanation of the adaptive processes of species amongst themselves and within their environment. The process was based on prevailing philosophic thought, which equated man with animals and animals with violence. The perspective has since been shown by subsequent biologists to be one-eyed and vastly oversimplified.[15] Nonetheless, Darwin crystalized the prevailing social and economic theories that pervade today in our universities, in our aid agencies, in our banks, and even in our life-styles.

Instead of struggle, we should talk about mutual dependence. For a basic theme in nature is cooperation, not simply competition. We see this in history in the failure of the Greek city states to unite against a changing external environment (Rome). We see this in modern industry, where cooperative management is the only way to make a big organization work. We see this in the physical sciences, where even electrons, let alone atoms and animals, need each other. Finally, we see this in development theory, where the so-called Law of Comparative Advantage has served to render destitute a large portion of the human race.

FROM HOBBES TO DARWIN TO MARX AND RETURN

In Charles Darwin, the Hobbesian universe came full circle. Our kingdom of the mind is converted into a kingdom of violence. As we know, Darwin has taught generations of sociologists, political scientists, bankers, diplomats, economists, even clerics, that nature is "red in tooth and claw."[16]

Darwin the biologist, however, forgot to tell us, or even note for himself, what we now know about nature from empirical evidence. In a commentary on Darwin's universe, Ashley Montagu cautions that "man is the only creature which makes organized attacks upon its own species."[17] Montagu writes, "The wars of apocryphal ants and other creatures are purely imaginary."[18] We might do well to recall these simple observations of nature, these facts, when we give a naturalistic or Darwinian justification for current trade and growth models.

The theoretical foundation of the Hobbesian worldview that Darwin elaborated with such credibility received additional reinforcement through the balance of the nineteenth and twentieth century. This reinforcement came from our major political philosophers on the right and on the left: on the right from Herbert Spencer to Friedrich Nietzsche to Hitler and on the left from Karl Marx to Lenin to current Soviet rhetoric.

We will recall that for Herbert Spencer, any policy aiming at social or economic improvement by the state stands condemned in advance to failure as it interferes with natural selection.[19] Nietzsche tells us that violence is the "wet nurse" of history. Accordingly, "Man must become better and eviler"[20] (*Thus Spake Zarathustra*). Nietzsche's prophet, Zarathustra, also tells us in his descent from the mountain: "Lo, I am weary of my wisdom,"[21] which he was.

Hitler extended these theories into the political arena in what turned out to be the bloodiest war in history, what we might call logically sound neo-Darwinism. Unhappily, Darwinian social theories seem to have been accepted by both sides of the war, if we care to compare Dresden with Coventry, or Nagasaki with Stalingrad. The theories continue to mark our geopolitical profile North-South and East-West. They likewise have formed the common ground of meaning in the education of political and business leaders for six consecutive generations.

Equally ironic, the Hobbesian, and by extension the neo-Darwinian worldview, underpins nearly every major tenet of communist philosophy. By a curious turn of history, Engels reminds us in *The Role of Violence in History* that Karl Marx wanted to dedicate his first book of *Das Kapital* to Charles Darwin. Marx writes to Engels in 1860, "Darwin's book is very important and serves me as a basis in natural science for the class struggle."[22] Later Lenin justified the terror of the Soviet revolution in more simple terms: "The State is power, violence and constraint." To believe that the state could somehow disappear once violence created order is even more illogical than Darwin's theory of Natural Selection. Both theories started with Hobbes' definition of nature.

Not only has the Hobbesian worldview come full circle, but it has formed a sort of double helix.

Both capitalism and communism are drinking from the same fountain. Hence, the North looks southward in the shape of a Leviathan. Judging from available figures, the Leviathan appears thirsty indeed. The problem, however, might well be that the fountain is running dry.

If this happens, then our systems could panic. In fact, this will surely happen if the leviathan continues to be moved by instinct rather than by reason. For the time being, instinct leads us to our mistaken belief that growth equals development and that competition is the sole source of progress, both manifest errors in judgment and in fact.

We would argue going forward that the goal of politics, like the goal of economics, should seek a synthesis between mechanism and ethos, between growth and development, and between survival and meaning. Without some adjustment to our current method of problem solving, we can hardly hope for a more satisfactory world order let alone for a banking or trading system that works. What we can expect is more of what we have seen to date, redoubled by virtue of our increasingly refined technology.

During World War I 14 million people perished as a direct result of the conflict. This figure increased to 53 million people during World War II. Since World War II, economic growth in the North has been possible in large part due to, and in spite of, growing trade and financial ties with the South. The overall structure of the North-South relationship, however, has been based on the worldview that we have come to describe. Unless we are able to reverse this bias as it inspires our geopolitical and financial strategies, the next global conflict will make the first two look parochial, let alone modest, in the dimensions of their destructive capacity. In other words, the second holocaust will surely become the first unless something can be done to help us recognize the root cause of both—and then to translate this recognition into a plan of action. First, the cause, then a plan of action.

13
Homo Rationalis
versus
Homo Economicus

Despite modern man's clearly immoderate distaste for metaphysical reasoning, we should realize that the fundamental crisis confronting the West today is ontological in nature before it is political, economic, or financial. What Thomas Hobbes, his successors, and his followers have been manipulating are causal realities, that is, a deeper metaphysical order. We need to do the same in an effort to understand our current social, economic, geopolitical, and financial strategies vis-à-vis the Third World and vis-à-vis ourselves.

Without an understanding of causal reality, we are unable to make sense of our current world order. Further, we would argue that our current world order did not come about by chance. The same can be said of the world's attendant disorder.

The reader will recall that in problem solving, we can look at an object of study from four different points of view, that is, from four distinct causes, in order to grasp its intelligibility. We can define the formative properties of reality based on quite specific criteria. The weight that we give to these differing criteria are at the heart of our worldview. This point has been well understood by our most important post-Renaissance political thinkers, notwithstanding their stated contempt for metaphysical speculation.

The criteria or necessary causes are as follows: the material cause (the matter with which we are dealing), the formal cause (the form that the object has or is taking), the mechanical cause (the power that gives movement), and the final cause (the end or purpose to which the other causes are directed).

In our Western tradition, the final cause, the telos, is the cause of causes. The final cause constitutes the goal or purpose as well as the point of departure not only in our thought processes but, by extension, in our inventions whether of a scientific, political, or even artistic order. This simply means that there is motive behind action.

Thus, the universe and its parts are deemed to be intelligible by virtue of intention. In the rapport between the various causes, it is final cause that gives direction or meaning to process. Without final cause, there is chaos.

Viewed from a slightly different perspective, when the Ancients suggested that art imitates nature, the corollary was that nature could not establish itself by chance nor by hazard. Harmony and order could not spring from force nor from efficient, mechanical causes alone unless efficient cause had purpose. This means that unless efficient cause were guided by a higher final cause, force would be wasted in a vast array of nothingness. Force would have no form.

As we have shown, we seem to have forgotten these elementary laws of nature, particularly in the social sciences, in economics, and in politics.[1]

To posit, however, final cause as the cause of causes risks to contaminate our thinking with a sort of abstract reasoning that could eventually lead to the door of natural theology. Alternatively, to deny final cause is to banish mind from the universe.

To banish mind from the universe is precisely what Thomas Hobbes and his spiritual heirs have set out to do. They might yet succeed if we are to extrapolate in a logical way the economic and social theory that underpins our two major political systems.

Both capitalism and communism are dangerous for the Third World. Both systems promote production over purpose, force over thought, and quantity over value. For both systems spring from an identical worldview. For the past three hundred years, our major political theorists have excluded final cause, telos, or reason from their explanation of what makes the world turn. Accordingly, it should not come as a surprise that the most fundamental problem facing modern man, both in the First World and in the Third World, is not his weapons nor his poverty but his rapid dehumanization. This rapid dehumanization is pregnant with consequent political, economic, and financial fallout. Modern man no longer believes in final cause, that is, in purpose. As a result, his systems are coming undone by his own doing.

In economic development theory and in the financial resources brought to bear on same, our logic encourages a specific reasoning process that creates a bias against measuring actual long-term costs. For example, we systematically ignore human satisfaction (or real social costs) in the type of production, let alone food and housing, that we promote. Modern decision makers forget the human person, namely, because we do not consider the person as entirely human. Here we are not making a moral judgment. Rather, we simply are addressing the logic of the thought process that makes up our current world order. By virtue of our understanding of causes, we are convinced that man is moved *by* something rather than *for* something.

George Bernard Shaw argued that modern Western man has been "intellectually intoxicated with the idea that the world could make itself without design, purpose, skill, or intelligence, in short, without life."[2] We are now on the threshold of canceling life itself in order to make our political and economic theories consistent with our worldview. We have assumed a mechanistic posture in a living, rational universe.

Indeed, it is by no means a coincidence that our two major political alliances are mutually prepared, in their own calculations of expenditure and of foreign policy, to destroy in a nuclear holocaust not only themselves but the entire human species. The arrogance, the size, and the waste of what has been called the "radical evil" built into the strategies of our respective military-industrial complexes represent an intolerable misapplication of available resources, human and material. The cost of the program per year will soon represent the approximate size of all outstanding Third World debt.

The waste takes on added dimension when measured against the bare statistics of world starvation—that is, against the lives of the 25 children in the world dying of hunger in the approximate time that it takes to read this page.

The waste, diseconomies, the mindless terror making up the fabric of our present world order are but symbols of a deeper reality. We enjoy, as we always have, the technology to address the worst examples of maldistribution and exploitation. By example, in the Third World, one jet aircraft would support 40 rural pharmacies and one tank 1,000 classrooms for 30,000 students. One nuclear bomber equals about 75 clinics of 100 beds each.[3]

The mindless terror that we have been talking about is structural. It is based on our notion of causal reality. For this reason, the dimensions of our current disorder take on a specific qualitative profile. In a commentary on our age, the poet William Butler Yeats intuited the crux of the problem in a lyricism that defies conjecture in prose.

> Turning and turning in the widening gyre
> The falcon cannot hear the falconer
> Things fall apart; the centre cannot hold;
> Mere anarchy is loosed upon the world,
> The blood-dimmed tide is loosed, and everywhere
> The ceremony of innocence is drowned;
> The best lack all conviction, while the worst
> Are full of passionate intensity.
>
> Surely some revelation is at hand;
> Surely the Second Coming is at hand.
> The Second Coming! Hardly are those words out
> When a vast image out of *Spiritus Mundi*
> Troubles my sight: somewhere in the sands of the desert
> A shape with lion body and the head of a man,
> A gaze blank and pitiless as the sun,
> Is moving its slow thighs, while all about it
> Reel shadows of the indignant desert birds.
> The darkness drops again; but now I know
> That twenty centuries of stony sleep
> Were vexed to nightmare by a rocking cradle,
> And what rough beast, its hour come round at last,
> Slouches towards Bethlehem to be born?[4]

The beast is the Leviathan. Yeats identifies what it means to live by mechanical cause alone.

We noted earlier that power (efficient cause) unless guided by a higher or anterior reasoned goal (final cause) would dissipate in a vast array of nothingness. This is exactly what has happened within metaphysics and political theory from Thomas Hobbes to twentieth-century existentialism. Jean Paul Sartre's, *Being and Nothingness*, condenses in a single phrase our current worldview, our paradigm. Reason co-equals unreason; being, nothingness; nature, chaos; power, order, existence, absurdity.

Our source of motion resides in an external opposition where being is powered by nonbeing, order by chaos, and vice versa. Our notion of cause remains entirely mechanical. Expressed differently, all unity originates in force rather than in thought. Unity occurs without reason, that is, unity is gratuitous. This shift in criteria, the emphasis on mechanical cause at the expense of all others, explains the abject nihilism with which we are confronting the twenty-first century.

Political and economic options no longer are determined by our objectives. They are dictated from behind the perceived, innate hostility of all that is. Existence is understood to originate in an arbitrary conflict between being and nothingness. In the end, our worldview staggers behind both our technology and our science.

In efforts to create a more stable global system, let alone guard homo sapiens in his personhood, modern man will need to believe once again in nature, that is, in final cause. Our one-sided confidence in mechanical cause gives us not only a partial understanding of reality. Our confidence accounts for the sorry state of our economic development efforts and explains the high-stake poker being played by the nuclear super powers.

Our little bit of knowledge degrades man and nature equally. If we are as a species to make even a timid step towards the twenty-first century, we will need to agree with Einstein when he said that he did not believe that the universe was created by a sort of "toss of the dice." Without purpose, without design, there is no unity. Neither the whole nor the parts exist.

In other words, without final cause there is no global development. In fact, there is no development at all. There remains only what we call blindness or fate, a "big push" or a "take-off" to nowhere.

UNDERSTANDING AND COMMUNICATIONS

Following the logic of final cause one step further, we should recognize its usefulness in political, economic and financial risk analysis. So often we describe a society in military, fiscal, monetary, demographic, even anthropological terms in order to understand with whom we are dealing. The facts, however, that we are so capable of assembling stand without order or priority. They are as tangible as they are self-evident. The problem is that the facts are by no means comprehensive. More often than not, they represent but the image, the prejudice of our own measuring devices. The facts give us but the shadow of a more palpable, more complex reality. Particularly, in Third World analysis, our numbers usually serve to obscure the very subject that is under examination. In other words, the numbers reflect appearances that are created by our own worldview. For this reason, facts do *not* make their own decision.

To speak with a wider conception of cause, in order to understand a given political or economic entity we are required to investigate, if not understand, the ends to which a given people aspire and not simply their existing state of being. Likewise, in economic development planning the goals—and not simply the complexities that all too often we describe in sociological terms—describe a given society, its identity, and, in large measure, its comportment.

Thus, if we are to reduce the analytic process to its fundamental unity, we need to understand a society, its economy, and its government according to its goals or according to what the philosophers call "causa finalis." Without *causa finalis* the very term, "society," becomes but a fiction held together by money, by force, and by economic constraints as temporary as they are unrealistic.

In the *City of God*, St. Augustine, the bishop of Hippo, argues in essence that a society is a group of rational beings, united among themselves because they love with concord the same ends. We would do well to note that St. Augustine does not dictate in his understanding of a society a precise goal that corresponds to his own wishes.[5] He simply argues that the members be at once rational and that they share a common purpose. This definition we have forgotten in the conceptualization of the great majority of our Third World development schemes, and in the money and trade that follows.

It is well understood in the *City of God* as in the more detailed dreams of Auguste Comte's horizontal Utopia that the ultimate end of each society should be justice, proportion, and the realization of individual potential. Nonetheless, in his own definition of society, the bishop of Hippo did well not to include his own final cause. His logic simply premised as a fundamental given that a society defines itself according to its goals and that a society by definition is made up of rational, that is, human beings.

Our multinational banks, our aid programs, and our governments have a tendency today, in their analysis and in their subsequent strategies, to forget—at great cost, it should be noted—the antique and universal definition of the term, "society." Firstly, we confuse our goals with those of others and second—an even bigger mistake—we do not search out the viability of alternative objectives. Oftentimes we assume that other objectives simply do not exist. In the process, we deny a society its past, its present, and its future.

For instance, in finance, the big banks provide funds to Third World countries for the construction of glass towers and elaborate hotel complexes in clear contradiction with real economic needs and with flagrant ignorance of local aspirations. Thus, it should not come as a surprise that the mountain of Third World debt now outstanding resembles vaguely a volcano about to rupture.

In food relief, our aid agencies donate production processes and nutritional habits that create a costly dependency rather than raise food production and intake. The dependency syndrome is further reinforced, as we have demonstrated, through subsidized export credit programs. The taxpayer in the North thereby participates in the erosion of Third World stability and contributes to hunger.

In geopolitical strategies, our governments increasingly fail to analyze correctly the cause and the direction of Third World political foment. The only cause that our leading political theorists can recognize, even in others, is mechanical and therefore is defined in economic terms. Eventually, aid and arms become a cure-all for Third World poverty. Our analysis—and, by extension, our action—is as one-dimensional as it is short-sighted.

The most recent example of the failure of our analytic process is the Middle East and more specifically, Iran. There will be others. Since the early 1960s, Iran was considered a most reliable ally and one of the best bank credit risks among all Third World countries. According to available statistics, the Shah's army represented one of the best equipped in the world. In economic terms, the country's foreign debt never exceeded the quite modest amount of 3 percent of annual export receipts.

With the exception of Russia, for obvious historic reasons, the world's major industrial powers were committed for large sums of money to the economic and social development of ancient Persia. Equally interesting, the country's government made it known at every available public forum that its model for development conformed and would conform to established international norms.

In the end, Iran in 1979, like France at its revolution two centuries earlier, opted for an alternative system, the only one that was not credible to the outside world.

Why was the upheaval in Iran not suspected even two months in advance by the most prestigious, well-endowed, strategic think tanks in the world, including the Hudson Institute, the World Bank, or Chase Econometrics? Perhaps the reason can be found in a common failure to identify the differences between efficient and final cause, between means and ends, between current realities and desired options.

In sum, we in the West have been trapped in a common logic that has reached the limits of its usefulness. This is obvious in the North, in United States-Soviet relations. We have 50,000 nuclear warheads peering down on us to prove the point. We remain convinced that mechanical force alone (power) can give direction to movement. Yet the argument enjoys equal credibility looking North-South.

We attempt to judge all of our problems mechanically because we judge all of the causes as efficient. In finance and aid circles, the solution is money. In economics, the remedy is specialized production according to comparative advantage. In politics, the response is arms. In every instance, force replaces design and unlimited conflict, reason.

In the end, purpose, measure, and identity—whether in banking, in development theory, or in geopolitical practice—have fallen victim to a worldview that admits no quarter, no meaning, and ultimately no profit. As a result, history, if we are to believe our figures on planetary debt, on Third World starvation, and on First World defense expenditures, would seem to be running away with itself, leaving man confronting the next century with little left save his logic. Perhaps with his logic, modern man will be able to defend himself against the Leviathan and, thereby, avoid what we have called the senseless destruction of a second Troy. For this time around, there is no Rome, no new frontier.

A shift in logic or in worldview would not require a Pascalian leap of faith but rather an expansion of our notion of cause to include purpose. With a notion of purpose in nature and especially in the organization of human society, man once again would discover his own identity as *homo rationalis* versus *homo economicus*. On a practical level, reason and subsequent method in Third World development would leave a place for cooperation and limit as the basis for growth. Our international aid organizations would be regionalized, competition rendered compatible with basic human needs—both cultural and material. Free trade would be made proportionate to personhood and economics recognized, in international planning, as an art and not as a science. In other words, meaning and responsibility would be restored to global resource allocation, trade, and finance.

Once the notion of final cause or of goal-values were restored, then politicians, their bankers, diplomats, and advisers, could be held accountable for bankruptcy, whether material or national. Abject poverty would be understood as a failure of the community and not of nature. Value would replace the violence of blind competition, and judgment, the iron law of survival.

In the financing of the development process, export credits and bank loans would be measured on the merit of their meaning and not just size. The organization of the multinational banks would be rendered consistent with a bank's purpose or identity and deflated accordingly. Corporate culture would promote a sense of consciousness of what a bank is, if not conscience. The nationalized banks would be privatized. Their bureaucracies broken and judgment restored. The largest private sector banks would be reduced to a size permitting their collapse if judgment is erring. Their deflation would return the banks to the market, where they belong. Thus, the secular temple would be restored to its proper vocation, to its telos, or its end. Our financial system as a whole would admit measure and value. The financing of the development process would be made compatible with the new mandate proposed for the World Bank and the IMF. The hedonistic principle and comparative advantage would yield to more sane global management based on the premise that direction is at least as important as force.

A shift from a blind belief in power to the inclusion of purpose would bring the West back to an ancient but reliable symbol of Apollo Victorious over the Phython, Apollo defenseless save an arrow representing his logic and a bow his force. This, then, is what we mean by the Western Question. Can reason be restored to the Third World question: Western Question? The resolution to this problem will determine not only the outcome of the debt crisis but also of the world order that we will be leaving to our own children and to theirs.

Should the shift in paradigm be accomplished by about five heads of state, the leaders of two international aid agencies, and the chairmen of some 50 banks, then the development process North-South and East-West would begin to make for a safer, less precarious human condition. The method would change the models, the models that have led us to our present fate.

Homo Abyssus Occidentalis

As the poet says: "It is silly to refuse the tasks of time." Hence, we must pardon and leave the Age of Anxiety, the booth in the bar where we began the discussion of the Western Question. Three centuries of midnight have passed. The starving children are witnesses. To return to daylight, we will need to reclaim intention to our understanding of cause. While justice and proportion will not automatically result, at least we will have restored man to his measure. On this basis, action will have meaning.

14
An Action Plan at
"The Edge of History" or
on Getting From Power to Purpose

In Part I of the preceding text, we discussed the external economic environment in which the multinational banks and their poorest clients have operated since World War II. As we noted, this external environment has been shaped, almost single-handedly, by a trading system based on the Law of Comparative Advantage. The law has been enshrined in the charters of our international aid agencies and has determined subsequent trade and financial flows. These flows have functioned to *mal*develop the world economy.

Worse yet, like a number of other economic axioms, the Law of Comparative Advantage has been understood to enjoy scientific validity, that is, the law commonly is thought of as universally valid, unchanging, and even necessary for growth. Accordingly, its application (a small error in the premise) has been extended to the rich and to the poor, to the strong and to the weak—indiscriminately.

The now manifest results of the Law of Comparative Advantage should have been (and were) predictable. They include growing destitution in the Third World matched by a corresponding fracture in our global financial system. Both problems threaten world stability. Famine is on the increase, while the banks are no longer capable of assuring minimum international credit flows. Not surprisingly, political tension mounts East-West and, more ominously, on the periphery, where the geopolitical ground rules are less well understood. As a result, increasingly frequent IMF riots could lead to a larger, more consuming global conflict.

Nonetheless, the Law of Comparative Advantage continues to inspire the economic growth models that determine the so-called

173

development process. The models (big push, creative destruction, takeoff, and unbalanced growth) all rely, in the end, on a system of feigned free trade, operative between the defended and the destitute. This schema holds firm not only as a theoretic leitmotiv or as an abstract nicety but as a source of finance. The schema has been endorsed by the United Nations planning process for three consecutive development decades. The machine now operates on its own fateful momentum.

Initially, the models were constructed (funded) with World Bank and with bilateral aid money. As the free trade paradigm came under increasing pressure due to the violence and contradictions of its own internal logic, First World export agencies and commercial banks joined the growing chorus of Third World aid donors. As demonstrated, the system of export credit not only falsifies the very principle of competitive advantage but has led to systemic abuses within the banking sector generally e.g., the Inga-Shaba transmission line, the Ivory Coast sugar program, the Korean nuclear power projects, not to mention the subsidized sale of other big-ticket items throughout the Third World such as airplanes, high-tech steel mills, and overpriced supertankers. The result?

In the North, industrial policy and agricultural production have been merged with a system of export sales. In the process, trade and financial credits have been extended to increasingly impoverished debtor countries. The instability of Northern trade and financial exposure in the Third World is matched by extreme social discontinuity in the South. The discontinuity starts with economic extroversion and ends in an ontological loss of self, i.e., a case of national schizophrenia. Production since the start of the First Development Decade has preceded as well as succeeded purpose. As a consequence, the world economy today is more than superficially awry. Yet the structural problems cannot (and will not) be addressed until the international community is able to gain some perspective on itself, that is, until its development model, and the premise on which the model rests, can be viewed objectively.

Meanwhile, the International Monetary Fund stands by in a vain effort to maintain the system of comparative advantage operating North-South. As a result, like a majority of Third World debtor countries, the big banks are living, albeit sometimes indirectly, on borrowed money from international aid agencies, or, on credit from First World governments. The banks likewise are living on borrowed time. Similar to Damocles, the legendary courtier of ancient Syracuse, our financiers appear seated at a banquet beneath a sword hung by a single thread. On the outside, the system has become increasingly tenuous. On the inside at a banquet paid for by the taxpayer, it is business as usual. This business-as-usual is leading us to the precipice of financial disorder on a worldwide basis.

In Part II, we reviewed the ideological substructure that has formed the economic models according to which the Third World has been developed. At every level of global systems management, competition has been confused with progress. Competence, let alone threshold cooperation, have suffered accordingly. Nuclear weapons measured in terms of megatons and emergency financial relief measured in terms of megadollars are but the two-faced symbol of modern man's loss of purpose and of proportion.

It remains to tie together the Third World Question (Part I) with the Western Question (Part II). In doing so, we will make concrete recommendations on how the international community might exit the financial crisis best exemplified in the tremendous size of Third World debt. For the debt crisis, or better, the debt bomb must be diffused if the comity of nations is not to experience a political rupture of perhaps permanent dimension. Indeed, the debt bomb and the real bomb cannot be entirely dissociated in calculating the principal variables that could account for the unmaking of our future. For as the popular expression would have it, money talks and money is, for better or worse, at the core of the Western World's global development efforts. When money and ideas fail, arms and technology become the unhappy but inevitable substitute. We are beginning to witness this verity at the edge of the world's two major empires. In the process, modern man seems to be flirting with the edge of history.

CONFRONTING THE PRECIPICE

The central bank for the Western Alliance, the Bank for International Settlements, notes that "the world today faces two major, immediate policy challenges: how to enable the emerging recovery in the Western industrial countries to proceed smoothly and how to keep the international debt situation within manageable bounds."[2] Obviously, the two problems are interrelated. Even in the short run they both hinge on the solvability of the big banks, that is, on the solvability of their poorest clients. "It is hard to envision," writes the management of the BIS, "a broadly based and lasting recovery in the western world as long as the fear of the potentially damaging financial consequences of a world debt crisis is not fundamentally allayed."[3]

Let us take the management of the BIS at its word and attempt to provide a set of solutions that might *fundamentally allay* the debt servicing problems of the Third World and their bankers. The solutions can be arranged into two categories: the temporary or technological fixes, and the permanent ones.

First, the technological fixes. Begrudgingly, the taxpayer in the North must be willing to pay more money, a lot more, to make up for the bankers, their regulators, and the international civil servants who did not cry "wolf" loudly enough and when they did it was too late. The big banks and their major Third World clients clearly need a costly and long-term bailout, say, a minimum of six years to a decade. In the case of the banks, the bailout might best come in the form of loan guarantees from multilateral aid agencies and from temporary equity participation from their respective central banks. Over the next half decade, the loan guarantees of existing plus new commercial credit could cost up to $100 billion, or about 0.1 percent of the First World's GNP, not a large price to pay for minimum financial stability on the planet. This $100 billion represents about 10 percent of outstanding Third World debt or about 2.5 times the capital base of the world's top 50 banks. We should recall in passing that the world's 50 largest banks hold about 60 percent of all Third World debt. The loan guarantee scheme would serve to sanitize the balance sheets of these banks and free up additional bank assets for more productive lending into the Third World. The simple rollover of existing principal outstanding plus interest only magnifies the problem. New bank credit, even if induced, is necessary to help reorient the economies of those debtor nations that effectively have dropped out of the system due to national bankruptcy.

Where does the money come from? In addition to modest participation from the banks, say, $20 billion per annum in new loans, the IMF statutory lending requirements already could go to SDR 405 billion (about $450 billion) by year-end 1985 if a currently contemplated 50 percent quota increase takes place. These quota requirements should be doubled once again, despite the ongoing reluctance of a number of legislators. Likewise, the IMF and/or the World Bank should be given additional guarantee authorities. Next, the IMF should in the future be permitted to borrow on public markets, while the World Bank be allowed to increase its gearing ratio from 1 to 1 to 2 to 1, this would be in keeping with the recommendations of *Common Crisis*, the Brandt report update for 1983.[6] Lastly, the World Bank should be encouraged to finance development where it is taking place, that is, *locally* rather than under the guise of export credits from the North. This would mean more program or indigenous lending as opposed to project finance. The lending would be tied to regional development, and not just growth in the context of a world economy.

Against an IMF/World Bank takeout on the order of $100 billion in guarantees, the world's top multinational banks should be prepared to accept a board member from either of these two multilateral institutions. This would increase everyone's awareness level as to the nature and duration of the crisis. The strategy likewise would give the taxpayer some additional protections against the $100 billion rescue operation.

In addition to loan guarantees, the world's major banks currently operate on a desperately thin equity base of less than 5 percent of total liabilities. This equity base is nonexistent if one were to give a true market value to the banks' Third World receivables. The problem already presents itself as a veritable nightmare for bank accountants and regulators.[7] As a first step away from the precipice of wide-scale financial instability, the central banks of the major industrial countries will need to go considerably further than recent steps to shore up the manifest capital inadequacy of the banking sector generally. As a temporary solution, the central banks of the Western Alliance nations should take immediate measures to at least double the shareholder component of the top multinational banks. As a worse case alternative, this increased equity might come from the governments themselves—with a fixed repurchase agreement from management and private shareholders. The doubling of the capital of the world's 50 largest banks would send the right signals to the market and cost the taxpayer, at least temporarily, another $20 billion. The *quid pro quo* would be a constellation of measures to assure more sound banking practices. The most important of these measures might be coordinated legislative action to keep the banks in the banking business rather than ignoring it through expansion into peripheral nonbanking industries. We will discuss other measures at the end of this chapter. Meanwhile, the bailout does not stop with the banks.

The World Bank and the International Monetary Fund already are spending about $45 billion annually in emergency relief to member states. To this amount should be added the overall cost of what the BIS appropriately calls the "combined firefighting actions" of lender governments, their central banks, lending banks, and other international organizations—about another $20 billion in 1984. For instance, Brazil alone cost the U.S. government $3 billion in emergency central bank credits, and Argentina nearly another half billion. Mexico doubled these figures.

Nonetheless additional "combined firefighting actions" in the Third World cannot be avoided for the foreseeable future if the world community wishes to assure the proper functioning of the international financial markets. The rollovers will need to continue, along with bilateral and multilateral government help, if the system is not to short-circuit. Obviously, the so-called "spontaneous bank flows" for additional high-priced financial or general purpose loans as well as subsidized nonpurpose export credits should be curtailed, that is, considered as an abuse of the depositor's and/or the taxpayer's money. Rollovers and additional bailout money must be conditioned on keeping the borrower—and the lender—honest. In the case of the Third World borrower, this means appropriate domestic policy measures to be monitored, as is happening, by a neutral third party, i.e., by the IMF. The IMF, of course, needs a different set of ground rules which might allow for development not just survival within an increasingly competitive, at times predatory, world market.

In the case of the lender, i.e. the banks, conditionality would be better assured by a change in reporting requirements to include purpose, not just size by country and by economic sector. The BIS or some like institution might be made responsible for verifying loan quality not just quantity. The so-called prudent spread of risk would be changed to include the prudent use of proceeds. New reporting requirements combined with a shift in the complexion of the board of directors at the major banks might serve to keep the banks, their regulators, and export agencies honest as well as alert. Public interest groups should be the first to address both of these issues. This is especially true since the estimated cost of the overall bailout described above quite easily could exceed $200 billion over the next half decade —no small sum, particularly if it is squandered. The estimated $200 billion represents the minimum necessary to keep the banks and their poorest clients afloat.

No Forgiveness

Oftentimes, it is suggested by well-meaning donors in the North and by their constituencies in the South that the rescue operations currently being put into place include a significant amount of debt forgiveness as part of the package. While a seemingly attractive solution (especially for the poorest Fourth World countries), the remedy functions ironically to mortgage not only the future credibility of the borrowing country but, more importantly, the future reliability of government. The solution quite probably would render the status quo permanent and thereby sentence future generations to more of the same, to wit, careless local government reinforced by continued careless borrowing and even more careless spending. Unfortunately, a loan workout should mean just that, for lender and for borrower alike. Charity without effort and some notion of justice is also without meaning and hope as explained by every philosopher from antiquity to Paul Tillich.[8]

In addition to yet greater taxpayer participation in a First World/Third World financial bailout, other technological fixes include a series of measures to bring the bubble down slowly so that it does not pop in midair. Here the technological fixes blend into the permanent ones.

Admittedly, the free trade paradigm cannot be changed overnight. In the meanwhile, it is imperative that further protectionist measures in the North not advance those in the South. A vital breathing space is needed while a conscious change in the development model works its way through those multilateral agencies responsible for trade and financial flows worldwide, i.e. the World Bank, the IMF, Gatt, and the OECD. Accordingly, changes in industrial and agricultural planning policy in the North must await a shift in development goals in the South. Without a gradualist approach on the part of both parties, with the North leading the way, systems maintenance will be impossible. In other words, the locomotive cannot simply stop dead in its tracks. In declining degree, Northern markets must continue to be assured to Southern exporters—especially to the most vulnerable countries, that is, to those that have played by the rules of the game and, in a tragically limited sense, won—for example, Brazil, Mexico, the Philippines, South Korea, even Japan and certain East European countries. Adjustment to a more balanced, less extroverted trading system would be the goal of future trade negotiations at Gatt and at similar UN planning sessions, especially UNCTAD. This gradualist approach to rendering trade flows more consistent with development should take about a decade to 15 years to start to work. In the meanwhile, the international community—now about to fall in on itself if current debt and trade figures can be believed—should be put on notice that the development paradigm has shifted.

In the South, the shift should start among those nations causing the most labor displacement in the North. In addition to those larger extroverted economies just mentioned, Argentina, Brazil, Mexico, South Korea, and so on, these countries would include, among others, Morocco, Singapore, Taiwan, Tunisia, Turkey, Yugoslavia, and, to a growing extent, China. The *quid pro quo* would be systems maintenance on the part of the North.

Meanwhile, in the North, the locomotive is clearly overheated. Fiscal and monetary policy, especially in the United States has done as much to underdevelop the South as have export credits and spontaneous or purposeless bank loans. Despite vigorous official reporting in the North to the contrary, inflation in the major industrialized countries has preceded Third World commodity price hikes, especially when one abstracts out of the charts the most fundamental of indicators, i.e., currency values. First World inflation not only has hurt fixed income families in the North and displaced the ultimate day of reckoning to future households, the same sleight of hand has impoverished the poorest members of the world community. In nearly every case, IMF riots are foreshadowed by an insupportable loss of purchasing power on the part of those people living already at the extremes of the poverty line. While inflation usually finds it origins in mismanagement by local government, it also has been imported, in large quantities, enough to overwhelm the system.

Likewise, careless monetary and fiscal policies in the North have created the huge dollar overhang on the international financial markets. In turn, the dollar overhang has promoted the ceaseless currency speculation and the spontaneous money flows coming out of inflated multinational bank balance sheets. As a result, systems management has turned into the firefighting measures now costing taxpayers billions of dollars annually in lost talent, time, and money.

Here again, the United States, one of the least vulnerable of Northern economies, has a special responsibility. Not only do U.S. monetary authorities need to control the banks, but they also need to control the dollar, the basic unit of account in international trade. The post-war *Pax Americana* can only be sustained on the basis of honest management by government of its money. Without a more stable dollar, the terms of trade will continue to vacillate at the edge and below the poverty line, leaving in its trace not only a severely weakened financial structure but a collapse of minimum solidarity among trading partners. In this regard, a resurrection of the barbaric relic, the gold standard, might be the least damaging of all alternatives. A return to gold would certainly introduce minimum sobriety to trade, currency, and international reserve movements. The return will become inevitable if U.S. fiscal policy, with its attendant monumental budgetary deficits, cannot be brought under control.

THE FUNDAMENTAL FIX: A POLITICAL ACTION PROGRAM

Advancing beyond the transition period between the technological and the permanent solutions to the North-South trade and debt crisis, it remains to propose an action plan that might bridge the precipice that both the North and the South steadfastly are approaching. It is hoped that the concrete action plan will appear as a necessary extension of the logic that we have pursued thus far.

At the start of the First Development Decade, it was the World Council of Churches that initially recommended that the rich countries of the Western Alliance put aside 1 percent of GNP as an allocation for foreign aid. While the World Council of Churches proposed the *money*, the politicians, economists, ex-colonial administrators, and bankers designed the *method*. It is now time for those private, nonprofit lobbies concerned with Third World poverty to recommend a change in the development paradigm. There exists more than 150 Private Volunteer Organizations (PVOs) registered with the U.S. State Department that are directly concerned with Third World poverty. These organizations oftentimes are closer to what actually is happening in the Third World than are the banks and aid agencies that fund the bulk of the development program. The PVOs range from church-related groups such as the American Friends Service Committee, Catholic Relief Services, Church World Services, and the United Israel Appeal to nonsectarian organizations such as Food for the Hungry Inc., Global Outreach, and Progress for Productivity (PFP). Together these special interest groups represent a formidable Third World lobby. They also represent the majority of the American people. Together, the PVOs should set out to address the most important systemic problems in North-South relations, starting with the free trade paradigm according to the Law of Comparative Advantage.

For effective political action, the PVOs might ally themselves with the so-called sunset industries in the North: steel, shipbuilding, textiles, apparels, other light manufacturing, home appliances, and electronics, to name but the principal sectors. The alliance might be productively extended to include the National Federation of Independent Business and organized labor. Each of these vested interest groups suffer from unloyal labor and investment competition in the Third World. This competition has been promoted by the North.

For example, in the case of steel, world production has been specialized, with concomitant social and financial vulnerability, largely in Brazil, South Korea, Taiwan, and Yugoslavia. In the case of textiles, electronics, or home appliances, one might add to this list Hong Kong, Mexico, Tunisia, Singapore, and the Philippines. The short-term advantages of this overspecialization have gone to export lobbies in the North—a rather small number of multinationals—and to the new elite in those economies, where the "big push" has led to de facto national bankruptcy and/or to extreme vulnerability to Northern markets.

In the case of the Third World, a different growth model would yield to the development of national resources—human, material, and technological—and not just to an artificial or misdirected increase in output. In the case of the big banks, the spontaneous flow of capital would move to where it could be used to everyone's best advantage, not simply to big government, to the new elite, or to a handful of multinationals operative in and selling to the Third World. The strategy makes good sense for yet another reason.

Increasingly in the North, it is the medium- and small-size businesses not the big, export-oriented multinationals that have been creating the necessary net new employment to keep the Northern economies from sliding even further into stagflation or economic paralysis. In the United States, for instance, government studies show that over the past decade, small- and medium-size business has created nine out of every ten new manufacturing jobs in the private sector.[9] On the whole, these companies stand to gain, along with U.S. labor, from a development paradigm that excludes overspecialization of production and predatory trade practices. They would also gain from a halt to subsidized finance of capital goods to the Third World (the boomerang effect) that has so damaged large sectors of America's heavy industry to which the smaller companies sell.

In brief, there would appear to be sound cause on economic, business, and humanitarian grounds for an active coalition between the PVOs, small- and medium-size business, the sunset industries, labor, and the world's poor. The multinationals would follow quickly for they are the most nimble at picking up changes in market policy. Ironically, the catalyst for more sane global development could come from where it originated, the World Council of Churches or like lobbies.

In terms of carrying the new development paradigm (the model) into production, the most obvious starting point is found in those UN organizations already responsible for financing the development process, the World Bank and the IMF plus the bilateral aid agencies of the OECD member states. Indeed, there is no lack of money, mechanisms, and talent for halting the drift toward anarchy in North-South relations. What is needed is the political will. This gap might be filled by the Third World lobby proposed above. The new coalition, however, needs a clear-cut mandate—and method!—if their collective political will is not to fragment in the process of shifting the global development paradigm from its collision course with history. We now shall set out to schematize the mandate.

Let us propose a chart outlining the distinctions between the old mandate and the new as it evolves from method or theory to model and money. To paraphrase Paul Tillich, mandate and method cannot be separated from content.[10] We now shall see how both are interrelated in a proposed plan of action.

Old Paradigm	**New Paradigm**
Mandate: growth —based on the premise that movement originates in force to the exclusion of purpose or proportion. The "how" precedes the "why".	Mandate: development —movement without design, purpose, or finality is not only unthinkable but intolerable, i.e., lifeless. The "how" and the "why" are inseparable.
Method: The Law of Comparative Advantage operative North-South. —international division of land, labor, and capital. —centralized development planning and the centralization of multilateral aid agencies, e.g., the World Bank, the IMF, etc.	Method: Competition or free trade among approximate equals. —regional development with goal of safeguarding self-sufficiency and, by extension, self-identity. —regional development planning boards and decentralization of World Bank Group and Gatt, with coordination but not absolute control remaining at headquarters.
—standardized adjustment programs within the free trade model.	—regional adjustment programming to protect against economic extroversion.
—increase output.	—allow for basic human need, material as well as normative or cultural.

	Old Paradigm		*New Paradigm*
Model:	Big Push, Takeoff, Unbalanced Growth, and Creative Destruction. —based on the assumption that economics is a science. *Homo economicus.*	Model:	Creative construction, balanced growth, threshold protection. —based on the understanding that economics is an art. *Homo rationalis.*
Money:	Official Development Assistance as a percent of GNP for OECD member countries taken as a group averages about .36 percent of GNP or some $35 billion per annum in net official flows (foreign aid) to developing countries, some of which passes through the multilateral aid agencies. —The bulk of these monies serve to finance capital-intensive First World exports, grains, or technical services designed to connect the Third World economies with the First.	Money:	ODA as a percentage of GNP should reach 1 percent as first suggested by the World Council of Churches, i.e., a 300 percent increase in foreign aid above current levels. The greater portion of this aid should run through the proposed decentralized multilateral development agencies so as to depoliticize the aid package, to curtail costly export credits, and to promote regional development with largely regional means. The overall goal would be to render the Third World market solvent for eventual reintegration into a global economy. Solvency, however, assumes a minimum degree of self-sufficiency. Once this self-sufficiency is obtained, foreign aid would no longer be needed. In other words, the funding of regional development could solve two problems at once: insolvency and the repetitive, growing need to shore-up the weakest links in the world economy with ever increasing amounts of foreign aid and bank credit.
	Officially supported export credits and guarantees are used		Suppress government-subsidized export credits as an

Old Paradigm	*New Paradigm*
Money: to (1) promote foreign trade (2) export employment (3) buy markets, and (4) displace excess industrial production. Net disbursements of subsidized export credits by OECD member states average about $6 billion annually and support the sale of an additional $20 billion of overpriced Northern exports, a large portion of which are counterguaranteed by First World governments.	Money: unfair trading practice for it promotes bogus buying and bogus finance. The bulk of these credits could best be used sponsoring development rather than feeding the ongoing trade credit wars between First World supplier nations. The suppression of export credits would also reorient First World production back to the First World. In the end, the credits represent a distortion of the market, North as well as South.

The Commercial Banks

Commercial bank credit exposure to the Third World increased from less than $15 billion in 1969 to over $300 billion in the late 1970s and then leaped to over $600 billion by year-end 1982. Credit exposure plateaued in 1983/84 representing a de facto freeze on net new bank lending to those governments that speak for two thirds of the world's population. Nevertheless going forward, a change in the development paradigm must involve at its very center the major multinational banks. And this for two reasons. First, the commercial banks have effectively replaced the multilateral and bilateral aid donors as the Third World's largest source of offshore investment. The balance cannot be redressed before the end of this century. Second, the big banks cannot hope to rationalize, let alone improve, their own balance sheets without a significant improvement in the creditworthiness of their Third World debtor nations. This means more than just a non-stop rollover of existing debt. The workout also means more reasonable but continued participation by the commercial banks in Third World development. Any coalition of Third World interest groups, including the banks, must be prepared to confront this elementary reality. Hopefully, the big banks, along with their major multinational clients (about 400 companies), will join the right lobby, the proposed Third World coalition, and thereby avoid the chasm, a violent economic discontinuity, between the past and the future.

In this same context, let us continue to elaborate a new development mandate bringing into focus the core issue that can hold the whole together, namely, money. At the start, we mentioned our concern for the impact of multinational banking in the Third World. Subsequently, we argued against conventional wisdom by demonstrating that the impact of the banks was not in fact spontaneous but structural, even inevitable. The so-called spontaneous megadollar money flows into the Third World that the BIS seems to be at a loss to explain have a specific cause. As Aristotle noted some 2,400 years ago in *Physica Bk. II*: "Spontaneity and chance are posterior to intelligence and nature." This is to say simply that results have a specific cause and that hazard, chance, magic, and wishful thinking represent a lack of knowledge. It is imperative that the international community recognize the intelligibility of the errors that have been made to date in Third World lending. The chart outlined earlier details the intelligibility, the ineluctable consequence of our existing development logic. The chart also lists the contradictory nature of the investment that has followed. The banks have been lending into a highly volatile world economy in which some of their clients get richer but the market gets poorer. In fact, the banks and their favored First World exporters should recognize, along with their most impoverished Third World clients, the immediate, short-term rationale for participating in a change in the development model.

For their part, the banks thus far have defended their actions by arguing that they have served as a mere vehicle for allocating (recycling) excess international liquidity. This passive brokering element has steered the banking community, some important First World clients, and nearly all of their Third World clients toward a condition of disguised insolvency. In the end, systems maintenance has come to mean systems corrosion.

If the banks want to help their biggest First World and Third World customers and, in the process, salvage their own balance sheets, they will need to join the Third World coalition, not *passively* but *actively*. How can they do this? How can the banks align themselves with the PVOs, business, and labor to change the global development paradigm? More money (although inevitable) is but of secondary importance. In fact, the banks can (and might) use more money simply to sidestep the most fundamental of issues.

Externally, the big banks will need to redefine, or better, rediscover the community that they are serving. To paraphrase the BIS, in the current crisis, the four players at the debt table include the borrower, the lender, the lender's government, and the IMF/World Bank Group. While the banks have not played out their hand, they have threatened, even attempted, to walk away from the table leaving the chips to the other players.

We see this in the scramble of the U.S. banks, in particular, shifting money and talent from the Third World to nontraditional domestic markets. In the United States, commercial banks have set out to dilute their overseas problems by expanding, with the consent of the government, not simply across state boundaries but into other industries. Daily the financial press reports on expensive takeovers by banks of finance companies, household savings institutions, and insurance societies. Meanwhile, the capital base of the banking industry fails to improve in meaningful terms while the equity support in the peripheral industries is weakened because of the takeovers. In the end, talent, decision-making authority, and responsibility to local markets suffer as a result of the dilution of bank investment and interest. This dilution will only make the debt trap more diffuse rather than solve it.

The big multinational banks cannot address their problems by ignoring them. In competing with Sears Roebuck, Shearson/American Express, and Blue Cross, corporate culture within the banking industry dissipates. Commercial bank lending blends into brokering and eventually inflationary speculation. Accordingly, the central banks of the OECD countries as well as the Third World coalition should assure continued bank participation in the North-South debt crisis that they, the big banks, helped to create. One important way of doing this would be to keep the commercial banks where they belong, that is, in the banking industry. A real change from the finger-in-the-dike approach to the Third World debt crisis would include a cleanup (not dilution) of bank balance sheets according to the terms of a First World government bailout, as described earlier, plus a predefined limit on bank activities. Both the Third World lobbies and central bank authorities should work to keep the banks close to their vocation as a storehouse of value and regulator within a private market system. An inevitable, temporary slowdown combined with a reorientation in commercial bank lending to the Third World must be matched by a reassertion of bank identity and purpose.

A second way to assure this reorientation would be to bring the really big banks back to size. This important second step would provide additional corrective remedy to blatant misallocation of credit both North and South. In the case of the U.S. banks, the inordinate, inflated expansion of the largest banking houses could be gotten under control through orderly disinvestiture as well as through the division of the largest banks into units of no more than $20 billion in assets. The United States already enjoys a commendable history of antitrust action, thus assuring balanced and proportionate competition within certain key industries, for example, steel, energy, and, more recently, communications. This balance urgently needs to be brought back to banking. More reasonable size would improve credit judgment, identification of customer needs, and better internal control. Second, the measure would bring the biggest banks back to market discipline, where mismanagement would be rewarded with bankruptcy rather than a bailout.

In the case of not a few European countries, the problem has become yet more complex, especially in France, Italy, Austria, Sweden, and, to some extent Germany. Government ownership and excess protection has placed the biggest banks at the mercy of government administration, if not manipulation. Over the long run, the concentration of power and money deprives individual bank management of the necessary sense of responsibility to themselves and to their clients. The nationalization also saps vitality out of the economy, leaving the state with unchecked economic power, indeed, with enough power to disguise its own economic mismanagement. Inevitably, state ownership of the banking sector not only removes the banks from salutary market discipline but the state as well. Meanwhile, the liberties of the depositor and client are blended into those of the taxpayer.

A movement toward the privatization of nationalized banking could be negotiated within the framework of Gatt or the BIS. Ideally, these negotiations should take place in parallel with a gradual rationalization of the United States and European banking industries. The rationalization should take place in the context of further central bank regulatory assymetry and include three key topics: bank size, the Eurodollar market, and Third World lending. In today's shrinking world, regulated assymetry in finance as well as regulated free trade by region are to be hoped (and lobbied) for. The goal would be a more balanced trading system between the rich and the rich and between the rich and the poor. The first step might start with the banks. Smaller, more coherent banks in private hands would make for a larger, more coherent world economy, not to mention world order.

The banks not only need the staying power in the Third World, they likewise need to understand their mandate in the First World. By understand, we mean the rediscovery of private initiative, proportion, purpose, and the policy guidelines that go with them. Small is not necessarily beautiful, but the proportionate is.

The Internal Bank Adjustment Process

We have come to restate the external or macroeconomic environment in which the banks today operate. We have suggested a number of strategic changes that might make for a more sane and durable international economic order. Corresponding internal changes in bank organization are equally vital. New internal policy guidelines certainly would include some mix of the following. First, the large commercial banks should be encouraged to establish specialized operating units concerned with Third World developmental issues. These units might be institutionalized in the form of development committees and be made responsible for overseeing both debt workouts and future Third World impact loans of significant size, say, 20 percent of bank capital. The chairman of the committee should be appointed by the board of directors and be accountable both to the board and to outside regulators.

Second, Third World loan officers not only should be judged over a longer reporting period but trained to understand the developmental issues at stake when a country borrows hard currency from abroad. Some training might take place at those multilateral agencies responsible for the development process. The IMF and the World Bank already have work/training programs designed for Third World government planners. These programs should be revised to account for a different, more balanced development model and extended to include commercial bankers from the First World.

In like manner, international civil servants and Third World planners should do some in-house training at the major banks in order to understand better private sector banking technique. The exchange resulting from such programs would aid substantially the North/South dialogue at the action level. Needless to say, bank regulators should participate in the work programs so that they stop playing catch-up football with borrowers and lenders alike in an ever changing marketplace.

Third, we mentioned earlier that the World Bank Group and central banks should participate on the boards of the world's largest 50 or so multinational banks in return for what has become an ever recurrent Third World bailout. Going in the other direction, leading commercial bankers, on a rotational basis, should participate formally in policy formulation at the principal aid agencies. This tactical measure would promote a needed parallelism in public and private sector Third World finance. The strategy might also direct attention, talent, and money at the banks away from insurance, travel, brokering, and other activities all peripheral to lending into productive enterprise. Risk analysis and purposeful business loans once again might take the central position at the banks over money changing, government subsidized export credit, and speculative (the BIS would say "spontaneous") lending in the First and the Third Worlds.

Finally, the Third World lobby also enjoys a place at the banquet of international finance. Would it be too much to ask that community leaders be elected by a coalition of PVOs to serve on the boards and/or on the proposed development committees of the big banks and aid agencies. This action should be considered as a minimum *quid pro quo* against a Third World "take out" paid for by the taxpayer. Likewise, the action might lend a voice, although distant and filtered, to the ever growing number of desperate and destitute citizens of the Third World. The big banks stand at the very center of the Third World debt crisis. The solution to the crisis should be a shared one, if it is to be both lasting and self-generating.

The policy proposals mentioned thus far, both external and internal to the banking industry itself, will not, even if applied collectively, release easily the debt trap along with its associated dangers. Despite frequent and sometimes careless assurances to the contrary, the First World and the Third World citizen should realize that, in a figurative sense, there exists no Prince Charming armed with a new ideology nor with enough money to make the debt problem go away, especially in the short term. The mistakes of today have and will continue to be paid for by the rich and the poor alike, with the poor suffering the most. The technological fixes cited earlier in this chapter should provide some breathing space, if one were able to make an abstraction of those currently suffering from malnutrition and death. But aside from a temporary respite, the fundamental policy initiatives relate to a new direction, or better, to a new beginning, a way of looking at the world.

These policy initiatives are inconsistent neither with the origin of Western man's intellectual heritage nor with sound government and banking practice. Faithful to one of the central themes of this book, we simply would insist that purpose advance change and, in like manner, development growth. In sum, the intention of the international community should be to restore intentionality to local and to world development. First World governments and the proposed Third World coalition might best start by imposing intentionality on the banks and their regulators. Herein we address the source as well as the solution to banking technology and lending practice. We likewise address an essential element, perhaps the most essential, for pulling the development process off its current trajectory, a trajectory that leads to violent discontinuities, if not to a final collision course with itself. Witnesses, North and South, must ask themselves whether or not this collision course is inevitable—and then act, however modestly, as a function of this choice.

Moving from banking to trade flows, the proposed Third World lobby should make apparent for policy makers the abject folly of our free trade paradigm when applied, without significant modification, to Third World development. As we have shown, the dynamic of such a scheme is predatory by nature. The Law of Comparative Advantage promotes neither growth nor progress when operative between the hyperdeveloped and the destitute. Instead, the parts merely distance themselves in such a way that the center cannot hold.

Trade flows need to be made coherent within the context of the new development paradigm proposed above. The model presumes both regionalization and protection of the weakest members of the world community. As the psychologist, Werner Wolff points out, "Man selects his material of reality."[11] This is nowhere more apparent than in the structure of today's trading patterns, or better, in the markets that have been created as a function of these patterns. The trade flows themselves are leading the system in its entirety toward a seemingly premeditated disintegration. Regional, national, and local cohesiveness, not to mention food security, have been sacrificed to an economic imperative that incarnates the self-destructive logic of Thomas Hobbes' *Leviathan*. The Leviathan is now on its last legs. Comparative advantage has led to an unsustainable balance of terror between bank lenders and borrowers and between aid donors and recipients. The unstable relationships that have developed in world finance and trade could unbalance the yet more mindless terror that makes up the logic of our military machinery.

Confronted with all three realities—banking, preemptive trade flows, and the politico-military standoff that sustains them—the world community not only needs to create time for debtors and creditors to recover their balance but, more importantly, measure in the organization of international commerce and development. For the moment, our limited notions of what makes the real world run precludes measure in trade patterns and purpose in credit and aid flows. On this basis, the PVOs themselves are rendered ancillary and the technocrat given sole charge of our destiny.

For this reason, the PVOs not only must lobby for *more* but for *meaning*. Indeed, the prime necessity in any future Third World/First

World development model will be to add to the subtitle of Thomas Hobbes' *Leviathan*, "Or the Matter, Forme, and Power of A Common-Wealth," the key phrase, *Purpose*. Without common purpose, banking, trade flows, and the geopolitical mechanisms that support the whole will stop turning in their gyres.

This book has sought to restore meaning to the machine. The method and the money, as we have explained, will follow in kind. For in the end, the debt trap is no more than a mental trap. The trap reflects, in aberrant dimensions, modern man's unthinking acceptance of power over purpose or of matter over meaning.

Any future Third World development model will need to reverse this order of priorities. Only then will banking, trade, and world development generally reflect mankind's needs rather than mankind's instinct. Expressed differently, *Homo abyssus* must be restored to his complete nature, a nature that admits not simply feeling in man's definition of himself and in the organization of world affairs but thought as well.

Alexander Zinoviev tells us that civilization is effort; communality is taking the line of least resistance. Since the Second World War, the North—whether East or West—has taken the line of least resistance in the creation of a global civilization. Growth, production, and profit have overwhelmed purpose, design, and meaning. Civilization has given way to communality. The proof of this assertion is the way in which Northern growth models have been franchised on a global basis. In the West, the banner is free trade, which serves to reduce man and society to a least common denominator, that is, to an economic imperative of mere survival instead of to a political imperative of choice and of civilization. In the East, the banner is a secular man-god that eventually turns into Big Brother.

In both instances, *Homo econimicus* evolves into *Homo abyssus*. Production becomes more important than product while feeling prevails over the freedom to create a civilization relative to man's real needs as *Homo sapiens*. Thinking man turns out to be subordinate to an economic system. To turn around this headlong reach to nowhere, this mental lethargy leading to disaster, man himself will need (as he will do) to think through an appropriate definition of himself and of his heirs. The definition that springs from this thought process hopefully should deliver man from the Leviathan, or, from the faulty logic in which he currently is embedded. Re-thinking development logic is equivalent to re-thinking man's purpose, his potential, and, by extension, his responsibility at this, the possible edge of history. This book has attempted to demonstrate the importance firstly of the thought process and, secondly, of the action which follows.

Notes

NOTES TO INTRODUCTION: THE SECOND HOLOCAUST

1. Teilhard de Chardin quoted by Louis Sabourin in "Critical Issues in Development in the '80's" (The Development Center of the Organization for Economic Co-Operation and Development, Paris, 1981), Liaison Bulletin, No. 7 New Series, p. 20.

2. See Anthony Sampson, *The Money Lenders* (Hodder and Stoughton, London, 1981), p. 283. In an interview with the author, Walter Wriston is quoted as follows: "Facts make their own decisions." The ex-chairman of Citibank, Walter Wriston, continues, "If you look at the same facts, it would not be unusual to come up with the same answer."

3. For example, see Pierre Drouin, "Un Autre Holocaust," *Le Monde*, June 16, 1982, p. 2.

4. Robert S. McNamara statement before the United Nations Conference on Trade and Development, 1972, Santiago, Chile.

5. Rene Habachi, "Critical Issues in Development in the '80's," p. 25.

6. G.W. Friedrich Hegel (1770-1831) was the first modern metaphysician to give equal weight to existence and non-existence as the source of all being and movement. As one of his disciples on the left, Lenin, aptly pointed out, "rational unity becomes a unity of contradictions." Meanwhile, Hegelian dialectics denies the central philosophical insights of both the Platonic and the Aristotelian traditions in Western thought, and falls back on a pre-Socratic definition of reality. This definition has inspired on the left Marx's notion of historic change through incessant conflict and, on the right, Nietzsche's inverted morality of the "Superman." Anyone who thinks that ideas do not precede facts need but look at Hegel's political and historical legacy.

7. David Ricardo, stockbroker, self-made millionaire, and ardent student of Thomas Malthus first proposed in 1817 the theory of Comparative Advantage, which some economists prefer to call a "law." To simplify, the theory posits that production and subsequent trade based on competitive natural endowment or specialization will produce optimal economic efficiencies and thereby render globally everyone better off. As we shall demonstrate shortly, wide-open competition based on comparative advantage has become the ideological leitmotiv behind international trade, output, and growth on a world-wide basis. Put differently, comparative advantage explains the international division of labor North/South. With Malthusian consequences, the South has borne the brunt of the logic. University students in the United States might recall Paul A. Samuelson's quaint explanation of the Ricardian theory of exchange: "A traditional example used to illustrate this paradox of comparative advantage is the case of the best lawyer in town who is also the best typist in town. Will he not specialize in law and leave typing to a secretary?

How can he afford to give up precious time from the legal field, where his comparative advantage is very great, to perform typing activities in which he is efficient but in which he lacks *comparative* advantage? Or looked at from the secretary's point of view. She is less efficient than he in both activities; but her relative disadvantage compared with him is least in typing. Relatively speaking, she has a comparative advantage in typing." Paul A. Samuelson, *Economics: An Introductory Analysis*, 6th ed. (McGraw-Hill, New York, 1964), pp. 266-67. And so goes the North-South dialogue.

8. Willy Brandt et al., *North-South: A Program for Survival*. Report of the Independent Commission on International Development (The MIT Press, Cambridge, 1980).

9. For an update/comparison with these figures see: Mohammad Abal-Khail Statement before the Board of Governors of the World Bank, Annual Meetings, 1980, Washington, D.C. Sheikh Abal-Khail remarks: "The latest *World Bank Development Report* projects a per capita growth rate of 2.5 percent growth after 1980 in the industrial countries, as compared with 1 percent per annum in low-income countries. It should be realized, however, that in 1980 the industrialized countries have a per capita income of $9,684, while that of the low income countries is $216. Therefore, the per capita income of the first group would increase by $242 per year, while that of the other would increase by a mere $2." Thus, by 1980 the annual projected increase in per capita income in the West exceeded the average annual base income of the average wage earner in the poorest countries. Since 1980, real income per capita in the large majority of Third World countries has actually decreased.

10. Willy Brandt et al., *Common Crisis*, North-South Co-Operation for World Recovery (Pan Books, London, 1983), p. 9.

NOTES TO CHAPTER 1/THE RICH NATIONS AND THE POOR NATIONS REVISITED: A MACROECONOMIC OVERVIEW

1. Louis Sabourin, "Critical Issues in Development in the '80's," p. 20.

2. Maurice Guernier, *Tiers-Monde: Trois Quarts du Monde*, Rapport au Club de Rome (Dunod, Paris, 1980), p. 20.

3. Mahbub ul Haq, *The Poverty Curtain* (Columbia University Press, New York, 1976), pp. 5-22.

4. Barbara Ward, *Progress for a Small Planet* (W.W. Norton, New York, 1980), p. 225. The author writes: "after thirty years of consistent economic growth, the richest 10% of the people take nearly half of the national income, while the share enjoyed by 90% of the Brazilians actually fell between 1960 and 1970." Ibid.

5. Mahbub ul Haq, op. cit., p. 39.

6. Presidential Commission on World Hunger, *Overcoming World Hunger: The Challenge Ahead* (U.S. Government Printing Office, Washington, D.C., March, 1980), pp. 89-90.

7. Jerry Lewis, "Assistance for Debt Woes," *Wall Street Journal*, April 3, 1984.

NOTES TO CHAPTER 2/THE ORIGIN OF THE DEVELOPMENT PROCESS: THE PARADIGM

1. Thomas Hobbes, *Leviathan*, ed., with Introduction by C.P. Macpherson (Penguin Books, New York, 1980), p. 395. As we shall explain, this Hobbesian premise premises Third World development policy.

2. A.W. Clausen. Remarks to the International Monetary Conference, Vancouver, Canada, May 25, 1982.

3. Ibid.

4. Ibid.

5. Rutherford, M. Poats et al., *Annual Report* of the Development Assistance Committee (The Organization for Economic Co-operation and Development, Paris, 1983), p. 179.

6. Barbara Ward, op. cit. p. 247.

7. Ibid.

8. By 1982, the World Bank lent quiet but official endorsement to the theme under consideration. In the World Bank's *World Development Report* (World Bank, Washington, D.C., 1982), p. 55 we read: "The food crisis taught some painful but important lessons." The *Report* continues, "Much greater emphasis has been given to increasing food production, the essential, long-term source of food security." Ibid and passim. See also: FAO, *The World Food Problem: Proposals for National and International Action* (Rome, November, 1974). Or, more recently, FAO, *Agriculture Toward 2000* (Rome, 1981).

9. See, for example, Sidiki Diakité, "Elements Pour Une Theorie et Une Praxis du Developpement," Philosophy Department Monograph (University of Abidjan, 1983).

10. See, for example, the Brandt Commission reports noted above. In addition to a number of well-known First World leaders, members of the Brandt Commission or, the Independent Commission on International Development Issues, included A.Y. Al-Hamad, an influential Minister of Finance from Kuwait, L.K. Jha, one-time Ambassador to the U.S. from India, and, until his death in 1982, Eduardo Frei Montalva, President of Chile, 1964-70. Other Third World countries represented on the Commission by high level politicians or civil servants were Algeria, Columbia, Indonesia, Tanzania, and Upper Volta.

11. Rutherford Poats et al., Op. cit. p. 41.

NOTES TO CHAPTER 3/THREE DECADES OF GLOBAL DEVELOPMENT

1. John F. Kennedy, address before the UN General Assembly, September 25, 1961. Available in *Public Papers of the Presidents of the United States* (U.S. Government Printing Office, Washington, D.C., 1962), p. 623.

2. As President Kennedy explained to the UN General Assembly, "New research, technical assistance and pilot projects can unlock the wealth of less developed lands and untapped waters." Op. cit. While President Kennedy was perhaps over-optimistic as regards the prospects for Third World development the same cannot be said for his projections on the dangers of the nuclear arms race. On this issue, the same General Assembly speech should be consulted.

3. For example, see Herbert Kahn with the Hudson Institute, *World Economic Development: 1979 and Beyond* (Westview Press, Boulder, Colorado, 1979, pp. 53-70 passim.

4. John F. Kennedy, op. cit.

5. Between 1970 and 1974, the poor nations, with 70 percent of the world's population, received less than 4 percent of the international reserves created during that period. The reserves in question were created mostly in dollars and sterling and led to the worldwide inflationary spiral that followed thereafter. For instance,

between 1970-73 more monetary reserves were created than in the entire history of the world since Adam and Eve. See: Mahbub Ul Haq, *The Poverty Curtain*, p. 158 and Table 10.

6. See *World Development Report* (World Bank, Washington, D.C., 1982) Figure 5.1.

NOTES TO CHAPTER 4/FROM METHOD TO MODEL: THE BIG PUSH

1. W. Arthur Lewis, *Development Planning* (George Allen and Unwin, London, 1966), p. 26. The big push theory was first articulated in quantitative terms by the economist, Ragnar Nurske, in *Problems of Capital Formation in Underdeveloped Countries* (Oxford University Press, New York, 1953). At the World Bank, the "big push" was referred to alternatively as "balanced growth" and effectively promoted by Paul N. Rosenstein-Rodar, an influential in-house economist and development theoretician.

2. Simon Kuznets, *Economic Change* (W.W. Norton, New York, 1953), Chapters 6 and 7. Development economists sometimes refer to the U-Curve as "Kuznets's Law."

3. Albert O. Hirschman, *The Strategy of Economic Development* (Yale University Press, New Haven, 1964), pp. 205-206. The author explains further: "Whatever the reason, there can be little doubt that an economy to lift itself to higher income levels, must and will develop within itself one or several regional centers of economic strength. This need for the emergence of 'growing points' or 'growth poles' in the course of the development process means that international and interregional inequality of growth is an inevitable concomitant and condition of growth itself." (Pp. 183-184.)

4. Herbert Kahn, *World Economic Development*, p. 65.

5. W. W. Rostow, *The Stages of Economic Growth: A Non-Communist Manifesto* (Cambridge University Press, Cambridge, 1961), p. 4.

6. Ibid., p. 7.

7. Ibid., p. 26.

8. Ibid.

9. The simplest and best known consistency model for development planning is the Harrod-Domar growth model, developed independently in the 1940s by Roy Harrod and Evsy Domar. The underlying assumption of the model is that the output of an economic unit, whether a firm, an industry, or a country depends on the amount of capital invested in that unit. While the model was developed to help explain the correlations between growth and employment in modern capitalist societies, it subsequently was used extensively in developing countries as a simple, or better, simplistic, way of looking at the relationship between growth and capital requirements.

10. W. W. Rostow, op. cit., p. 88.

11. Ibid., p. 20.

12. T.H. Huxley quoted in Floyd W. Matson, *The Broken Image*, (Anchor Books, Doubleday, Garden City, 1966), p. 21. For anyone who wants to know 'up from down' in the history of ideas since the Seventeenth Century, Prof. Matson's, *The Broken Image*, a too little known book, might serve as the start and the finish.

NOTES TO CHAPTER 5/THE SECOND AND THIRD DEVELOPMENT DECADES

1. *International Development Strategy for the Second United Nations Development Decade* (*the 1970s*) (Office of Public Information, United Nations, New York).

2. For comparisons of Third World debt figures see, especially, World Bank, *World Debt Tables* and *Borrowing in International Capital Markets* (various issues); OECD, *External Debt of Developing Countries*, (various issues); and Bank for International Settlements, *Quarterly Press Releases* and *Annual Reports*. Perhaps the most usable source on private nonguaranteed debt is derived from publications by the OECD's Development Assistant Committee (DAC), which reports information, collected mostly from creditor sources, on the debt of 143 developing countries and territories. World Bank and IMF debt figures come largely from debtor reporting countries.

3. Jean Loup, *Le Tiers Monde Peut-Il Survivre?* (Economica, Paris, 1981), Chapter IV.

4. Halfdan Malher, the managing director of the World Health Organization, quoted in *Le Monde*, March 25, 1979.

5. See *FAO Production Yearbook* (Food and Agricultural Organization, Rome) (various issues) and Jean Loup, ibid. Even more alarming figures can be found in Willy Brandt, *North-South: A Program for Survival*. The Brandt Commission projects food import requirements of the Third World exceeding 145 million tons by 1990, based on current growth rates in demand. While the Brandt Commission set out to show the seriousness of the situation and its attendent suffering, hopefully the exponential figures can be taken as a worse case scenario. See: Willy Brandt, *North-South: A Program for Survival*, p. 159.

NOTES TO CHAPTER 6/THE THIRD DEVELOPMENT DECADE AND BEYOND

1. *International Development Strategy for the Third United Nations Development Decade* (*the 1980s*) (Office of Public Information, United Nations, New York).

2. See John W. McDonald, Jr., "The North-South Dialogue and the United Nations," Occasional Paper, Institute for the Study of Diplomacy (Georgetown University, School of Foreign Service, Washington, D.C., 1982), pp. 9-17 passim.

3. Albert Camus, *The Rebel* (Vintage, New York, 1958), p. 210.

4. For a recent, vigorous, orthodox defense of post-war Third World development planning, see: Herbert Kahn, op. cit., or, alternatively, Malcolm Gillis et al., *Economics of Development* (W. W. Norton, New York, 1983). This latter work was written under the aegis of the Harvard Institute for International Development and is expected to become a textbook classic. To paraphrase Alfred Whitehead, both books advance in detail while "fundamental novelty is barred."

5. This theory has been effectively challenged by a number of modern demographers and medical historians who, in the face of popular wisdom, are now emphasizing the insignificance of medical and hospital contributions as regards population growth. For a preview of what may become the new orthodoxy, see: Thomas McKeown, *The Modern Rise of Population* (Academic Press, New York,

1976). See also: Morris D. Morris, *Measuring the Conditions of the World's Poor: The Physical Quality of Life Index, for the Overseas Development Council* (Pergamon Press, New York, 1979) Chapter 4.

6. For a practical summary of more elaborate World Bank projections, See: Barbara Ward, op. cit., pp. 230-243 and passim. See also: *World Development Report 1982* (World Bank, Washington, D.C.), Chapter 4, Table 4.3.

7. Barbara Ward, op. cit., p. 258.

NOTES TO CHAPTER 7/AID POLICY AND THIRD WORLD DEVELOPMENT

1. In 1983, financial flows to the Third World from the World Bank Group totaled $11.1 billion and SDR 35 billion from the IMF, a near doubling of previous highs for this second category of fund flows. The World Bank/IMF Group accounted for an additional $2 billion in net flows, acting as a catalyst for other lenders, mostly under the World Bank's Cofinancing program. A much higher figure could be counted if one were to include the *induced* commercial bank "rollovers" for which the IMF, in part, can be credited.

2. IMF Articles of Agreement, Article I, p. 16.

3. Maurice Guitan, "Fund Conditionality and the International Adjustment Process," *Finance and Development* (International Monetary Fund, Washington, D.C., December, 1980, p. 16.

4. Anthony Sampson, op. cit., pp. 334-35.

5. "External Debt of Developing Countries, 1982 Survey," (OECD, Paris, 1982), pp. 11-12.

6. IMF Staff Papers, Vol. 25, No. 2 (International Monetary Fund, Washington, D.C., June 1978).

7. George Schultz, Testimony before the Senate Foreign Relations Committee on February 15, 1983.

8. Willy Brandt, *Common Crisis*, Chapter 2.

9. Maurice Guernier, op. cit., pp. 98-100.

10. Ibid., p. 34.

11. Edward Mason and Robert Asher, *The World Bank Since Bretton Woods*, (The Brookings Institution, Washington, D.C., 1975), p. 1.

NOTES TO CHAPTER 8/THE WORLD BANK: FROM PROCESS TO PROJECT LENDING

1. The agricultural economist, Alan Berg, observes, "The mathematically precise growth models that have been in vogue since the 1940's seldom take explicit account of the notion of investment in human beings. Increases in tomorrow's income are assumed to result primarily from today's additions to material capital, and since consumption displaces capital investment, it becomes an enemy of growth, not a handmaiden. Consumption in the form of educational services, clothing, and eating have an instrumental impact on productivity but since the effects of such consumption are difficult to identify, all growth in income is imputed to those more easily measurable factors included in the model. Expenditures on health and nutrition are also classified as consumption and thus fail to

show up as factors affecting national growth." *The Nutrition Factor* (The Brookings Institution, Washington, D.C., 1975), p. 1.

2. The total amount of World Bank loans to agriculture at June 30, 1967 was $802 million versus $8.7 billion in overall Bank lending—i.e., less than 10 percent. (See: World Bank *Annual Report*, 1967). The balance of the Bank's lending activity concerned electric power, transportation, communication, and heavy industry. This investment strategy was, of course, in keeping with the various development models then in vogue: big push, take-off, unbalanced growth, creative destruction, and the like.

3. Herbert Kahn, op. cit., p. 448.

4. Ibid., p. 487.

5. Robert S. McNamara, Address to the Board of Governors, Copenhagen, September 21, 1970.

6. Robert McNamara quoted in John L. Maddox, *The Development Philosophy of Robert McNamara* (The World Bank, Washington, D.C., June, 1981), p. 43.

7. The World Bank *Annual Report* 1981 (The World Bank, Washington, D.C.).

8. Robert McNamara, Remarks before the United Nations Conference on Trade and Development (UNCTAD III) Santiago, Chile, April, 1972.

9. Robert McNamara, Remarks before Columbia University Conference on Development, Columbia University, New York, February, 1970.

10. *Summary Proceedings, 1976*, Annual Meetings of the Board of Governors (The World Bank, Washington, D.C.), p. 9.

11. Quoted in John L. Maddox, op. cit., p. 42.

12. Ibid.

13. Ibid., pp. 42-43 and passim.

14. John Maynard Keynes, *Essays in Persuasion* (W.W. Norton, New York, 1963), pp. 371-72.

15. Quoted in Anthony Sampson, op. cit., p. 299.

16. The concept of addressing basic human needs as a precondition to growth was first put forward by the International Labor Office. See: International Labor Organization, *Employment, Growth and Basic Needs: A One-World Problem* (Praeger, New York, 1977).

17. Quoted in John L. Maddox, op. cit., p. 42.

18. Willy Brandt, *Common Crisis*, p. 18.

NOTES TO CHAPTER 9/FROM THIRD WORLD PROJECT FINANCE TO GOVERNMENT EXPORT PROMOTION

1. Walter Wriston, "Banking Against Disaster," *New York Times*, September 14, 1982.

2. Wriston argues, "We have some chips in every game in town." He then continues, "In a spectrum of 156 countries there are always going to be two or three or four in trouble." Quoted in Anthony Sampson, op. cit. p. 162. In the case of Brazil and/or Mexico, Citibank not only has a chip in the game but its suit and wallet as well. The same is true in other countries but in less spectacular fashion.

3. The concept has been widely reported (and repeated) within Citibank management hierarchy. EVP, George J. Clark told *Business Week* in slightly different terms: "There is no Chapter 11 for countries. We think we're going to

collect." See: "A Rift Over Shaky Foreign Debt," *Business Week*, November 29, 1982, p. 80.

4. "The Largest U.S. Non-Industrial Corporations," *Fortune*, July 2, 1983, p. 134.

5. *U.S. Government Agency Directory* (U.S. Government Printing Office, Washington, D.C., 1982, p. 113.

6. M. Peter McPherson, testimony before the House Committee on Foreign Affairs, March 19, 1981.

7. Mahbub ul Haq, "Tied Credits—A Quantitative Analysis," in John H. Adler ed., *Capital Movements and Economic Development* (Macmillan, New York, 1967), p. 326 and passim. This remains, in economic development literature, the only available "quantitative analysis" for public view. Price "mark up's" are more than a trade secret. They have become a secret of State.

8. Nathaniel McKitterick and J. Middleton, "The Bankers of the Rich and the Bankers of the Poor," Monograph Series (Overseas Development Council, Washington, D.C., 1972), p. 12.

9. Gordon Hurlbert, testimony before the Senate Subcommittee on Appropriations, June 10, 1982.

10. Ibid.

11. T.A. Wilson, Testimony before the Senate Subcommittee of International Trade, March 5, 1981.

12. Walter Wriston quoted by Sanford Rose in "Why they Call it 'Fat City'," *Fortune*, March, 1975, p. 110.

13. Willard Butcher, quoted in *Euromoney*, October, 1981, p. 30.

14. Paul Volker, Testimony before the Joint Economic Committee on November 24, 1982.

15. Internal Memorandum entitled "Global Debt and its Implications," (Morgan Guaranty Trust Company, New York, April, 1983), p. 3.

16. Ibid., p. 4.

17. Ibid.

18. George J. Clark, "In Our Own Interest," *The Global Financial System and LDC Debts* (Citibank, New York, n.d.), p. 17. The article is a transcript of Mr. Clark's testimony before a House Banking Subcommittee. While not asking for help, Mr. Clark argues, "The IMF has played a significant role in the past and its effectiveness should be maintained if we hope to restore health to the global economy. The quota increase is significant to that effort." Ibid. In other words, the IMF is to step in where the banks now fear to tread. This is fine but Mr. Clark should not then claim to be an angel. . .instead of a welfare case.

19. Hans H. Angermuller, "LDC Debt—The Bailout that Isn't," Ibid., p. 8.

20. Financial Accounting Standards Board Rule 15.

21. "Giant Sugar Project Turns Sour," *Daily Telegraph*, May 28, 1981.

22. Department of the Interior, *Sub-Sahara Africa: Its Role in Critical Mineral Needs of the Western World* (Government Printing Office, Washington, D.C., 1980), p. 44.

23. Lester B. Pearson et al., *Partners In Development*, Report of the Commission on International Development (Praeger, New York, 1969), p. 121.

24. Ibid., p. 120.

25. See: "External Debt of Developing Countries," (OECD, Paris, 1982), Table 3.

26. Malcolm T. Stamper, testimony before the Senate Subcommittee on Appropriations, June 10, 1982.

27. By 1981 Boeing Aircraft Company accounted for more than 40 percent of Eximbank's direct credit loans to foreign buyers.

28. Malcolm T. Stamper, testimony before the Senate Subcommittee on Appropriations, June 10, 1982.

29. Wilson Committee, Evidence, Vol. 3. p. 46. Cited in Jean Pearce, "Subsidized Export Credits," *Chatham House Papers, VIII* (The Royal Institute of International Affairs, London, 1980.), p. 26.

30. Verle Lanier, Acting Administrator for Export Credits in testimony before the House Committee on Foreign Affairs, March 19, 1981.

31. William E. Brock, "Trade and Debt: The Vital Linkage," *Foreign Affairs*, Summer 1984, p. 1045.

32. Francois Partant, "The System is Beginning to Strangle itself," *The Guardian*, December 20, 1981.

33. R. Peter DeWitt, "The Crisis in International Debt Management," *Contemporary Crisis*, February 1980, Vol. 4., No. 2., pp. 144-159. For similar analysis see: Thomas Hanley, *U.S. Multinational Banking: Current and Perspective Strategies* (Salomon Brothers, New York, 1976) and various issues.

34. Robert A. Bennett, "Less Risk, More Worry for the Banks," *New York Times*, October 10, 1982.

35. "External Debt of Developing Countries" (OECD, Paris, October, 1981), p. 4.

36. A.W. Clausen, "Third World Aid Must Not be Cut," *The Times*, April 22, 1983. See also: *World Development Report, 1982* (The World Bank, Washington, D.C., 1982), p. 5. Here we read: "Economic growth is the ultimate remedy for rural poverty."

37. Jeffrey E. Garten, Remarks to the International Monetary Conference, The Hague, October, 1982.

38. "Worry at the World's Banks," *Business Week*, September 6, 1982, p. 56.

39. Alfredo Phillips et al., *Joint Ministerial Development Committee Task Force Study on Third World Indebtedness* (World Bank, Washington, D.C., March, 1982).

40. Felix Rohatyn, "The State of the Banks," *The New York Review of Books*, November 4, 1982.

41. See: Lawrence Malkin, "The Debt Bomb Threat," *Time*, January 10, 1983, pp. 4-11.

NOTES TO CHAPTER 10/THE IMPACT OF MULTINATIONAL BANKING IN THE THIRD WORLD

1. "Bankers Feel the Earth Move Under Their Feet," *The Economist*, October 16, 1982, p. 2.

2. Walter Wriston et al., *The Citicorp Concept: The Emerging Financial Services Enterprise* (Citicorp, New York, 1982), p. 30. Theobald's chairman, Walter Wriston, eventually was to dream of what he called a "Bank'n'Burger." Instead of diluting the capital base of a number of insurance and finance companies, Citibank would have rendered perhaps a better service to the economy by purchasing MacDonald's or Burger King. This would have been more consistent both with

Citibank's changing vocation (or vocations) and with its identity crisis. The Wriston idea of a "one-stop Bank 'n' Burger" is discussed briefly in Michael Moffet, *The World's Money* (Simon & Schuster, New York, 1983), p. 238.

3. Walter Wriston quoted in "The Glory Days Are Over at Citibank," *Business Week*, November 7, 1977, p. 67. Not only does Mr. Wriston's remark ignore the existing structure of international finance, it likewise ignores the numbers. By the time of the first OPEC oil price increase in 1973, the big U.S. banks had already become dependent on purchased funds from abroad. For instance, in 1964 the top ten U.S. banks had only six percent of their total deposits from abroad. By 1973, foreign deposits had increased to about a third of total deposits. Even before the first oil shock in 1973, Citibank, Chase Manhattan and Bank of America had 49 percent, 37 percent and 35 percent respectively of its deposits at overseas branches.

4. Lord Harold Lever, "Chain Letter Banking," *The Times*, July 7, 1982.

5. Walter Wriston, *The Citicorp Concept*, p. 10. What Mr. Wriston really set out to do was to separate "making money" from banking. This he achieved.

6. Ibid., p. 11. Citibank and others have argued that they should be allowed to expand into non-banking activities in order to compete with non-bank banks. Until the Continental Illinois fiasco, the Comptroller of the Currency with the backing of the Reagan Administration, endorsed the schema. Then it was realized that nonbank banks, unlike non-dairy dairy products, crossed an invisible threshold that could rupture the internal workings of the private sector economy. A non-bank bank is just that, a *non*bank or financial broker as opposed to a guardian of wealth or regulator in a free market economy. We will discuss these distinctions at more length throughout the balance of the Chapter. Meanwhile, to allow the biggest banks to expand out of the banking business represents a sort of disguised rescue operation for those banks that cannot make it in their own industry. In a parallel sense, what policy holder would want his insurance company in the credit card, travel, or computer business? What we are dealing with here is the structure of the economy not a simple sharing of markets. We likewise are dealing with the protection of the economy, something some bankers have forgotten. The Citicorp Concept, we would note in passing, is not a bank concept but a rationale for ignoring a bank's fiduciary responsibility and, by extension, its identity.

7. Anthony Sampson, op. cit., p. 291.

8. Henry Wallich, Remarks before the Allied Social Sciences Association, San Fransisco, December 29, 1983.

9. Benjamin J. Cohen and Fabio Basagni, *Banks and the Balance of Payments* for The Atlantic Institute, Paris (Allan Held, Osmun, Montclair, NJ., 1981), p. 126.

10. "Nigeria Suspends Oil Aides," *New York Times*, April 19, 1980. See also, "Nigeria Oil Billions 'missing,'" *Financial Times*, April 19, 1980.

11. "Have United States Banks Provided Enough," *The Banker*, April, 1983, p. 7.

12. Henry Wallich, op. cit.

13. Lord Harold Lever, "International Banking's House of Cards," *New York Times*, September 21, 1982.

14. Felix Rohatyn, op. cit. The idea of a federally funded Reconstruction Finance Corporation which would buy LDC loans from banks at a discount is vigorously opposed by Citibank's George Clark in Senate testimony cited earlier.

Clark argues the familiar line that the debtor countries simply face a temporary liquidity or funding problem. Clark wants to keep his LDC loans as earning assets while the IMF provides the cash to pay down the banks. Clark argues that the proposed RFC ". . .is not the appropriate remedy for the liquidity problem the debtor countries face today." Op. cit., p. 19. Like his regulator, Henry Wallich, Clark simply wants more of the same, i.e., more money from the IMF.

15. "Not with a Bang But a Fonda," *The Economist*, September 18, 1982, p. 91.

16. For an elaboration of these themes see: R.W. Lombardi, "Multinational Banking and the Third World," *International Herald Tribune*, March 18, 1981, and "The World's Mountainous Foreign Debt," *International Herald Tribune*, November 10, 1981.

NOTES TO CHAPTER 11/FIRST ANALYTIC TO THE WESTERN QUESTION: ECONOMICS AS SCIENCE

1. Aristotle, *The Nicomachean Ethics*, translated with Introduction by R. W. Browne (Henry G. Bohn, London, 1853), p. 4.

2. Xenocrates division of learning likewise parallels that of the Bible. See, for instance, Book of Wisdom.

3. See: Aristotle's *Posterior Analytics*, Loeb Series (Harvard University Press, Cambridge, 1968) Bk. II.

4. *The Nicomachean Ethics*, op. cit., p. 155.

5. Montesquieu, *De L'Esprit des Lois* (my translation) (Editions Social, Paris, 1977), p. 50.

6. David Hume, *An Enquiry Concerning Human Understanding and Other Essays*, ed., with an Introduction by Ernest C. Mossner (Washington Square Press, New York, 1963), p. 21.

7. Ibid., pp. 52-53.

8. In a related sense, as Edmund Husserl points out, without "conscience" the world is contingent and relative. Conscience, then, is a condition *a priori* of the possibility of objectivity. The ethical implications here are obvious. For Husserl, the ethical springs from his epistemological consideration that "conscience" or intuition, not static sense experience, is at the origin both of knowing and of creation. In sum, all primitive concepts such as unity, plurality, even objectivity or the objectivization of sense experience (raw data) are based on intuition in its broadest sense. Husserl stands against Hume, even Kant as well against the very foundations of the behavioral and social sciences in arguing that sense impressions are captured by the human mind to be made human. They do not determine the human mind. In *Fact and Essence*, Husserl writes: "Each physical property draws us toward the infinite." In other words, without intuition or judgment, all knowledge borders on chaos or leads us to the brink of absolute scepticism, i.e., moral anarchy. Economists should be aware of this, but too few are.

9. Adam Smith, *Theory of Moral Sentiments*, (Bohn's Standard Library, 1853), p. 470.

10. Joseph Schumpeter, *Economic Doctrine and Method* (George Allen & Unwin, London, 1954), p. 154.

11. Ibid., p. 161.

12. The concept was first elaborated by the Physiocrats in France in the early Eighteenth Century, notably by Francois Quesnay in *Tableau Economique*. See: R.L. Meek, *The Economics of Physiocracy* (Harvard University Press, Cambridge, 1963).

13. Eugen von Böhm-Bawerk, *Capital and Interest*, translated by George D. Huncke (Libertarian Press, South Holland, Ill., 1959), Bk. I, Ch. 3. pp. 31-32.

14. Ibid., p. 32.

15. Ibid.

16. Adam Smith, *An Inquiry Into the Nature & Causes of the Wealth of Nations* ed. by R.H. Cambell and A.S. Skinner (Clarendon Press, Oxford, 1976), Vol. II, iii, p. 337. Smith adds: "It is by means of additional capital only that the undertaker of any work can either provide his workmen with better machinery, or make a more proper distribution of employment among them." He draws the following conclusion based on the pre-concept that savings *always* pays: "...every prodigal appears to be a publick enemy, and every frugal man a publick benefactor." Ibid. p. 347. Smith's preconcept served as a working assumption in classical and neo-classical economics until the appearance of Keynes' *General Theory*.

17. John Maynard Keynes, *The General Theory of Employment, Interest, and Money* (Macmillan, London, 1936), p. 368. Earlier in the same volume, Keynes argues: "capital is not a self-subsistant entity existing apart from consumption. On the contrary, every weakening in the propensity to consume . . . must weaken the demand for capital." p. 106.

18. Karl Marx quoted in *A History of Economic Theories* (Langland Press, New York, 1952), p. 2.

19. Ibid., p. 11.

20. Thomas Hobbes quoted in Karl Marx, *Salaire, prix et Profit* (Editions Sociales, Paris, 1962), p. 130. For original of quotation, see: Thomas Hobbes, op. cit., p. 151.

21. John Maynard Keynes, *General Theory*, p. 33.

NOTES TO CHAPTER 12/ECONOMIC DEVELOPMENT VERSUS ECONOMIC DETERMINISM

1. Thomas Hobbes, op. cit., p. 699.

2. It is revealing to note that Thomas Hobbes served as the private secretary to Francis Bacon. While Francis Bacon introduced the inductive method of reasoning to science, his friend and disciple, Hobbes of Malmesbury, introduced a purely empirical method of reasoning to the study of man and the State. Hobbes represents nothing less than the inversion of the Aristotelian tradition in Western thought and action. For instance: "Good and evil," Hobbes argues, "are names that signify our appetites and aversions." Ibid., p. 97. The ethics that stem from this premise (definition of man) are as materialistic as they are simplistic. In the end, sense impression overwhelm thought, discipline, and *conscience*.

3. Etienne Gilson, *D'Aristote A Darwin et Retour* (J. Vrin, Paris, 1971), p. 14.

4. Albert Camus, op. cit., p. 113.

5. Thomas Hobbes, op. cit., p. 151.

6. Ibid., p. 126. Likewise, for Hobbes free will is the "last Inclination" or "Appetite in Deliberating." Ibid., p. 128. Or, a mere inclination making "No action voluntary." Ibid., p. 88. As an accomplished tennis player Hobbes seems to have forgotten the important phenomenon of "the will to win."

7. Ibid., p. 88.

8. David Hume, "Of the Independence of Parliament," in *Essays, Moral, Political and Literary* (Oxford University Press, Oxford, 1963), p. 31.

9. Thomas Malthus, *An Essay on the Principle of Population*, ed., with an introduction by A.F. Harmondsworth (Penguin Classics, Baltimore, 1970), p. 68.

10. Ibid., p. 118.

11. Ibid., p. 72.

12. Charles Darwin, "Autobiography," in *The Life and Letters of Charles Darwin*, ed. by Francis Darwin (John Murray, London, 1898) Vol. I, p. 83.

13. Charles Darwin, *The Descent of Man and Selection in Relation to Sex*, (D. Appleton, New York, 1896), p. 6.

14. Readers interested in looking at an alternative to Darwin's war of nature as an explanation to evolution might consult the following eminently readable studies: Peter Kropotkin, *Mutual Aid: A Factor of Evolution* (Penguin, London, 1939); Ashley Montagu, *Darwin, Competition and Cooperation* (Greenwood Press, Westport, Conn. 1973), and George G. Simpson, *The Meaning of Evolution* (Yale University Press, New Haven, 1949).

15. As George G. Simpson explains regarding the evolution of species, "Struggle is sometimes involved, but it usually is not, and when it is, it may work against rather than toward natural selection. Advantage in differential reproduction is usually a peaceful process in which the concept of struggle is really irrelevant. It more often involves such things as better integration into the ecological situation, maintenance of a balance in nature, more efficient utilization of available food, better care of the young." *The Meaning of Evolution*, p. 53.

16. Yet as Martson Bates reasons: "I think there has been an increasing tendency in biological writings to stress the cooperative rather than the competitive aspects of relations among various kinds of organisms. But this tendency has not been adequately reflected in the thinking of the social philosophers (sic), who have tended to confine their biological explorations to the post Darwinian or Thomas Huxley period. I don't think the social philosophers are entirely to blame for this. The biologists have failed to make their growing knowledge, their accumulating facts and concepts, easily available to philosophers." In fact, most philosophers worthy of the name are one step ahead of the biologists among whom Mr. Bates figures. This is not true of the so-called social scientists or those to whom Mr. Bates refers to as "social philosophers." *The Nature of Natural History* (Scribner, New York, 1950), p. 123.

17. Ashley Montagu, *Darwin Competition and Cooperation*, p. 46.

18. Ibid.

19. Darwin's "natural selection" became Herbert Spencer's "survival of the fittest." Darwin showed how evolution worked in nature according to the presumed "law" of the "struggle for existence" while Spencer developed similar theories for human society. Spencer's doctrine, much to his chagrin, came to be known as "social Darwinism." Simultaneously, however, Spencer and Darwin both were providing a pseudo-scientific rationalization for colonialism, industrialization, 19th century morality, and the class struggle based on the premise that nature advances by a sort of unlimited warefare within the biosphere. This "rationalization" has been brought whole into the twentieth century, with the results that are before us.

20. Friedrich Nietzsche, *Thus Spake Zarathustra*, translated by Thomas Common, Modern Library edition (Random House, New York, n.d.), p. 322.

21. Ibid., p. 3. Nietzsche adds: "Dead are all the Gods: now do we desire the Superman to live." Ibid., p. 83. He did. In the figure of Adolf Hitler.

22. See: *The Correspondence of Marx and Engels* (International Publishers, New York, 1935), pp. 125-26.

NOTES TO CHAPTER 13/HOMO RATIONALIS VERSUS HOMO ECONOMICUS

1. To borrow an observation from Ilya Prigogne, the ambition of Post-Renaissance science has been to model or "form" the world, not to understand it. See: I. Prignone and I. Stengers, *Order Out of Chaos* (Bantam, New York, 1984).

2. George Bernard Shaw, "Preface," in *Back to Methuselah, A Metabiological Pentateuch* (Brentano's, New York, 1921), p. 1ii.

3. Comparisons are those of Willy Brandt et al., *North-South: A Program for Survival*. See sub-section of Introduction, entitled "Destruction or Development?"

4. "The Second Coming," reprinted with permission of Macmillan Publishing Company from *Collected Poems of W.B. Yeats* by W.B. Yeats, p. 185. Copyright 1924 by Macmillan Publishing Co., Inc., renewed 1952 by Bertha Georgia Yeats.

5. The analysis comes from Etienne Gilson, *Les Metamorphoses de La Cite de Dieu* (J. Vrin, Paris, 1952), p. 258 passim.

NOTES TO CHAPTER 14/AN ACTION PLAN AT "THE EDGE OF HISTORY"

1. Title of chapter is taken from William I. Thompson's remarkable little book, *At the Edge of History: Speculations on the Transformation of Culture* (Harper & Row, New York, 1971).

2. Fifty-third *Annual Report* (Bank of International Settlements, Basel, June, 1983), p. 179.

3. Ibid.

4. Ibid., p. 108.

5. Ibid., p. 122.

6. Willy Brandt et al., *Common Crisis*, Chapter 2.

7. See, for example: Robert A. Bennett, "Strict U.S. Ruling to Slash Profits of Banks That Lent to Latin America," *Wall Street Journal*, June 19, 1984.

8. Paul Tillich, *Love Power and Justice* (Oxford University Press, New York, 1960).

9. These seemingly unreal figures can be explained by the fact that for the past 20 years the major multinational companies have been able to take advantage of a global labor pool not only on their own initiative but by virtue of increasingly easy credit (private and government subsidized export facilities), First World tax incentives, and outward bound industrial policies especially in the Far East. Thus the largest U.S. manufacturers have been displacing labor intensive U.S. plant facilities—and jobs—to the Pacific Basin and, to a lesser extent, Mexico, Brazil, and Central America. In addition, U.S. heavy industry, steel, chemicals, and automobiles have lost market share to foreign producers specialized in production for U.S. markets and supported by (1) an undervalued currency (Japan), (2) unequal labor costs, including social costs (South Korea/Mexico/Singapore/Hong Kong, etc.), (3) a nationwide industrial policy keyed on U.S. markets not on their own regional ones, and, (4) hard work. Meanwhile, double-digit inflation in the U.S. or a general

over-heating of the economy has caused its own labor displacement out of capital intensive industry into the government and service sectors. The cumulative effect is that the U.S. economy, like most Third World economies, has become overly dependent on increasingly unstable foreign markets, labor, and supply. The only manufacturing sector in the U.S. which is able to defy the rule is "defense" and the high-tech industries on its periphery. This is why defense spending maintains an ineluctable momentum. Politicians would rather opt for an easy, punctual solution to employment problems instead of attempting a structural, long-term correction. In the end, we prefer to export not only our production but our decision making capacity as well.

10. Paul Tillich, op. cit., p. 24.
11. Werner Wolff quoted in Floyd Matson, op. cit., p. 310n.

Selected Readings

(The primary source material dealing with the topics on which this book concentrates have been cited in the text. Others are listed below.)

Adelman, Irma and Cynthia Morris. *Economic Growth and Social Equity in Developing Countries*. Stanford, Calif.: Stanford University Press, 1973.

Anderson, Tim and Peter Field. "The Tremors That Threaten the Banking System." *Euromoney*, October 1982, pp. 17-31.

Aristotle. *Politics*. New York: Modern Library, 1943.

Aronson, Jonathan. *Debt and the Less Developed Countries*, Boulder, Colo.: Westview Press, 1979.

Brockway, George. "How Our Sun May Rise Again." *The New Leader*, July 12, 1982.

Brown, Lester and Erik Eckholm. *By Bread Alone*. New York: Praeger, 1974.

Brasmeer, Karl, et al. "International Debt, Insolvency and Illiquidity." *Journal of Economic Affairs*, April 1983.

Cassirer, Ernst. *The Philosophy of the Enlightenment*. Boston: Beacon Press, 1955.

Champion, George. "Regulators and Bankers Are to Blame." *New York Times*, June 10, 1984.

Chenery, H. B., et al. *Redistribution with Growth*. London: Oxford University Press, 1974.

Cline, William and associates. *World Inflation and the Developing Countries*. Washington, D.C.: The Brookings Institution, 1981.

de Castro Andrade, Regis. "Brazil: The Economics of Savage Capitalism." In *The Struggle for Development*, edited by Manfred Bienefiel and Martin Godfrey. New York: John Wiley, 1982.

Delamaide, Darrell. *Debt Shock*. Garden City, N.J.: Doubleday, 1984.

de Rougement, Denis. *L'Avenir est Notre Affair*. Paris: Editions Stock, 1977.

Drake, P.J. *Money Finance and Economic Development*. New York: John Wiley, 1980.

Erb, G. F. and V. Kallab, eds. *Beyond Dependency: The Developing World Speaks Out*. Washington, D.C.: The Overseas Development Council, 1975.

Galbraith, John Kenneth. *The Nature of Mass Poverty*. Cambridge, Mass.: Harvard University Press, 1979.

Georgescu-Roegen, Nicholas. *The Entropy Law and the Economic Process*. Cambridge, Mass.: Harvard University Press, 1971.

Gilder, George. *Wealth and Poverty*. New York: Basic Books, 1981.

Gran, Guy. *Development by People*. New York: Praeger, 1983.

Guenon, Rene. *The Reign of Quantity and the Sign of the Times*. Baltimore: Penquin, 1972.

Hansen, Roger et al. *U.S. Foreign Policy and the Third World*. For the Overseas Development Council. New York: Praeger, 1982.

Kissinger, Henry. "Debt: Developing Nations Can't Pay." *Baltimore Sun*, June 24, 1984.

Lutz, Mark A. and Kenneth Lux. *The Challenge of Humanistic Economics*. Menlo Park, Calif.: Cummings, 1979.

Macfarlane, John M. *The Causes and Course of Organic Evolution*. New York: Macmillan, 1918.

Maritain, Jacques. *The Dream of Descartes*. New York: Philosophical Library, 1944.

_____. *Humanism Intègral*. Paris: Fernand Aubier, 1936.

Meier, Gerald M., ed. *Leading Issues in Economic Development*, 3rd ed. New York: Oxford University Press, 1976.

Mattis, Anne, ed. *A Society for International Development Prospectus*. Durham, N.C.: Duke University Press. Annual.

Mayer, Martin. *The Bankers*. New York: Ballantine, 1974.

_____. *The Fate of the Dollar*. New York: Time Books, 1980.

Oppenheimer, J. Robert. *Science and the Common Understanding*. New York: Simon and Schuster, 1954.

Organization for Economic Cooperation and Development. *World Economic Interdependence and the Evolving North-South Relationship*. Paris, 1983.

Partant, Francois. *La Fin du Developpement: Naissance d'une Alternative*. Paris: F. Maspero, 1982.

_____. *La Guerilla Economique*. Paris: Seuil, 1976.

Randall, John H. *The Making of the Modern Mind*. Boston: Houghton Mifflin, 1940.

Rohatyn, Felix. "A Plan for Stretching Out Global Debt." *Business Week*, February, 28, 1983.

Shapiro, Harvey D. "What is John Heimann Up To?" *Institutional Investor*, June 1978.

Thayer, Frederick C. *Rebuilding America*. New York: Praeger, 1984.

Jan Tinbergen et al. *Reshaping the International Order*, A Report to the Club of Rome. New York: E. P. Dutton, 1976.

United Nations Industrial Development Organization. *Proposals for Reform of the International Financial System*. Vienna: 1984. Doc. UNIDO/IS. 432.

Volcker, Paul A. "How Serious Is U.S. Bank Exposure?" *Challenge*, May-June 1983.

Weiskopf, Walter. *Alienation and Economics*. New York: Dell, 1973.

Whitehead, Alfred N. *Science and the Modern World*. New York: Macmillan, 1925.

World Food Conference. *The World Food Problem: Proposals for National and International Action*. Rome: Food and Agricultural Organization, 1974.

Index

About the Author

RICHARD W. LOMBARDI, Vice President, The First National Bank of Chicago, took leave from the bank in 1981 for purposes of preparing this book. Until 1981, Mr. Lombardi was responsible for First Chicago's lending activities in Sub-Sahara Africa. While on leave of absence, Mr. Lombardi has served as a Research Associate and Thursday Fellow at the School of Foreign Service at Georgetown University.

Mr. Lombardi has published a number of journal and newspaper articles on the debt crisis. His writings have appeared in the *Baltimore Sun*, the *International Herald Tribune*, and in more specialized trade journals. This is his first book.

Mr. Lombardi has guest lectured at universities in the U.S. and in France. He holds a B.A. from John Carroll University and an M.A. from the University of Maryland.